THE
FIRST TIME
SUPERVISOR

THE
FIRST TIME
SUPERVISOR

A Guide for the Newly Promoted

Second Edition

Elwood N Chapman

KOGAN
PAGE

First published in the United States of America
in 1986 by Crisp Publications Inc, 1200 Hamilton Court,
Menlo Park, California 94025-9600, USA.
Revised edition 1992.

First published in Great Britain in
1988 by Kogan Page Ltd, 120 Pentonville Road,
London N1 9JN. Second edition 1994.

British Library Cataloguing in Publication Data

A CIP record for this book is
available from the British Library.

ISBN 0-7494-1296-8

Typeset by DP Photosetting, Aylesbury, Bucks
Printed and bound in Great Britain by
Clays Ltd, St Ives plc

Contents

Preface

Improving the quality of first line supervision has always been considered essential by successful executives because of the immediate impact on employee productivity. As a result, training directors allocate a sizeable portion of their budget to new supervisor training. A common problem, however, has been that because of factors such as geographical dispersion, or the time of year, considerable time may elapse before a new supervisor receives help. This can lead to costly mistakes or the formation of poor habits before formal training takes place. *The First Time Supervisor* was developed to remedy this training delay problem.

The First Time Supervisor should be considered Phase 1 of any training programme. It was primarily designed as a helpful resource to be given to a new supervisor or an acting supervisor as soon as practical following promotion.

To complete the *First Time Supervisor* programme, all that is required is a pencil, a chair and some time. Once completed, this programme should help a new supervisor to get off to a successful start. Later, following an on-the-job adjustment period, the individual will be better prepared for Phase 2 – a more formal supervisory training programme.

About This Book

The First Time Supervisor is not like most books. It has a unique self-paced format that encourages a reader to become personally involved. Designed to be read with a pencil, there is an abundance of exercises, activities, assessments and case studies that invite participation.

The objective of this book is to help a person recognise the traits that lead to successful supervision and then make any required behavioural changes that apply to the concepts presented in the book.

The First Time Supervisor can be used effectively in a number of ways. Here are some possibilities:

- **Individual study.** Because the book is self-instructional, it can be introduced at the point of promotion. By completing the activities and exercises, a person should receive not only valuable feedback, but also practical ideas about steps for self-improvement.
- **Workshops and seminars.** The book is ideal for a workshop or seminar. It can also be effective as a self-study reference.
- **Distance learning.** Copies of the book can be sent to those unable to attend head office training sessions. It is ideal for organisations that have a number of remote branches.
- **Informal study groups.** Thanks to the format, brevity and low cost, this book is ideal for lunch-time seminars or other informal group sessions.

There are other possibilities that depend on the objectives, programme or ideas or the user. As you will soon learn, it is a hands-on approach to learning the basics of supervision.

To the Reader

Congratulations on becoming a supervisor. In approximately 50 minutes you will know many secrets of good supervision. What you learn, and any positive changes you make in your behaviour, are far more important than the time it takes to finish, so please *do not read so fast that you miss something.*

To benefit fully, be honest, especially when you rate yourself on factors such as attitude and self-confidence. It is not what you are now, but what you can become as a successful supervisor that will help you to progress in your organisation.

CHAPTER 1
Developing a Managerial Attitude

Your attitude to being a supervisor

Attitude is the way you look at things *mentally*. You have the power to look at your new position in any way you wish. If you look at it in a positive, enthusiastic manner you will communicate to your employees that you are ready to accept your new responsibility and they will enjoy working for you. If you are tentative or insecure they may interpret your attitude as negative and you may receive less cooperation.

As a new supervisor, you will be watched by everyone and no matter what you may do to hide it, your attitude will show.

If you have not already done so, now is an ideal time to read a book entitled *How to Develop a Positive Attitude* (Kogan Page). This simple publication will provide the human relations foundation you need to become a superior supervisor.

To measure your attitude, complete this exercise. Read each statement and circle the number where you feel you belong. If you circle a 5, you are saying your attitude could not be better in this area; if you circle a 1, you are saying supervision may not be for you.

	Agree			*Disagree*	
I seek responsibility.	5	4	3	2	1
Becoming a respected supervisor is important to me.	5	4	3	2	1
I enjoy helping others do a good job.	5	4	3	2	1

I want to know more about human behaviour.	5	4	3	2	1
I want to climb the management ladder.	5	4	3	2	1
I am anxious to learn and master supervisory skills.	5	4	3	2	1
I like leadership situations.	5	4	3	2	1
Working with a problem employee would be an interesting challenge.	5	4	3	2	1
I intend to devote time to learning motivational skills.	5	4	3	2	1
I'm excited about the opportunity to become a supervisor.	5	4	3	2	1

TOTAL ☐

If you scored above 40, you have an excellent attitude to becoming a supervisor. If you rated yourself between 25 and 40, it would appear you have a few reservations. A rating under 25 indicates you probably should not pursue becoming a supervisor.

Attitude and productivity

Nothing will improve relationships with those you supervise more than a consistently positive attitude. *Your* attitude sets the pace and the tone in your department. If you are late arriving at work, it will be reflected in the attitudes of your staff; if you discuss the negative aspects of your organisation with employees, your comments will eventually be reflected in their attitudes. *Every thing you do and every position you take will be reflected in the attitudes of your employees.*

1. Attitudes are caught, not taught!
2. Your attitude speaks so loudly, employees can't hear what you say.

There is a direct relationship between your attitude and the productivity of those you supervise. When you are upbeat, your employees will respond in positive ways that will enhance productivity. When you are negative, a drop in productivity can be expected.

Productivity gaps

In the diagram below, you will notice that there is a gap between what a hypothetical *department* is producing and what it *could* produce. We call this a departmental productivity gap. You will also notice there is a gap between what the *employees* are producing and what they *could* produce. Such gaps are normal and to be expected.

So how do you close the departmental productivity gap? The answer is to build such good relationships with your employees that they are motivated to close their individual productivity gaps. Of course, as a working supervisor, what you produce yourself is important. But it is the sum total of all producers that narrows the departmental gap, not what you can do yourself.

All successful managers will tell you that it is what others produce for you that makes the difference. It is a lesson some first-time supervisors fail to learn.

The challenge ahead

Supervision is a special challenge that can help you to reach new career and lifestyle goals. But becoming a successful manager is not as easy as some people imagine. Three factors will require you to be a different kind of person on the job.

1. Those in your department will expect you to lead where in the past you have been, like them, a follower. This means they will be watching your actions in the hope that you will make quick and good decisions that will lead the department in the direction that is best for the organisation.
2. Your new role will put you in the position of being a buffer between your superiors and those you supervise. This means you must satisfy your superiors and, at the same time, keep

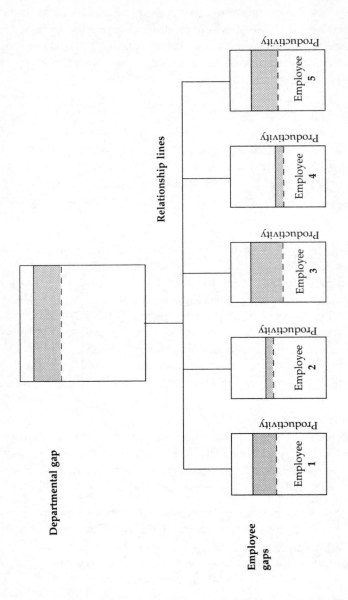

your employees happy so they will maintain high productivity. At times this may mean it is best for you to absorb pressure from above rather than pass it on to your employees.

3. You will be setting standards rather than living up to those set by others. This means you will be responsible for creating a disciplined environment where employees do not violate company standards or those set by you. When violations occur, some sensitive counselling on your part may be necessary.

All of this should be accepted as a challenge that will help you to grow into a stronger person. And, of course, there are special rewards, as listed on the next page.

What can success as a supervisor do for you?

Many good things can happen to you once you become a successful supervisor. Ten statements are listed below. Three are false. Tick the square opposite the false statements and match your answers with those on page 17.

As a supervisor you will:

- ☐ 1. Increase your earnings potential.
- ☐ 2. Have opportunities to learn more.
- ☐ 3. Develop an ulcer.
- ☐ 4. Position yourself for promotion to higher management.
- ☐ 5. Have less freedom.
- ☐ 6. Increase your self-confidence.
- ☐ 7. Try out your leadership wings.
- ☐ 8. Have fewer friends.
- ☐ 9. Learn and develop human relations skills.
- ☐ 10. Have better feelings of self worth.

As you contemplate making your transition into a supervisory role, it is often a good idea to model your behaviour on a successful supervisor you respect.

You will discover that highly successful supervisors have much in common. If the opportunity presents itself, discuss some of the characteristics and principles of good supervision with your manager. Some of these characteristics are presented below.

Make your choice now

Successful supervisors
Supervisors who remain positive under stress.

Those who take time to teach employees what they know.

Those who build and maintain mutually rewarding relationships with their employees.

Supervisors who learn to set reasonable and consistent authority lines.

Those who learn to delegate.

Those who establish standards of high quality and set good examples.

Individuals who work hard to become good communicators.

Leaders who build team effort to achieve high productivity.

Add your own:

_____

_____

_____

Failures
Supervisors who permit problems to get them down.

Those who rush instructionss to employees and then fail to follow up.

Individuals insensitive to employee needs.

Those not interested in learning the basic supervisory skills.

Those who fail to understand it is not what a supervisor can do but what supervisors can get others to accomplish that is important.

Supervisors who let their status go to their heads.

Those who become either too authoritarian or too lax.

Add your own:

_____

_____

_____

_____

_____

_____

False statements on page 15
3. There is no evidence that supervisors have more ulcers than non-supervisors.
5. Supervisors normally have more freedom because they control their actions more than employees do.
8. Good supervisors develop new friends and keep the old ones.

As an employee, you have had the opportunity to study mistakes supervisors make. List three you do not intend to make.

1. _____

2. _____

3. _____

Along with a positive attitude, it takes personal confidence to become a successful supervisor. When you first start out, like others, you may not have *all* the confidence you would like, but *do not lose faith in yourself.* As a supervisor, you will slowly build your level of personal confidence. That is one of the advantages of becoming a supervisor in the first place.

As you work on this goal, keep in mind that you need not be a highly verbal extrovert to be successful. Quiet, sensitive people become excellent supervisors even though they may not show their personal confidence on the outside.

You have the 'right stuff' or your superiors would not have given you the opportunity to become a supervisor in the first place. In management circles, the 'potted plant' theory is often expressed. Sometimes, like a plant that is root-bound in a pot too small to permit growth, an employee outgrows his or her position and only through a promotion into greater responsibilities (larger pot) can growth continue. This may be the best way to view your move into a supervisory role.

Self-confidence scale

This exercise is designed to help you discover your level of self-confidence. Read the statement and circle the number where you feel you belong.

	Agree				*Disagree*
I'm not easily intimidated.	5	4	3	2	1
Complex problems do not overwhelm me.	5	4	3	2	1

If necessary, I can discipline those who require it.	5	4	3	2	1
I can make a decision and stick to it.	5	4	3	2	1
I am strong enough to defend a deserving employee with a superior.	5	4	3	2	1
I have enough confidence to be a good teacher.	5	4	3	2	1
Speaking in public does not frighten me.	5	4	3	2	1
Superiors are basically people like me.	5	4	3	2	1
I won't avoid confrontations, when required.	5	4	3	2	1
I can say 'No' when necessary.	5	4	3	2	1

TOTAL ☐

If you scored 40 or above on both attitude and self-confidence, you have a winning combination as far as being a successful supervisor is concerned. If you scored lower on self-confidence than attitude, it is a signal that you need to learn to take a firmer stand on those items relating to supervision.

Case 1
Who will survive?

A case study is designed to provide insights you may not possess. Five problems are included in this book. Please give them your careful attention.

The case below will help you to understand some of the things involved in making the transition to a successful supervisor. You can benefit from expressing your views and comparing them with those of the author.

Assume that Joe and Mary are equally qualified to take on the role of supervisor in the same department. Further assume that they adopt different attitudes towards their new challenge. Which one, in your opinion, stands the best chance of surviving after six months?

Joe received news of his promotion by throwing a party for his close friends. Although he received two weeks' advance notice, he did little to prepare for the new assignment. Joe reckoned he had worked under enough supervisors to know what to do. He would model his behaviour on what he had learned from observation. Why bother to study techniques and principles in advance? Why get stressed needlessly by too much preparation? Joe believes that personality and good common sense are all that is needed.

His only strategy will be to set a good example by personally working hard, staying close to the group and doing a lot of listening. Joe has complete confidence in his ability to succeed.

Mary was delighted with the announcement of her promotion. She decided to use the two-week period to prepare for her new responsibilities. She quickly found some good books on supervision and started to make a list of recommended techniques to follow. How to demonstrate authority? When to delegate? What changes in behaviour would be required etc? Mary accepted the premiss that she had much to learn about becoming a successful supervisor. Although she believes in herself, she does not have Joe's level of confidence.

Mary has decided on the following strategy. Although she intends to remain friendly, she will slowly pull back from too much personal contact with former fellow-employees. She feels this will be necessary to demonstrate her authority. Next she will concentrate on creating a good working environment so that workers are more relaxed. Everything will be planned and orderly. Everyone will know where they stand and what is expected.

Which individual has the best chance of survival? Will Joe with his outgoing, confident approach do a better job than Mary with her more scientific attitude? Or will Mary, with her less confident but more deliberate strategy, overtake Joe? Tick the appropriate box below and compare your decision with that of the author on page 55.

☐   Joe will survive.

☐   Mary will survive.

☐   Both Joe and Mary will survive.

Supervisors are 'in-charge' people. As leaders, they use their sources of power in sensitive but effective ways. When you assume your role as a supervisor–leader, you have three sources of power to tap:

First, you have 'knowledge power' because of what you know about the department you lead. In most cases, you *know* more than those who work for you. When you teach them what you know, you make the best use of your 'knowledge power'.

Second, you gain power from the role you occupy. Just being the supervisor gives you authority which you must use gently and wisely.

Third, you have 'personality power'. You can persuade or motivate others through your positive attitude, friendly manner, patience and other personal characteristics.

Although you must be sensitive in the way you use your power (do not let your new position go to your head), properly used, the three sources of power can help you to become the kind of supervisor you want to be.

Convert to a stronger image

It is important that a new supervisor learns to communicate a 'take charge' image. She or he must let everyone know (co-workers and superiors) that things are under control – that decisions are being made and that the role of supervisor is comfortable. All this must be accomplished without giving an impression that the new position has gone to the individual's head. It must be a natural transition.

Why is a stronger image necessary? Among other reasons, your employees want you to be a leader. They will produce more if they know they are part of a cohesive group with established standards. In contrast, a weak supervisor will cause employees to be confused and unproductive.

How do you communicate a stronger image? Here are some suggestions. Tick the square if you agree.

☐ *Improve your appearance.* Don't overdo it but look the part. Dress for success.

☐ *Make firm decisions.* In making decisions, do it with confidence. Demonstrate you can handle decision-making.

☐ *Set a faster tempo.* Move about with more energy. Become a model of productivity.

☐ *Handle mistakes calmly.* When things go wrong, collect the facts, and develop a solution. Show your inner strength.

☐ *Share humorous incidents.* Balance your authority with a sense of humour. Help everyone to have a little fun.

☐ *Demonstrate your ability to communicate with superiors.* Employees will feel more secure and produce more when they know you can represent them.

☐ *Be a positive person.* Stay in touch with members of your team in a positive manner. Keep in mind that their positive attitudes are dependent upon yours.

Above all, be organised!

Some individuals fail in the role of supervisor because they are poor organisers. Some are unable to organise themselves or their departments. They move from one activity to another without a plan. They assign work on a haphazard basis without giving employees a chance to finish one assignment before a second is due.

Result?
Employees feel frustrated, insecure and they do not live up to their productivity potentials.

The answer?
As a start, it is vital to set daily goals as outlined below.

Set daily goals

Planning is simply the thinking that precedes doing. Planning means setting goals and objectives for yourself and your employees that support larger organisation goals received from above. Most employees respond to properly articulated, achievable departmental goals in a positive way. This is especially true when employees have been involved in the goal-setting process and participate in the excitement when objectives are reached.

Before you became a supervisor, the chances are that you could do your job without much serious planning. You basically react and adjust to goals that have already been agreed. Your supervisor probably gave them to you. As a supervisor, it is essential that you have a daily plan that can be reviewed and implemented *before* the working day begins.

Supervisors are always planning. Planning goes with the territory. Most successful supervisors operate with a daily checklist. The smart ones:

- Keep a list of 'to do' projects that is prioritised.
- Use a star or other symbol to designate projects with the highest priority.
- Write daily goals in their personal notebooks, planners or desk diary.
- Enjoy the process of drawing a line through goals as they are reached.
- Recognise and reward others who help to reach significant departmental goals.

Use your own system! Select your own style! But supplement your long-term departmental objectives with daily goals. It will make you feel much better on your way home each day.

CHAPTER 2

Weaving Four Irreplaceable Fundamentals into Your Style

Establishing and maintaining fair, open, and healthy relationships with all employees is the key to good supervision. This includes the establishment of authority or a *discipline line*. This line is a well-defined, well-communicated set of behaviour standards that you expect all employees to maintain. It tells an employee what is expected and what is not permitted.

Most employees enjoy working in an environment that has high but achievable standards. They feel more secure about their jobs when their supervisor is an 'in-charge' person who does not permit one employee to 'get away' with recognised violations.

It is important to set a reasonable and *consistent* discipline line. As you learn to do this, keep in mind that there is nothing incompatible about showing compassion and maintaining high standards at the same time.

Demonstrate your authority and style

First you must demonstrate that you are in charge and know what you are doing. You need to establish a style of your own. As you do this, give your team time to adjust. You are more interested in long-term, sustainable productivity than immediate results that may not last. This means the establishment of a sound working relationship with your employees.

In making your transition, consider these tips:

1. Set high (but attainable) standards at the outset. The lower your standards at the beginning, the more difficult it will be to improve productivity later.

2. Make an effort to establish a good relationship with each individual employee as soon as practicable. This means working to get to know each employee personally and letting them know you care. It is not a sign of weakness to show understanding. You can be a sensitive supervisor and still be a disciplinarian.
3. Quickly counsel those who are not meeting your standards, so they have no doubts about what is expected.
4. Keep in mind that a few important standards (or rules) are better than a list of complicated directions. Do not be a 'picky' supervisor. Instead, set basic terms that all understand and can attain.

Nothing undermines your authority faster than playing favourites. Employees need to be treated equally – especially if some are personal friends.

It is not business as usual

In order to remain competitive in a difficult environment, most organisations are streamlining their operations. This often means:

- Fewer employees to meet the same or higher productivity standards.
- More on-the-job training to help employees reach higher personal productivity.
- Tighter schedules.

Achieving such goals throws more responsibility on the shoulders of front-line supervisors. In other words, supervisors are expected to operate in a leaner, more efficient way that will result in higher productivity. On top of this, higher levels of quality will also be expected.

Some people, especially executives, call this running a 'tight ship'. This does not mean that the demands on employees will be excessive. It does not mean that employees will become rebellious or unhappy. Just the opposite is often true because employees like to reach goals, perform efficiently and belong to an organisation that can win in tough times.

Are you prepared, as a supervisor, to accept this higher tempo of productivity? The exercise below will help you find out.

Tight ship exercise
This exercise is designed to start the process of deciding just how prepared you are to run a tight ship.

	Yes	No	Not sure
1. Can you keep strict control over your employees without stifling their self-motivation?	☐	☐	☐
2. Can you quickly spot and correct unacceptable behaviour in a subordinate without becoming upset yourself?	☐	☐	☐
3. Do you consider it a compliment when someone says you run a tight ship?	☐	☐	☐
4. Can you spot a problem in its infancy and make a correction before it grows into a major problem?	☐	☐	☐
5. Can you keep discipline among your employees without becoming heavy-handed?	☐	☐	☐
6. Can you prove that there is less employee theft in your department than there is in similar sections?	☐	☐	☐
7. Have you set up the right kind of financial reporting (systems) so you can spot trends quickly when corrections are easier?	☐	☐	☐
8. Do you enjoy spending time analysing financial reports?	☐	☐	☐

9. Can you approach a sensitive, problem–employee in such a way that she or he makes a behavioural change while respecting you for helping?

□ □ □

10. Can you run a tight ship without being so picky that employees consider you a fuddy-duddy instead of a good manager?

□ □ □

TOTAL □ □ □

Seven or more 'Yes' answers indicate you may have your operation under proper control. Seven or more 'No' or 'Not sure' answers suggests you may have problems running a lean, productive department.

Setting the right discipline line

As you become a supervisor you must draw a disciplinary line that employees understand. The establishment of a framework of values will allow your employees to operate securely. Supervisors must set disciplinary lines based upon their own special work environment and individual style.

Case 2
Which strategy should Henry use?

Although sensitive to the needs of fellow-workers, Henry has always set higher standards for himself. He is never late, seldom absent and, once on the job, all business. Henry attributes his work style to his upbringing and religious training. Henry is respected more by management than fellow employees.

Yesterday Henry was promoted to supervisor of his own department. When they informed him of the promotion, Henry's superiors said: 'You were selected because we think you can put some discipline back into the department. It won't be easy, but we have faith in you, Henry.

Last night Henry sat down and developed three different

strategies to consider. Which one would you recommend Henry to employ?

Strategy 1
Set a good example and give employees time to adjust to it.

Strategy 2
Call a departmental meeting and, in a low-key manner explain the mission you have been given by your superiors. Explain that the higher standards you will impose will not only protect their jobs in the future but will give them more pride in what they are doing now. Tell them you will be hard but fair.

Strategy 3
Do the same as strategy 2 but on an individual counselling basis. Call in each person and explain the changes that will be made and why.

Write out your answer below.

I would recommend Henry to employ strategy _____ for the following reasons:

_____

_____

_____

Compare your answer with that of the author on page 55.

The need to delegate

Delegating is the assignment of tasks and responsibilities to help employees make their best contribution to the overall productivity of your department. When you delegate you become a teacher. You tell an employee how to perform a new task effectively, show how it is done, and then ask that he or she demonstrate that the task has been learned. Delegating takes time, patience, and follow-up to ensure it is done correctly.

A supervisor must learn how to distribute tasks evenly, tap the special creativity of each individual and, when appropriate, rotate responsibilities among different employees. Proper delegation keeps employees motivated, increases productivity, and frees the supervisor for more important activities.

The contributions of others make you a good supervisor

After setting a fair, consistent disciplinary line, the next big lesson is that you cannot do all the work yourself. You must delegate, and allow others to have responsibility to complete tasks which meet the expectations of your organisation. This means that intelligent delegation is more important than the actual work you do yourself. Building good relationships with employees helps to motivate them to do the work. It is a great thing for employees to like you, but respect is more important. These tips will help you to meet the second challenge. Tick each square as you go through the list.

☐ Nothing builds respect better than demonstrating to employees that you know what you are doing. Knowledge gives you power, and when you share it, you earn respect. Teach those who work for you everything you know to help them become more efficient.

☐ Set a good example. It is smart to pitch in and work from time to time to demonstrate your competence. But don't overdo it. Your skills are more valuable as a supervisor than as a worker.

☐ Create a relaxed but efficient working climate. People make mistakes and produce less when supervision is too close and constant. People should be able to enjoy their work within your disciplinary line.

☐ Circulate and communicate. Give your employees every opportunity to do a good job and when they do, follow up with compliments. Give credit freely when it is due.

☐ Keep an 'open door' policy. That is, be accessible to employees. Welcome their suggestions and complaints. If you set a disciplinary line that is too tight you will destroy the environment employees need to produce at an optimum level.

When Molly was only 20 years old, she became an instant supervisor without training. Although she was capable, enthusiastic, and did many things well, instead of delegating work Molly tried to do too much herself. As a result, she became ill through overwork and decided that supervision was not for her. Later, at 25 (after taking a course in beginning management), Molly had a second opportunity to be a supervisor. Realising that she would be judged by what her staff did (productivity) more than what she did herself, she delegated as much as possible so she would have extra time to build good relationships, communicate, and plan. Today, at 35, Molly is a successful executive and still developing.

Quality delegation takes planning. You must analyse all the tasks that need to be performed – before you start the process. Haphazard delegation can do as much harm as good.

How to delegate: steps to take

A supervisor who learns to delegate effectively achieves two goals at the same time. First, more time is available to plan, organise and maintain relationships with other employees and co-workers. Second, employees become more versatile and valuable as they learn new tasks.

Below are ten typical steps in the delegating process. As you tick the list, assume you have been working overtime and need to hand over tasks you have been doing.

☐ **Step 1** Analyse your tasks and identify one you feel will provide you with additional freedom as well as benefiting the employee to whom you assign the responsibility.

☐ **Step 2**   Select the most logical individual for the task you identify and delegate it. Be careful not to overload one employee.

☐ **Step 3**   Instruct the individual selected how to perform the task. Do this in detail by both explaining and demonstrating. Explain why the task is important to the total operation.

☐ **Step 4**   Solicit feedback to ensure the employee is prepared to assume the new responsibility. Provide opportunities for the employee to ask questions.

☐ **Step 5**   Allow the employee you selected the freedom to practise the new assignment for a few days. Over-supervision can kill motivation.

☐ **Step 6**   Follow up in a positive manner. When it is deserved, compliment the employee. If improvements are required, go through the instructional process a second time.

☐ **Step 7**   Consider the rotation of tasks: employees learn more and boredom is less likely when this is done properly. Also, an objective productivity comparison is possible among employees.

☐ **Step 8**   Delegate those assignments which prepare employees to take over in the absence of others – including yourself.

☐ **Step 9**   Give everyone an opportunity to contribute. Solicit employee ideas. Use their special talents and abilities.

☐ **Step 10** Discuss new assignments and rotation plans with the entire group to obtain feedback and generate enthusiasm.

If you are a sports fan, you know the primary job of a coach is to build a cohesive team. When everyone works together the team is more likely to win. Personality conflicts can destroy a team.

They can also destroy productivity in a department. A supervisor is a coach. She or he must keep harmony among workers to ensure productivity and win the game. The best way to do this is through good communication and counselling.

Become an effective counsellor

Counselling is sitting down in a private setting for an open discussion with an employee. Sometimes it is to pay a sincere compliment; sometimes it is to solve a problem that is reducing productivity; sometimes it is because an employee has violated company discipline and you need give a warning. There are many counselling skills. One of the most important is being a good listener. This will help you to find the *real* problem, and then help the employee to make a mutually rewarding decision. There is no magic to good counselling. Anyone can do it.

We communicate on several levels from individual to large groups. We also communicate both formally and informally. When you become a supervisor, communication of all types, at all levels, takes on new importance.

Communicating one to one, in private, is counselling or interviewing. Once you become a supervisor you will discover that counselling is one of the best 'tools' you possess. Until you understand what counselling can do for you, it will be difficult to move to the next stage.

Below are ten situations. Seven call for counselling by the supervisor; three do not. Tick the three that require no counselling. Check your answers with those given on the next page.

- [ ] 1. An employee violates your standards.
- [ ] 2. An employee is consistently late or absent.
- [ ] 3. You disagree with an employee's lifestyle.
- [ ] 4. An employee's productivity is down.
- [ ] 5. One employee behaves in such a way that the productivity of others is reduced.

☐   6. You are upset.

☐   7. Two employees have a conflict that is becoming public.

☐   8. You dislike the personality of an employee.

☐   9. You want to compliment an individual.

☐ 10. You want to delegate a new task.

If productivity in a department drops, action needs to to taken quickly. Time will not normally solve problems that must be addressed. Often action can take the form of counselling – either individual or group, or both.

Answers to exercise 3, 6, 8

To be an effective supervisor you need to know how to *create* and maintain relationships with members of your staff. Good relationships are created when you:

● Provide clear, complete instructions.
● Let employees know how they are doing.
● Give credit when credit is due.
● Involve people in decisions.
● Remain accessible.

The best way to maintain a relationship is through frequent communication.

Case 3
Will MRT counselling work?

Kathy learned about MRT counselling last week. As she understands it, the idea is to sit down with a problem employee and discuss rewards she can provide for that employee, as well as rewards that employee can provide for her. The technique is based on the Mutual Reward Theory (MRT) which states that a relationship between two people can be enhanced when there is a satisfactory exchange of rewards between them. When the exchange is considered balanced, both parties will come out ahead.

Kathy has been having trouble with George for over a month. In desperation, she decides to call him into her office and discuss the situation to see if the Mutual Reward Theory can be applied. Her hope is that she can give him what he wants in exchange for a better attitude on his part.

Kathy starts the counselling session by complimenting George on his consistent productivity and asking him to suggest any rewards she is not providing that are within her capacity. She informs George that she will, in turn, suggest three rewards she would like to receive from him.

Here are George's suggestions:
1. More opportunity to learn.
2. More recognition.
3. Less supervision by Kathy.

Kathy in turn asks for the following:
1. Continued high productivity.
2. More cooperation with co-workers.
3. Less hostility towards herself.

George and Kathy spend 30 minutes discussing the rewards each wants and how the other could provide them. George admits that he could be more cooperative; Kathy admits that she can provide George with more opportunity to learn and they discuss a number of ways this can be accomplished.

Will this kind of MRT counselling work for Kathy? Will it permanently improve the relationship between Kathy and George? Write your answer in the space below and compare it with that of the author on page 55.

_____

_____

_____

View yourself as a coach

Counselling is when you help an employee to solve a personal problem that is lowering his or her productivity. In most cases problems are solved because you understand how to be a good listener. Employees often discuss solutions they did not know existed until someone listened to their problem and asked meaningful questions.

Coaching is when you help people to win as individuals so the department (team) can also win. You help your employees win when you:

- Teach them a new job or skill.
- Explain procedures, standards, strategies and the rules of the game.
- Help them adjust to changes.
- Enhance their careers.

When you do an excellent job as a coach or teacher, the following benefits occur:

- You build your reputation as a people developer.
- The increased departmental productivity pleases your superiors.
- It becomes easier for you to delegate.
- You get more freedom to make significant decisions.

It is through good coaching techniques that winning teams are developed on athletic fields and in business offices. Many people claim that it is smart for a new supervisor to use her or his favourite coach as a model to develop a productivity team in the workplace.

Case 4
Can Sylvia keep her job as a supervisor?

Sylvia, without realising it, has been spending too much time on budget and administrative reports and not enough time communicating with her ten employees. As a result, morale is low, productivity is down and two good employees are thinking about submitting their resignations. Everyone feels frustrated and unappreciated.

The situation is so bad that Sylvia's boss called her into his office and informed her: 'Sylvia, you have committed a cardinal sin by neglecting your employees in favour of other responsibilities. Instead of delegating some of your work in order to free yourself, you locked yourself into your office and allowed things to fall apart outside. You could have great potential as a manager, but not until you learn to balance people activities with job tasks. You cannot have high productivity with low communication. All your employees feel you have been taking them for granted. A few have even talked to me about it. Your job as supervisor is in jeopardy. Be in my office at ten o'clock tomorrow with a plan to restore morale and productivity within ten days.'

What are Sylvia's chances of coming up with a plan that will turn things around?

Tick the appropriate box below and write out the reasons for your choice.

☐	☐	☐	☐
Excellent	Good	Long shot	Too late

_____

_____

_____

Turn to page 56 to compare your answer with the author's.

To be highly effective as a supervisor you will want to put more leadership into your style. Everyone likes to work for a supervisor who keeps them motivated and headed in the right direction. Just as football players build loyalty towards coaches that lead them to victory, employees like supervisors who lead them to greater achievements.

Leadership means stepping out in front of others with new,

workable ideas that save money and create greater productivity. Leadership means creating *followers* – employees who respect you to the point that they would like to follow you when you earn your next promotion. Becoming a supervisor is the best possible way to learn and practise leadership skills.

Become a good leader

Your job as a supervisor is to establish departmental goals and then lead your people to achieve them. Keeping good records and ensuring that everyone stays busy is more management than leadership. Another way of saying it is that managing is the protection of what is already in place. Leadership, on the other hand, is reaching for new heights. Managers keep things the way they are to avoid trouble. Leaders take prudent risks to gain greater productivity. *You want to be a good manager, but you also want to be a leader.*

To become both – and get home safely – consider these tips:

First, be a good manager. Ensure that your operation is conforming to your organisation's standards. Watch details. Get reports in on time. Achieve the good feeling that comes from having everything under control.

Next, become a positive influence. Set new goals and motivate others to reach them. Stay positive. Keep things stirred up. Don't permit employees to become bored.

Help your people to reach their goals. Help them feel better about themselves. Provide the rewards and recognition they deserve. The better they feel about themselves, the more they will produce.

Now and then establish your authority. Employees need to be reminded that a discipline line exists. One way to demonstrate your authority is to make firm, difficult decisions. Another is to counsel disruptive employees and expect continued improvements in productivity.

Share good news. Keep the bad news in perspective. Look for positive things to talk about, including individual and group achievements. Make everyone feel that they are on a winning team.

Leadership characteristics

As you view yourself as a manager/leader, keep in mind that most leaders develop these characteristics. Tick those that you feel you already possess.

- ☐ Communicate a sense of being in charge.
- ☐ Convert employees into followers.
- ☐ Strong track record on decision making.
- ☐ Prudent risk takers.
- ☐ Articulate an inspiring mission.
- ☐ Generate a feeling of pride in followers.
- ☐ Create active tempo.
- ☐ Highly energetic.
- ☐ Stand firm on principle.
- ☐ Turn a department into a team.

Leaders build winning teams

Excellent managers in all types of organisation often seem content with their group performance without trying to turn their group into a team. This may occur because they are satisfied with current productivity or have not considered what *could* be accomplished with a team approach. They refuse to accept that other managers doing similar tasks with the same technology are able to increase productivity by establishing a climate where people reach closer to their potentials and consider themselves as part of a team.

Team building is a little like football. The leader (coach) has the responsibility of selecting players, coordinating efforts, and, where possible, winning the game.

- Players must be committed to helping the team.
- Communication, trust and mutual support are essential.

- A reward system must be established.
- A game plan must be accepted.

Establish a productivity goal

'Management by objectives' is a system whereby supervisors submit their goals to higher management to be integrated with the organisation's goals. Supervisors are rewarded when their goals are achieved or surpassed.

Your organisation may not use this approach. If it does not, create your own goals (plans) on a weekly, monthly and annual basis.

Those who set goals are usually more motivated to reach them. Even if management does not know about your goals (and consequently does not hold you accountable for reaching them) you will benefit from having them.

Most people are goal-oriented. They like to be headed in a positive direction that will provide satisfaction.

Provide direction!

Everybody likes to be on a winning team. In your organisation, your department is a team which can win only if it reaches predetermined goals. *It is your responsibility as supervisor to help establish such goals and then motivate your people to reach them.*

Below are ten suggestions on how to motivate employees to reach a goal. Three are unacceptable because they will probably do more harm than good. Tick the squares opposite those that are counter-productive, and then compare your answers with those on page 40.

☐   1. Involve employees in setting goals.

☐   2. Make it easy for employees to motivate themselves by creating a relaxed and predictable working climate.

☐   3. At meetings, lay down the law. Tell everyone you are the boss, and things are to be done your way.

☐   4. Give employees credit when it is earned.

☐ 5. Circulate regularly and listen in order to discover the kind of rewards you can provide to improve productivity.

☐ 6. Act disappointed with everyone's performance as a method to get people to work harder.

☐ 7. Ask for suggestions from employees on how productivity can be improved.

☐ 8. Tell everyone that unless productivity improves their jobs are on the line.

☐ 9. Have a positive counselling session with each employee on a regular basis. Listen to complaints and, when possible, make adjustments to resolve the issue.

☐ 10. Through your own positive attitude create a more lively and happy work environment.

It is important that each member of a team shares in success. Communication is the only way this can happen.

Answers to exercise 3, 6, 8

CHAPTER 3
Dealing With Special Problems

Eliminating personal down periods

It is not always easy to be positive. The responsibilities of being a supervisor are often great and they can, without your realising it, turn you negative. The truth is, when you are positive, productivity is up; but when you become negative, productivity drops. So your challenge is to remain positive even if those around you are not.

The exercise below assumes three things: (1) You are generally a positive, outgoing person. (2) There are certain things you can do to remain positive. (3) Being aware of these activities will assist you in the elimination of 'down periods'. After reading the list, select the three that will do the most for you.

- ☐ Engage in physical exercise of some sort.
- ☐ Give yourself more attainable goals.
- ☐ Try to take life less seriously.
- ☐ Share your positive attitude with others.
- ☐ Take more week-end or 'mini' vacations.
- ☐ Maintain a better balance between work and leisure.
- ☐ Improve your grooming.
- ☐ Do more to help others.
- ☐ Talk with a more experienced manager you respect to find a way to eliminate down periods.

Others:

_____

_____

_____

Danger ahead

Gilbert is an outstanding producer, but he has a short fuse that often gets him into trouble. Maria is an excellent member of the department, but now and then she has a down period that requires great tolerance from her supervisor and co-workers. Craig is too chummy with all his co-workers but becomes upset when they prefer to not include him in their activities.

Q. With such characteristics, can Gilbert, Maria and Craig become successful supervisors?

A. Yes, but only if they can break those habits described above.

It is possible to tolerate such behaviour in an employee but it could spell disaster should the same behaviour surface in a supervisor.

After you hold down your job as a supervisor for about three months, you will start to feel comfortable with your new role. However, you may need to change some habits before this happens.

If you are prone to make any of the mistakes listed below, start to make corrections immediately or you will have trouble as a supervisor.

Six unforgivable mistakes

1. Treating individuals unequally because of sex, culture, age, educational background etc. Each employee is unique and should receive the same consideration as any other.
2. Not keeping trust with an employee. The fastest way to destroy a relationship is to make a promise and then break it.
3. Blowing hot and cold. Consistency is essential when manag-

ing. If you are positive one day and down the next, employees will not know how to react. Respect will disappear.

4. Failure to follow basic company policies and procedures. As a line supervisor, you must handle your relationship with each employee in a fair and legal manner. This may mean, for example, establishment of an 'improvement plan' before you ask for approval to terminate an employee's appointment.

5. Losing your composure in front of others. Everyone reaches their threshold of tolerance on occasion but, as a supervisor, you need to keep your temper in check. Blowing up can destroy relationships.

6. Engaging in a personal relationship with someone you supervise. When you become a supervisor, you change your role. It is not possible to be in charge of a person during the day and personally involved with them after work.

As concisely as possible, in your own words, write the six unforgivable mistakes in the spaces below.

1. _____

2. _____

3. _____

4. _____

5. _____

6. _____

Transition tips

● Stay warm and friendly but slowly back away. You can't be too friendly *and* a supervisor at the same time.

- Do not permit those who were co-workers yesterday to intimidate you today. If you play favourites you are in trouble.
- Do what you can to make everyone's job better than it was before you became supervisor. Do not make the same mistakes your boss made when you were an employee.
- Demonstrate to your previous colleagues that you are knowledgeable by teaching them in a sensitive manner new skills that will make their jobs easier.
- Seek more assistance from your superior in making your transition. Ask for suggestions. Be a good listener.
- Give previous colleagues credit when it is due.

Provide reinforcement

Employees like to know how they are doing. Take a few minutes every now and then to let your people know you appreciate their dependability and the contribution they are making. Many capable employees resign because superiors take them for granted.

You are only as good as the people who work for you. Make sure your employees regularly receive the reinforcement they need.

All supervisors must occasionally deal with a difficult employee. Some employees are consistently late or absent from work – others create false rumours that affect the productivity of workers; still others fail to follow safety rules or make mistakes that need to be corrected. In extreme cases, problem employees carry hostility towards another employee or his or her supervisor.

How you deal with such employees and convert them into 'team members' is a critical part of your job. The following suggestions are designed to provide you with the help you may need.

Reacting to the problem employee

Below are ten ways to react to an employee who is demanding, hostile and disruptive. Three are acceptable forms of behaviour. Tick the box opposite those you feel are appropriate behaviour for a supervisor, then match your answers with those further down the page. Remember, we are talking about your initial reaction – not action that might be taken later.

☐ 1. Stay cool. Let the employee express anger without an immediate reaction on your part.

☐ 2. Let the employee know that you consider him or her to be a problem.

☐ 3. Challenge the employee with a firm countenance.

☐ 4. Consider the employee as objectively as possible and refuse to take things personally.

☐ 5. Avoid the problem. Time will solve it.

☐ 6. Become distant and non-communicative.

☐ 7. Challenge the employee to stop giving you a problem.

☐ 8. Act uninterested and ignore the situation.

☐ 9. Get angry and give back the kind of behaviour you receive.

☐ 10. In a calm manner say: 'Let's talk in my office.'

Firm, friendly, and fair are the key words in maintaining your discipline line. But when a difficult situation arises, it is time to use your counselling skills.

Answers to exercise 1, 4, 10

Throughout this book you have learned that becoming a successful supervisor is a combination of many personal characteristics (positive attitude, personal confidence, patience etc) and the application of many tested skills and techniques (delegating, counselling, restoring relationships etc).

CAN YOU PUT ALL THESE REQUIREMENTS TOGETHER?

Of course you can – especially if you don't try to do everything at once! Keep in mind that, after all is said and done, the key to your success as a supervisor is how well you achieve improved productivity.

If your department is regularly noted for higher productivity than similar departments, your superiors will recognise this and you will be in a good position for future advancement.

Achieving greater productivity is a *human challenge*. As a supervisor, it is not what you can accomplish by doing tasks yourself but the quality of the working relationships you build with the people *who do the work for you*.

Develop your human skills

As an employee, your productivity was measured and compared with your co-workers'. Your superior normally did this through some kind of formal appraisal. Your promotion may have depended on these appraisals.

When you become a supervisor, you are measured by the productivity of your department or section. This means your future depends on how well your team performs. If you employ the human skills which motivate your staff to produce more, you will be recognised for doing a good job. If the opposite happens, your job may be in jeopardy.

It helps to contribute to productivity by doing a small amount of work yourself. This also helps to set the work pace. If you do too much yourself, however, your people may not get the supervision which will allow them to produce more.

To test your understanding, answer the following true and false questions. The correct answers are given below.

True   False

_____ _____ 1. Nothing should receive higher priority than helping an employee to reach his or her productivity potential.

_____ _____ 2. A drop in productivity by a reliable employee need not be dealt with immediately as it might cause resentment.

_____ _____ 3. Employees will often produce more for one supervisor than for another.

_____ _____ 4. A disruptive employee who reduces the productivity of co-workers must be dealt with immediately.

_____ _____ 5. Some employees with modest personal productivity can help the productivity of others so much that they are highly regarded by supervisors.

_____ _____ 6. Most employees have higher productivity potential than they realise.

_____ _____ 7. Generally speaking, the more employees produce, the better they feel about themselves.

_____ _____ 8. Human skills are easier to learn than technical skills.

_____ _____ 9. A smart thinking supervisor can do less personally and still have the highest producing department.

_____ _____ 10. A 'golden' employee is one who produces at a high level and, also, contributes measurably to the productivity of co-workers.

Answers to exercise:
1. T, 2. F, 3. T, 4. T, 5. T, 6. T, 7. T, 8. F, 9. T, 10. T

Keeping superiors happy

When you become a supervisor it is important not only to keep your employees happy and productive, it is also important to make sure that good relationships are maintained with your superiors. As mentioned earlier, you are the 'buffer' and must be concerned with relationships in both directions.

Here are three suggestions to assist you in developing and maintaining a healthy, open relationship with _your_ boss.

1. Tie your departmental goals to those of the firm as a whole. This means listening to changes that come down from above and bringing your section into line. Just as there are problem employees, there are problem supervisors. Don't be one.

2. Keep your superior informed. Share the good news (it is a good idea to have your superior compliment one of your deserving employees now and then) and openly admit any misjudgements you may have made.
3. Be a good team member. As a supervisor, you will need to build good relationships with supervisors and management other than your immediate boss. In doing this, see that your superior is placed in the best possible light with others. Do this even though she or he may not give you all the recognition you feel you deserve.

Case 5
Between a rock and a hard place

Grace did so well as a first-time supervisor for her departmental store that they invited her to attend an all-day management workshop. When she showed up for work the following day her superior, Mr Adams, called her into his office and questioned her harshly about the behaviour of her employees. Knowing Grace was absent, Mr Adams had dropped by her department at closing time and found her employees playing catch with some merchandise and laughing loudly. Grace, feeling let down by her staff, told Mr Adams it would not happen again and on the following day came down hard on everyone at an informal staff meeting. Then, after checking the sales figures, Grace discovered her group had such a great sales day – an all time record in fact – that they were simply celebrating their success. Mr Adams had misinterpreted their behaviour.

How, in your opinion, should Grace handle the situation? Write your answer below and compare with that of the author on page 56.

Repairing relationships

In becoming a successful supervisor, you will make your share of human relations mistakes. This is inevitable because your personnel responsibilities will be different. You will be exploring new human relations territory.

If you permit these mistakes to go unattended you may turn

out to be the victim. This can happen when employees become offended and cut back on their personal productivity, start rumours, etc. You did not intend to damage a relationship, but you become the victim anyway. To avoid this, you may wish to consider the following:

1. Apologise by saying you are still learning the ropes.
2. Engage in some personal counselling with the injured parties so that they can bring anything bothering them out in the open. Communication is not only the best way to restore a relationship, often it is the only way.
3. Without showing any favouritism, do something special to send the injured employee a signal that you know you made a mistake and that it won't happen again.

Problem-solving techniques

Many qualified workers refuse opportunities to become supervisors because they do not want to face the problem-solving responsibilities that go with the job. Some of these individuals are not aware that there are proven techniques to help them make good decisions. These skills can be learned.

For example, it is helpful to divide problems into four classifications:

1. Small, people-centred problems. Little requests that a supervisor can handle quickly according to acceptable practices. Sometimes, even making an exception to the rule.
2. Major, people-centred problems. An employee is hostile, refuses to be a part of the team, and is a negative influence on the productivity of others. Counselling and coaching come into play. Considerable time may be involved.
3. Small, job-centred problems. Little adjustments that need to be made to equipment, layout or processes. Minimum time and effort required.
4. Major, job-centred problems. Solving these problems requires time and a procedure. (1) Recognise the problem. (2) Gather data. (3) Analyse. (4) Discuss with others. (5) List options. (6) Make decision. (7) Follow up.

When a supervisor has a cool head, takes time to size up and classify a problem, and then makes a decision based on the impact the decision will have on productivity, he or she will develop a good decision-making track record.

The staffing challenge

As a manager, you may or may not be deeply involved in the staffing process. Some managers have complete control over who is hired or transferred into their departments. Others must select from those sent by the human resources department. Often they have refusal powers only.

Staffing includes much more than simply filling a vacancy with the best available individual. It also involves determining long-term personnel needs, induction and training, transfers and reassignments, rotation, performance evaluation and terminations. The moment a vacancy or personnel change is in the offing, experienced managers ask themselves these questions:

- Is the function performed by the departing employee absolutely necessary?
- Could the tasks be divided among other employees?
- What skills are missing among the staff that a new employee could provide?
- What kind of person will contribute most to greater productiity?
- Is someone being trained to eventually take my job?

The goal of every manager should be to recruit, develop and maintain the most cohesive and productive staff possible. Sex, race, age or handicaps cannot play a part in the selective process. The practice of first come, first hired should be avoided. Screening written applications and interviewing should be done studiously.

Pulling together

When you think of an outstanding coach you think of someone who designs strategies so the team can win. Excellent supervisors can develop strategies. They devise plans that keep productivity at the highest possible level. To make the plan work, each member of the team must produce near his or her potential. When everyone contributes, everyone wins.

So coaches (and supervisors) motivate their players to live up to their expectations and take pride in their achievements. In doing this, they:

- Maintain a sense of humour.
- Communicate and encourage involvement in the 'game plan' of the day, week or month.
- Seek a commitment to quality and performance from each individual.
- Provide support for each player, even when performance is not up to expectations.
- See that all players are rewarded, even though special recognition is given to one or two team members for unusual performance.

Someone once explained that a *group* is composed of people who try to push a giant rock through uncoordinated, individual effort. The rock seldom moves. A *team* is composed of individuals who have a single goal and coordinate their efforts to achieve it. They push together and the rock quickly moves in the right direction.

In the middle of any successful team is an individual who orchestrates the efforts of each individual. This individual can be called a coach or a leader. The most common name, however, is that of a supervisor.

It is important to remember that individuals who become good first-time supervisors become candidates for middle and upper management positions. Those who demonstrate their skills in the minor leagues (supervision) are often promoted to the major leagues. In supervision, as in football, it is extremely important to get started on the right foot. If you weave the strategies and techniques of this book into your behaviour patterns, you will be preparing yourself for a higher-paying, more challenging management role. Do not make the mistake of saying to yourself that excellent supervision is simply common sense. It is much more than that. That is why you should regularly review the skills you are learning so that you know and practise all the competences required to win the management game.

Demonstrate your progress

For each statement below, put a tick under true or false.

True   False

____ ____ 1. Negotiation is not a management function.

____ ____ 2. *The First Time Supervisor* should be considered as the first phase of a more extended supervisory training programme.

____ ____ 3. One way to become a successful supervisor is to do more of the actual work yourself.

____ ____ 4. Supervisors have less freedom than those they supervise.

____ ____ 5. Behavioural changes are not necessary for most people to become good supervisors.

____ ____ 6. Supervisors need not communicate a strong image.

____ ____ 7. You make a good start when you establish and maintain a fair and consistent discipline line.

____ ____ 8. Popularity is more important to the new supervisor than earning respect.

____ ____ 9. In setting a disciplinary line, it is better to start easy and get tough later.

____ ____ 10. It is easier to become a good supervisor when you are promoted within the same department.

____ ____ 11. Most supervisors are good at delegating.

____ ____ 12. Intelligent delegating takes too much time to be worthwhile.

____ ____ 13. Supervisors should remonstrate only as a last resort.

____ ____ 14. Most supervisors are better at managing than leading.

—— —— 15. Supervisors who stay in the background and control with a firm hand are usually the most successful.

—— —— 16. Coaching and counselling are not important enough to be two of the four basics in the football analogy.

—— —— 17. Counselling is the best technique for working with a problem employee.

—— —— 18. Unlike employees, a supervisor does not have the luxury of reporting to work in a negative mood.

—— —— 19. Failure to keep a promise with an employee is not an unforgivable mistake.

—— —— 20. Supervisors cannot afford to show compassion for employees.

TOTAL   Turn the page for answers.

Preparing for Phase 2 of your management training

What you have learned from this book should be considered Phase 1 in an ongoing plan of personal growth into higher management levels. Think of it as a strategy to get you up and running on the right foot. Later, perhaps sooner than you think, you may have the opportunity to attend a Phase 2 seminar offered by your organisation. Or you can enrol in a management course at a local college on your own. One thing is certain, the progress you make in more sophisticated programmes will depend upon your success with Phase 1.

As you look ahead to your future in management, please keep the following in mind:

1. Nothing can take the place of a positive supervisory experience at the very beginning. Some individuals who get off to a bad start return to non-supervisory roles and never try again.

2. The more you apply the basic principles and simple techniques of this book the better your start will be.

3. Once you can handle the basics you will automatically become confident and gain insight into more difficult management problems.

Answers to exercise

1. F
2. T It is possible you will be able to attend management seminars at a later date.
3. F A supervisor should *supervise*, not do actual work all the time.
4. F Supervisors have more freedom, especially if they learn how to delegate.
5. F Many behavioural changes are usually necessary.
6. F A stronger image is necessary but, of course, it should not be introduced too quickly or overdone.
7. T (See page 27.)
8. F
9. F Just the opposite; start out with a firm but fair line and relax to the proper point later.
10. F Just the opposite.
11. F
12. F It takes time at the beginning but releases time in the future.
13. F Counselling is a tool that can be used daily.
14. T
15. F Constant communication through circulation is required.
16. F Coaching and counselling constitute a basic supervisory tool.
17. T
18. T If the supervisor is down the entire team may be.
19. F
20. F There is nothing incompatible about being compassionate and still maintaining a strong, productive discipline line.

CHAPTER 4
Author's Suggested Answers to Cases

Case 1
Who will survive?

It is the opinion of the author that both Joe and Mary will survive, but the edge is with Mary. Joe will probably be better liked as a supervisor. Mary, however, will probably earn more respect. Joe ignores the fact that there are many sound techniques and principles every supervisor should learn. He will survive only if he learns them in time.

Case 2
Which strategy should Henry use?

The author favours strategy 2 but would also follow up the group session with individual counselling to avoid any misunderstandings and improve relationships. Henry should not expect 100 per cent compliance with his new standards quickly. He should, however, set his standards high enough to achieve the kind of productivity desired. Reachable standards are required, but employees should be given sufficient time to attain them. While doing this, Henry should also set a good example both as a supervisor and worker.

Case 3
Will MRT counselling work?

If both Kathy and George make a serious effort to provide one or more of the rewards wanted but not previously provided, the chances are excellent that the relationship will improve. MRT counselling frequently works because it opens up communication and both parties accept that there is something specific to do to make improvements. Care should be taken to announce in advance that there may be some rewards (such as an increase in pay) over which the supervisor does not have jurisdiction or complete control.

Case 4
Can Sylvia keep her job as a supervisor?

It is doubtful that Sylvia can turn things round. In fact, in similar situations, many experienced managers would transfer Sylvia to a non-supervisory position until she can demonstrate she is ready to assume the full responsibility of being a supervisor. Sylvia's boss is right in saying she committed a cardinal sin. The only way a supervisor can increase or maintain productivity is to establish and nurture good relationships with all employees. Once other activities take priority, morale begins to fall and trouble starts. Restoring relationships at this point is a long shot. Once relationships have deteriorated to a certain point, rebuilding them is almost impossible.

Case 5
Between a rock and a hard place

First Grace should go to Mr Adams and explain the reason for their behaviour and stand up for them and their high productivity. Second, she should tell her staff what happened at the meeting with Mr Adams. A supervisor's first responsibility is to stand up for his or her staff.

Further Reading from Kogan Page

Delegating for Results, Robert B Maddux, 1990
Effective Meeting Skills, Marion E Haynes, 1988
Don't Do, Delegate! The Secret Power of Successful Managers, James M
  Jenks and John M Kelly, 1986
A Handbook of Management Techniques, 2nd edition, Michael Arm-
  strong, 1993
How to Be an Even Better Manager, 3rd edition, Michael Armstrong,
  1990*
How to Communicate Effectively, Bert Decker, 1989*
How to Develop a Positive Attitude, Elwood N Chapman, 1988*
How to Make Meetings Work, Malcolm Peel, 1988
How to Motivate People, Twyla Dell, 1989*
Learning to Lead, Pat Heim and Elwood N Chapman, 1991
Project Management, Marion E Haynes, 1990

*Also available on cassette. Enquiries phone 071-278 0433.

C000132931

CHINA

BANGLADESH　**BURMA**

any as
)00 more are
ed dead in the
aman and
obar islands

Thousands are missing
from villages near such
popular coastal resort
areas as **Phuket**

Tsunamis are not tidal waves
because they are not
influenced by the
gravitational effect of
the moon. But their
appearance from
shore can be similar
to a rapidly rising or
falling tide, and the
severity of a
tsunami can be
affected by the
level of the
tide when the
waves hit
land

LAOS

EURASIAN PLATE

Andaman
and Nicobar
islands
(India)

ll Nadu　　*Bay of Bengal*

CAMBODIA　VIETNAM

Gulf of
Thailand

Extent of
earthquake

Banda
Aceh

Phuket

Colombo
Galle

*BURMA
PLATE*

Meulaboh

MALAYSIA

1 hour

2 hours

SINGAPORE

Borneo

dian Ocean

INDIAN PLATE

EARTHQUAKE EPICENTER

Sumatra

Java

Jakarta

AUSTRALIAN PLATE

I LANKA

namis lose their energy in shallow
er. The ocean off **Sri Lanka's**
stern coast is thousands of meters
ep just a few kilometers from
ore, so the tsunami hit with much
re force than it did in **Bangladesh,**
ere the shallow water extends
re than 160 km out to sea

INDONESIA

By far the highest death toll was
on the remote northern end of the
Indonesian island of **Sumatra,**
which suffered the double shock
of the quake and the earliest
strike of the tsunami. Tens of
thousands died in **Meulaboh** and
the provincial capital, **Banda Aceh**

Indicates locations of aftershocks

3 The waves spread in all
directions, moving as fast
as 800 km/h. In the deep
ocean, the waves may be
imperceptible, but they slow
down and gain height as
they hit **shallow water**
near shore

**Sudden movement
forces water up
and down**

The retreat of a tsunami
from land can be quick—
and just as dangerous
as its approach. The
waves often come
in a series

A GIANT JOLT

The Indian plate usually
moves northeast about
6 cm a year. Scientists
estimate that in last
week's quake, the
two plates slid about

In deep water tsunamis are very long,
shallow waves, which means they don't lose
much energy fighting gravity. Given enough
initial force, they will travel vast
distances until they are slowed
by resistance from the sea
floor near shore

Sources:
Vasily Titov,
National Oceanic and
Atmospheric Administration;
U.S. Geological Survey; AP;
Reuters; Globalsecurity.org;
University of Washington

TSUNAMI

TSUNAMI

7 Hours That Shook the World

To DAD

SHAUN 2019
XMAS

THIS BOOK WILL OPEN YOUR EYES TO
A NATURAL DISASTER THAT "IS BREAKING
NEWS."
THEN FORGOTTEN...

Satinder Bindra

ENJOY

HarperCollins *Publishers* India
a joint venture with

THE INDIA TODAY GROUP

New Delhi

First published in India in 2005 by
HarperCollins *Publishers* India
a joint venture with
The India Today Group

HarperCollins *Publishers*
1A Hamilton House, Connaught Place, New Delhi 110001, India
77-85 Fulham Palace Road, London W6 8JB, United Kingdom
Hazelton Lanes, 55 Avenue Road, Suite 2900, Toronto, Ontario M5R 3L2
and 1995 Markham Road, Scarborough, Ontario M1B 5M8, Canada
25 Ryde Road, Pymble, Sydney, NSW 2073, Australia
31 View Road, Glenfield, Auckland 10, New Zealand
10 East 53rd Street, New York NY 10022, USA

Typeset in 12/14.5 Meridien
Nikita Overseas Pvt. Ltd.

Printed and bound at
Thomson Press (India) Ltd.

To
all those
who are not with us

Contents

Foreword

...even television could not begin to comprehend the suffering of the people of South Asia. The screen was simply not big enough.

Chris Cramer

MANAGING DIRECTOR,
CNN INTERNATIONAL

THERE IS A CRUEL EQUATION IN THE NEWS BUSINESS THAT Christmas and tragedies go hand in hand.

And there are plenty of examples – like the bombing of Pan Am 103 over Lockerbie, Scotland, in 1988 or the Bam earthquake in Iran in 2003. So when the telephone rang at 3 a.m. in my house in Atlanta, USA, on the day after Christmas, I did what I have been doing during the twenty-five years or so I have been on call. I crossed my fingers and said a prayer.

There is a good reason that phones rarely ring during the night. People don't call at that time to offer congratulations or share gossip. There is never the sound of laughter at the end of the line. Only news of grief, or suffering, or death. CNN at this time had a large contingent of staff in Baghdad, living and working in the world's most dangerous city. We had already had two employees killed earlier in the year and several had escaped with their lives. Now I feared the worst.

'Chris. It's Parisa.'

I crossed both sets of fingers and said another prayer. Parisa Khosravi is CNN's senior director of international coverage and one of the most accomplished people in the global news business. She is also CNN's harbinger of bad news to nervous news executives.

'Sorry to wake you. There has been a huge undersea earthquake off the Sumatran coast and a tsunami. We are all over it and Satinder has broken his vacation and is filing from Colombo.'

I uncrossed my fingers and exhaled.

My first thought, one of relief, was that no CNN people were in trouble. My second, that although this was undoubtedly a tragedy for some people in the surrounding area, historically, undersea earthquakes, far out at sea, cause very little loss of life in remote areas of the world. I was reasonably confident that this would also be the case this time.

I could not have been more wrong.

Shaken from sleep I got up and went to my study area in the kitchen, switching on the television set on the way. CNN International was in 'breaking news' mode as the first reports of the tsunami damage came in, bringing news of casualties from countries as widespread as Sri Lanka, Thailand and Indonesia.

I flicked open the dictionary at the word 'tsunami', not a familiar one to someone brought up in Britain and yet a word which would soon become etched in the minds of everyone across the world. Its literal meaning in Japanese seems almost benign: 'tsu' for port or harbour, 'nami' for wave. Put the two together and you get the description for a submarine earthquake, subsidence or volcanic eruption, which can either be mild or, as we now know, have the most catastrophic effects on everything in its path.

◆

Nature has a cruel and devastating way of reminding us that it is mightier than man, and no more so than on 26 December 2004, when the worst disaster in half a century hit South Asia and killed almost 220,000 people in twelve countries as far apart as India, Sri Lanka, Indonesia, Thailand, the Maldives and Somalia.

The tsunami, caused by a 9.3 Richter-scale undersea earthquake off Sumatra, led to one of the world's largest-ever relief efforts as countries and governments across the globe pledged billions in aid to the shattered lives of those who had survived the tragedy.

More significant, perhaps, was the outpouring of sympathy from millions of private individuals for a third of the victims – the children of the tsunami, those who had died and those who were either orphaned or left with a single parent trying to rebuild their lives.

Eyewitnesses to the tidal waves report hundreds of giggling children running onto the beaches to snatch the teeming fish left stranded when the earthquake sucked the waves from the shores – only to be hurled to their deaths when the tsunami roared back again a short time later. Thousands more children were simply too tiny to outrun the water, which engulfed their villages and communities along the coasts of Sri Lanka, Thailand and Indonesia.

CNN's coverage of the tsunami and its aftermath was one of the most complex in its history – and involved nearly one hundred staff and more than a dozen separate reporting teams on the ground, with many hundreds more producing, coordinating, researching and broadcasting our coverage from CNN production centres around the world.

I am in no doubt that the coverage represented the most logistically challenging assignment in my forty years in journalism – and one of the saddest news stories I have ever played a part in.

Yet, even television could not begin to comprehend the suffering of the people of South Asia. The screen was simply not big enough.

On 1 June 2005 we mark the twenty-fifth year of our operation. This tragedy was to test even the huge news-gathering resources that CNN has put in place around the world since Ted Turner set it up in 1980. Unlike most other broadcasters, who have tended to close their overseas news operations in recent years because of the costs involved, CNN has maintained operations in Thailand, Indonesia, India and the Philippines. It also has well-staffed bureaus relatively close by in Hong Kong, Beijing and New Delhi. Fortunately, this book's author, Delhi Bureau chief Satinder Bindra, was on vacation in Colombo and Tokyo Bureau chief, Atika Shubert, was in Bali.

CNN has also invested in recent years in revolutionary new broadcasting equipment – Digital News Gathering – which enables its teams to transmit *live* or recorded images from anywhere on the planet where access to a satellite can be obtained via satellite telephone. This new technology meant that within forty-eight hours of the tsunami striking the shores of South Asia, CNN had teams of correspondents in every location possible, covering every angle of this terrible human tragedy.

Unusually for CNN, for much of the coverage it decided to simulcast its domestic and international channels, CNN USA and CNN International. CNN USA had just appointed a new president, Jon Klein, who felt strongly that the human dimension of the tsunami – the stories both of loss and of hope – required maximum focus. Four of the channel's seniormost anchors and presenters were flown from New York and Washington to hook up with CNN's chief international correspondent, Christiane Amanpour, for several days of *live* coverage.

Our coverage struck a chord with the millions of people who watched in the United States and around the world. They responded in the only way they could, with offers of money and help to the numerous charities set up to help the victims in the countries affected.

Viewers were moved most by what they saw on twenty-four-hour news channels, a concept which had drawn so much ridicule when Ted Turner first launched CNN in 1980. And yet without his vision the sheer magnitude of what happened in Asia on 26 December 2004 may not have been understood by hundreds of millions of people around the world.

Millions more turned to the Internet for information, for help in finding friends and relatives and for an explanation as to what had happened under the sea and on the coastlines of Asia. The

Internet and websites like CNN.com and many others became a pivotal tool in communication.

Most disturbing for the viewers was the huge death toll of children who had perished or those who had lost their parents. The stories of toddlers swept from the arms of their parents and eyewitness accounts from locals or tourists, both caught up in the tragedy, were the most heart-wrenching many veteran CNN correspondents had ever experienced in their long careers. It was impossible for most of them to stay detached from the story they were covering. Many joined in the rescue efforts, putting down their cameras and notebooks, to carry stretchers and attend to the injured. Or just offer a water bottle to a thirsty survivor.

The coverage of the South Asia tsunami by reporters and correspondents like CNN's Satinder Bindra, and hundreds of others from other news organizations across the world, was some of the finest in the history of journalism. It was significant and it was compelling and it told the stories of both the dead and the living with compassion and great sensitivity.

Readers, like me, who are told that the tsunami is an awesome reminder of Mother Nature's fury, might wonder why the ferocity of this tsunami should be associated with the caress of the female gender rather than the brutality of a man. Out of control, wicked and evil – Father Nature would be a more apt description of the force behind such terror and suffering, inflicted on so many people in its path.

Either way, it is impossible to be unaffected by the stories of those who died and those who lived in the wake of the angry sea.

April 2005
Atlanta, USA

Preface

My book tells a real story. My heroes are ordinary people. Yet, they jump out of the pages of the book and grab you because even with all that nature has subjected them to, they refuse to give up.

As one of the most awesome displays of nature's fury and the biggest news story of 2004, you must have read about the tsunami in newspapers and watched hours of its coverage on television. But this book won't remind you about what you already know. Instead, it will take you on a journey through the tsunami-ravaged countries of Asia and introduce you to its people, who showed unimaginable courage and dignity in the face of this cataclysmic natural disaster. My motivation to write this book wasn't to describe an event and its immediate aftermath, but to introduce you to dozens of warm, generous and selfless people who truly made a difference to their communities.

One of my favourite characters is nine-year-old Tharesh Liyanage, who was reading a book when the tsunami roared through his home in Galle, southern Sri Lanka. Within moments, the force of the water had hurled Tharesh out onto the street. His mother fainted and very soon died right in front of his eyes. But Tharesh clung onto life. And hope. A few days later, my reporting duties took me to Galle hospital, where I ran into Tharesh as he tried to identify his dead mother through pictures taken by forensic pathologist Dr Rohan Rowanapura. I couldn't imagine a more difficult task for anyone, leave alone a nine-year-old. But Tharesh presented a picture of calm. He identified his mother with a quick nod of his head and later talked about his plans to honour her memory by working hard at school and becoming a scientist. The experience choked me up, but stirred the writer in me. I wanted to share his story. *Tsunami: 7 Hours That Shook the World* is mainly about the resilience of survivors like Tharesh. It's a personal tribute to their courage and humanity.

My book tells a real story. My heroes are ordinary people. Yet, they jump out of the pages of the book and grab you because even with all that nature has subjected them to, they refuse to give up. Instead of being dispirited and depressed, they want to move on. One of the chapters focuses on the children of Peraliya in Sri Lanka, where a train was swept off its tracks by the tsunami, entombing more than 1000 people. The spot marked the single largest loss of life on the island and understandably the children were deeply distressed. But when a relief worker gave them cameras to record their feelings, the children's artistry shone through. They smiled and showed enough spirit to find the best things in life even though they had been through the worst.

I've written this book in the same manner in which the events unfolded. It is emotional and fast-paced. It's also a first-person account. I was vacationing with my family on the beach in Colombo when I watched the first waves roll in, flood the road and come right up to the wall of our hotel. Fortunately, all of us managed to scramble to high ground. This was close and personal. I feared for our safety and, from the onset, I was deeply involved. I was part of the story and quickly grasped the magnitude of what was happening. The experience was to scar me. How could nature, which I had always thought of as a benevolent force, be so cruel?

This is a story about two waves. The first, a killer; the second, a wave of compassion, which became the largest-ever relief operation launched in the world. So why did the world respond the way it did? First, the sheer scale of the tragedy had a profound effect on people across the world, and second, I do believe, TV coverage made a huge difference. People connected with our stories. They felt for the victims. They felt vulnerable because this could just as easily have happened to them. Imagine your entire family being swept away, your home and livelihood destroyed – all in a matter of minutes.

For the first three days I got no sleep at all. The story kept me going but everything else around me seemed to be a blur. I still hadn't really understood the depth of my own feelings till one night I came back to my hotel room and turned on CNN. The person on screen was a father describing how he had put inflatable armbands around his daughter, who was struggling to stay afloat in the swirling waters of the tsunami. 'Daddy,' she told him, 'I'm scared.' Those were the last words she uttered before she was swept away from her father's grasp. The girl was four years old – the same age as my older daughter who uses the same phrase every time she wanders away from my affectionate gaze. Suddenly, my composure, which had held up well for so long, broke. I collapsed and could feel tears flowing from my eyes. I stayed in my room for several hours before

I could walk out and once again face the all-enveloping atmosphere of grief. Other crew members also broke down, but we supported each other. We just had to tell the story. At that moment in time, it was bigger than anything else because we knew it was bringing Sri Lanka much needed help. It was also one way of coping with our own sense of helplessness for not being able to reach out more closely to share the people's pain and anguish.

The misery of the Sri Lankans was compounded by the fact that no one really knew what a tsunami was. Most people loved and trusted the sea, which has nurtured the island's tourism and fishing industries for generations. The last known major tsunami is supposed to have occurred in Sri Lanka in the second century B.C. Legend has it that King Kelantissa was so incensed over a love affair between his wife and brother that he executed a Buddhist monk. The king's violent temper angered the guardian deities of the sea who ensured that the waters rose up and poured out onto the west coast. The overpowering waves only subsided when the king placed his daughter in a boat and launched her into the sea as a form of sacrifice.

I eventually stayed on in Sri Lanka for several weeks. As the days went by I witnessed many inspiring incidents and reported so many uplifting stories that they seemed to energize me. Perhaps the most important lesson that I learnt during my stay was about the concept of karma. The Sri Lankans believe that every good deed is like making a deposit in a bank. Then, in times of adversity, the strength derived from this karma, *karmashakti*, pulls you through.

Judging by all the acts of kindness that I witnessed, Sri Lanka seems destined to overcome its troubles. Still, there will be challenges, not just for the island-nation but for all tsunami-affected countries. Although by April 2005, countries had pledged almost six billion US dollars for tsunami relief and rehabilitation, the UN has received only one billion dollars so far. For the sake of millions of people who have lost so much, these pledges need to be fulfilled.

As a journalist, I remain committed to this story and will soon travel to the region again with my team, whose trust and dedication are a constant source of strength to me. I am deeply grateful to my deputy Ram Ramgopal, Colombo stringer Iqbal Athas, correspondent Suhasini Haidar and staffers Rohit Gandhi and Prithwijeet Banerjii for all the hard work they put into the story as well as the help they gave me while writing this book. I would also like to acknowledge the efforts of cameramen Sanjiv Talreja and Rajesh Mishra and bureau manager Subramaniam Gopal.

The role played by Sumnima Udas in this project deserves a very special mention because without her drive and dedication this book would never have been ready on time. She researched, edited and proofed my copy, and lined up many important interviews, besides playing the role of the deadline policewoman with grace and charm.

Other than my own field notes, I have relied on over 600 hours of CNN programming and feel I owe a debt of gratitude to hundreds of CNN staffers across the system who put it all together. Almost all our field journalists – led by senior Asia correspondent Mike Chinoy – Hugh Riminton,

Aneesh Raman, Atika Shubert, Matthew Chance, Stan Grant and Phil Turner spent hours narrating their experiences to me and this book has been enriched by their contributions. The insight of deskers Eli Flournoy and Paul Ferguson helped me immensely as did their encouragement. My editor Ravi gets the credit for always being calm and composed. His laid-back style also got the best out of me. The work ethic and dedication of the other editors (Nandita Aggarwal and Ratika Kapur), the production manager (Arti Walia), the designers and the graphic artists helped complete this book in record time. It was a phenomenal effort and I consider it a privilege to have worked with such committed professionals.

At the CNN headquarters, Rick Davis and his team (Rebecca Conners and Marianna Spicer) spent hours poring over my manuscript and I want to acknowledge all their guidance and support. Tony Maddox, my immediate boss, was always generous with his time for interviews and allowed me to use the immense resources of CNN that I needed to put this project together. Managing Director Chris Cramer was quick to gauge my strong desire, in fact, passion, to write this book, and his understanding and blessings have truly meant the world to me. To my parents, wife and two children, I would like to apologize for my long absences; they egged me on to do this book and feel proud that the royalties from it will be used to help children orphaned by the tsunami.

◆

The vicissitudes of life sometimes make us cynical; when confronted by a tragedy of this magnitude we often question the very meaning of life. I truly hope that the stories in this book – of human compassion and fortitude, of the heroism of children and the inherent goodness of people – will rekindle hope and give reason to an existence that is threatened by forces that we don't necessarily understand.

April 2005   **Satinder Bindra**

1

The 'Angry' Sea

'Words defy description. It was a massive 30-foot wall of sea, you know, black in colour, stretching from one end of the beach to the other and the very sight of this mass of water rushing towards us, it was like a thousand freight trains charging at you, that thunderous roar itself petrified you with fear.'

Dateline: Colombo, 25 December 2004

I WAS FEELING SPECIAL AND COUNTING MY BLESSINGS ON Christmas Day, 2004. For the first time in years, I was not on assignment. I was on a holiday with my parents, in-laws, daughters Sacha and Megh and wife, Dolma, in Sri Lanka. We were staying at the Global Towers, a beach-side hotel in the capital, Colombo, just a short walk from one of my favourite eating places in the world – Beach Wadiya.

You enter the restaurant by actually crossing a railway track. A large beer advertisement then announces you are entering an eatery that prides itself on serving 'jumping fresh' seafood. Beach Wadiya is a simple, no-frills place. A few tables are located inside a cavernous hut, where the only piece of eye-catching décor is a glass aquarium. Sarong-clad barefoot waiters greet you with warm smiles and, if you are a regular here, you get a prized table outside the hut, right on the beach so that you can look out to sea.

The restaurant's simplicity and laid-back ambience attracts some well-heeled customers.

Among its patrons, one could count the late Princess Diana, Virgin Atlantic chairman, Sir Richard Branson, Hollywood stars and almost the entire diplomatic community of Colombo.

I first came to Beach Wadiya in 1989, when I started covering the civil war* on the island. Over the years, I've come back to this country more than a dozen times and always made it a point to come here so I could sit on the beach, dig my toes in the sand and enjoy the local brew, arrack, a coconut tree sap concoction.

On Christmas day, I was excited to bring my family here. Owner Olwyn Weerasekra offered us a large table underneath a palm tree. We admired the moonlit view of the beach and tucked into crab, steamed fish and shrimps. Arrack flowed freely, the atmosphere was relaxed and I barely noticed the conversation shifting to the sea. 'The sea's very loud,' pronounced Dolma. I was too mellow to care and hardly paid any attention to my mother's response: 'The sea', she announced, perhaps with a great sense of foreboding, 'is "very angry".'

Seven hours later, the world's most powerful earthquake in forty years rattled the ocean floor just off the Indonesian island of Sumatra. The energy released by the earthquake has been estimated to roughly equal that of a bomb packed with 32 billion tonnes of TNT. Such massive energy, once released from the bottom of the seabed, quickly transferred

---

* The civil war broke out in July 1983, when the Liberation Tigers of Tamil Eelam (LTTE) launched guerrilla warfare against the Sri Lankan Army, demanding a separate state for the Tamils in the northern and eastern parts of the island.

itself to the water, setting off a tsunami that began hurtling its way across the Indian Ocean at 800 km an hour towards unsuspecting tourists, fishermen and millions of ordinary people...

In just fifteen minutes, the tsunami swamped Aceh, the northernmost province in Sumatra. In Indonesia it killed more than 122,000 people. About 37,000 people were reported missing. The Andaman Islands were next to feel the brunt of the wave, followed by Thailand, Sri Lanka and the Maldives. Seven hours later, the waves crashed into Somalia, Africa, almost 5000 km away from the epicentre of the earthquake. No one received any advance warning of this global tragedy. By the time top international scientists pieced together the sequence of events, the world was a different place. More than 220,000 people were dead and around 50,000 were missing, forcing a stunned international community to launch its largest-ever relief operation. And a little-known Japanese word – tsunami – would quickly become part of everyday usage, finding its way into school textbooks and novels to symbolize the almost unspeakable horror of what happened on 26 December 2004.

It was 6:59 a.m. Sri Lanka time on Boxing Day when the seabed near Sumatra shook with the earthquake, which registered 9.3 on the Richter scale. Thanks to Christmas festivities, I was in a deep slumber and didn't get up till almost 8:30 a.m. By that time, it was too late to go jogging on the beach, so I promised my wife we'd all go shopping and familiarize ourselves with some local culture. Sri Lankans were marking 26 December as Poya Day, one of the holiest days in the year in this Buddhist-dominated country.

On Poya Day, Buddhists normally visit some of the country's stunning white-domed temples, where they offer special prayers and make offerings of freshly cut flowers. Devotees also light oil lamps to symbolize wisdom. The sweet smell of incense and the soothing, sonorous rhythm of hymns can all make for a spiritually uplifting experience, so we decided to try to soak up this atmosphere.

Just before leaving the hotel, I walked out to catch some sea breeze from the balcony of our sixth floor room. Our hotel was barely 500 metres from the beach and it offered a stunning view both of the sea and the city. To my right, I could see the famed World Trade Towers, home to Sri Lanka's stock exchange, the Hilton Hotel and government offices. Straight ahead of me were a partially sunken barge and the sea. As the breeze hit my face and tousled my hair, I noticed the waves gently curl towards the shore. Everything appeared normal, except that the water had crept inland, with the tide carrying out piles of garbage left on the shore. 'Nice local system of waste disposal,' I announced to my family, before we all took the elevator down.

Driving past the Beach Wadiya restaurant, I noticed the water creeping up towards some of the tables where we had celebrated Christmas dinner the night before. 'It must be high tide,' I mused, but as we motored along a small road parallel to the sea, I noticed small crowds with cameras and a great sense of energy and excitement rushing towards the shore. My curiosity was by now aroused, but I didn't feel the need to get out of the car. I was more intent on enjoying the sea breeze and soaking up the amazing 30 degrees centigrade temperature. The laid-back manner of Sri Lankans can be quite infectious and I had every intention of being the perfect tourist. Little did I know, nature had something else in store for me.

It was just past ten in the morning when my phone beeped. 'Please call me it's urgent,' read the text message on my cell phone. The message was from Iqbal Athas, CNN's trusted representative in Sri Lanka. Both of us had worked on several big stories in the past, such as Sri Lanka's civil war and the 1999 attempt by the Tamil Tiger rebels in the north to assassinate President Chandrika Kumaratunga. During the course of these assignments we had struck a deep personal and professional bond. I regard Iqbal as one of the best journalists I have ever worked with. With over thirty-five years of experience and legendary contacts, Iqbal is conservative and always on the money with his assessments. So when he called me on vacation, I knew it wasn't just to say hello.

I decided to call Iqbal as soon as we pulled into one of Colombo's most popular stores, Paradise Road, which sells scented candles, crockery and art pieces. But before I could return his call, the phone rang. It was Iqbal. 'Sat,' he said breathlessly, 'there is trouble. I'm receiving reports the entire coast has been hit by huge waves.' From ten that morning, Iqbal's phone had been ringing non-stop. One of the first calls he received was from a senior naval officer in Trincomalee, eastern Sri Lanka. 'Our mess hall is flooded. So are the other sailors' quarters,' he told Iqbal, who was quick to ask him what time the Christmas party had ended. 'Looks like you were the last to leave,' joked Iqbal. The joke didn't go down well. By this time Iqbal too realized that the force of the water must have been quite severe to have reached the mess hall, which he remembered from previous visits was located on high ground. His conclusion was clear: Sri Lanka was in the midst of a huge natural disaster.

Within seconds of hanging up, Iqbal's phone rang again. This time, it was his sister-in-law who was travelling along Sri Lanka's southern coast. She too told him of widespread flooding and described how she narrowly escaped death when a wall almost collapsed on her car.

Within minutes of these calls, Iqbal and I locked heads on the phone to make a quick and sobering assessment. Both of us believed the death count was probably already in thousands and having covered some of the biggest disasters in South Asia recently, such as the 26 January 2001 earthquake in western India and the 1999 supercyclone that flattened large parts of eastern India, my instincts as a reporter were telling me the toll would continue to rise.

It was time to act. I quickly called CNN headquarters in Atlanta to tell supervising editor Eli Flournoy on our International Desk that I was cancelling my vacation. With reports of casualties and damage coming in from everywhere, I called my own bureau in New Delhi to speak with the assignment editor, Prithwijeet Banerjii. By this time, New Delhi too was aware we had to move news-gathering resources to the southern Indian state of Tamil Nadu and the Andaman Islands. We reached a decision to deploy all three news teams from New Delhi. The time was just before 11:00 a.m. Prithwi was given the job of pulling all staffers off vacation and getting a crew to me in Sri Lanka on the first available flight.

With the logistical ends tied up, there was still a story to report and I raced back from our aborted shopping trip at breakneck speed to our hotel. I wanted to check the news wires, and, in my hotel room, waiting and prepared for any such eventuality, was my trusted trolley bag. I never left home without my gear and, just on the eve of this trip, I had spent over an hour fretting and fussing over my own professional equipment. Consulting a laminated checklist attached to the outside of my bag, I packed my computer, cables, a small satellite modem called a RB-Gan – this was to enable me to log into our mainframe in Atlanta and the Internet – a car phone charger and several spare batteries for my cell phone. As our car sped down Colombo's narrow alleys, I was glad I had taken so much effort to bring along my equipment. I was even more relieved that I had warned New Delhi staffers to stay on their toes, because past experience had taught me some of the biggest stories in South Asia somehow always happened during the Christmas break.

Meanwhile, back on the beach, the crowds continued to swell. As we drew up to our hotel, I saw thousands nervously watching the water and was fully aware I would soon be reporting one of the biggest stories of my life. With my adrenaline now pumping, I raced to my room to log in to the news wires, simultaneously instructing Iqbal on my cell phone that he should, for the next hour, take care of any 'beepers' or *live* phone interviews from Atlanta.

I set up the equipment on my sixth floor hotel room balcony and even before I had connected, the sea thundered into the swimming pool just an arm's length away from us, then surged across a road and came up to the wall of our hotel. My heart was in my mouth, my pulse quickened and journalism suddenly wasn't the priority any more. The safety of my children and the entire family was now paramount, but then, just as quickly as the sea had rushed onto land, it began retreating, creating such a powerful undertow, that I felt that I was watching the world's most powerful vacuum cleaner in action. Furniture from seaside restaurants, pieces of damaged homes and all kinds of debris were being pulled kilometres out to sea. I watched, horror-struck, unable to comprehend the situation. Wasn't I on vacation? As I struggled with my emotions, I also felt for a few fleeting seconds that this wasn't real perhaps I was just watching a disaster movie.

I was pulled back to reality by the ringing phone. It was my News Desk in Atlanta, USA, calling to tell me they needed me *live* in another few minutes. With very little information coming out of Indonesia at this time, CNN's coverage was being driven by events in Thailand and Sri Lanka. As I continued receiving reports mainly from eastern Sri Lanka about mounting casualties, I was reporting that 'this tiny island-nation of Sri Lanka is bearing the brunt of the tragedy'.

I talked of a ship that had sunk in Colombo harbour and a jail that had been smashed by the waves in the city of Matara, 160 km south of Colombo. Some 300 of the country's most-hardened criminals had escaped in the process. Close to Matara, hundreds had been killed when the open-air Sunday market in the town of Hambantota was hit by three successive 20-foot high waves. They tore into the market, smashing tents, shops and large concrete structures. Within minutes, a scene of merriment and holiday joy had been transformed into a landscape of mass hysteria. Thousands of petrified screams rent the air; people tried clutching and somehow holding onto their children, but it was all too late as a wall of water crashed down on them, killing hundreds.

More than 500,000 people live in the Hambantota district and according to official statistics, about one third of them are below the poverty line. In Hambantota harbour, which is just a few metres above sea level, the majority of inhabitants are Muslims. Some are fishermen, others work in the nearby salt industry and many are small traders, like Imtiaz Ahmed, who eke out a living selling toys.

On that Sunday, Imtiaz had pitched his tent to sell his wares, when he sauntered a few hundred metres away from the sea to his aunt's house to meet his brother. His relatives' home is located at a height and just as he got there, Imtiaz saw the first wave come in. His thoughts immediately turned to his sisters who were at home. But it was too late for them. They were killed instantly. Imtiaz told me he didn't feel angry with the sea, but he decided he would not come to the beach any more. He just couldn't cope with the memories.

Imtiaz also told me it would take at least five years for him and his community to put their lives back on track again. As I described these events, I was finding it hard not to get drawn into the developments of the past few hours. My training as a journalist had taught me to keep a studied distance from what I reported and not to get emotionally drawn into the story. On the other hand, I was human too and was struggling to cope with the burden of what was unfolding. I kept agonizing over how many lives could have been saved if people had received even a 20-minute warning. But with no notice of what was coming their way, it took just minutes to decimate entire families, smash their homes and sweep away their businesses. This could just as easily have happened to me and my family. It was a chilling thought.

Worse news followed. I started receiving calls from Galle, Sri Lanka's second largest city and a major resort, just south of Colombo. The first to call was CNN's distributor in Sri Lanka – Arthur Senanayake. He spoke breathlessly and in the manner of someone who had seen more than he could fathom. 'The sea just exploded,' he said, 'sending 30-foot waves hurtling at us.' With a population of about 100,000, Galle was in a shambles. The city's picturesque cricket stadium was virtually reduced to rubble and dozens of buses were floating on their sides at what was once a bus stand. 'The waves were so huge,' added Arthur, 'that several buses had even landed on the top of multistoreyed buildings.' The hospitals were also filling up with dead bodies and Arthur himself counted more than 400 at one hospital alone. This information I put on CNN immediately.

By this time, I was thinking not just of what I was reporting today, but how we would sustain our coverage in the following days. I had to get to what we journalists describe as the 'heart' of the story and some others call 'ground zero'. With so much carnage, it was obvious we had to have a strong reporting presence in Galle immediately. But the coastal road from Colombo to Galle was inaccessible and the only way to get in was by helicopter. I called the International Desk, to make my case to Eli. Permission was granted immediately.

With Galle lined up, I turned my attention to what was happening within Colombo itself. While the business district was unaffected, other parts of the capital suffered major damage. On the southern fringes of the city, the tsunami had virtually eaten into the coastline destroying homes, flipping over boats and flattening what were once thriving neighbourhoods. As far as my eye could see up and down this coast, misery and suffering were the dominant features.

Row upon row of houses had been smashed to smithereens. People's belongings were littered everywhere on the streets. There were soggy teddy bears, kitchen utensils, remnants of a baby's crib, shoes and clothes. Huge fibreglass boats had been lifted and tossed around like weightless toys. Tonnes of debris were littered onto a railway line connecting Colombo to the rest of the south. I figured it would be months before life here would be normal again.

None of the people living along this coast had any insurance. One of my scripts that day read: 'When it unleashed its fury, the sea targeted the poorest of the poor.' As I walked amongst the rubble I came across a survivor, Ajit Priyantha. Several members of his family had been killed and his home and business premises were reduced to rubble. He wasn't even thinking about rebuilding because all that was on his mind at that moment was a feeling of utter helplessness and isolation. It was an all-pervasive sentiment on the coast. I saw hundreds of residents just sitting outside their smashed homes, gazing vacantly into the distance. My training recognized such symptoms as post-traumatic stress disorder or deep psychological trauma. At the end of one of my beepers, I sat down on a piece of rubble feeling cold and numb, wondering how nature, something I loved so dearly, could be so cruel.

As the sun set, another fear started gnawing at the survivors. They all believed the sea would strike them again. Still, small clusters of people continued to hang around their homes and scattered belongings. With power cables washed away, several communities had no source of illumination, creating ideal conditions for looters. Some came from other communities. Hotelier David Gittins showed me two vans smashed and looted by people of his own community. The vans belonged to Western surfers, 300 of whom perished instantly because they were on the water, close to the shore, when the tsunami struck. The tourists were staying in Gittins' hotel, the White House, which he had finished constructing just a few weeks earlier. The hotel was spared by the tsunami, but it didn't escape the greed of looters, many of whom were Gittins' own neighbours. 'My immediate neighbours, everybody from the local community is walking onto my property,' he complained. 'They are stealing, taking property that does not belong to them. I find it a very despicable thing.' Gittins even caught people walking away with furnishings from the White House and turned them over to the police.

Dr Chandini, a psychologist examining the state of anarchy, explained the breakdown of social norms in this way: 'What we experienced was very traumatic, very stressful, unexpected, devastating. When people experience such a traumatic event, they react in all sorts of different ways. Some people will just withdraw, some people can become aggressive. These are the different ways personalities react to stress.' The police reacted to the breakdown in law and order by announcing a curfew and advising residents to spend the night at makeshift shelters, which had been created mainly in churches and Buddhist temples.

As night fell, I drove back to downtown Colombo. I checked in with my wife on the telephone, but didn't go back to my hotel. Instead, I drove to the Hilton to check on the state of Western tourists who, I was informed, were being brought back to the capital from across the country. When I arrived at the hotel, its brightly lit lobby was full of holiday-makers, discussing the day's events. A huge Christmas tree occupied most of the space in the lobby, intricately prepared decorations adorned the walls and small stalls were selling candy. The mood was in sharp contrast to the desperation and despair I saw on the streets, but it would be a while before those Sri Lankans who escaped unscathed would realize how the tsunami had ravaged their country or how lucky they had been.

It had been an exhausting day and it was now well past midnight. My crew would soon be arriving from New Delhi, so I decided to get a few hours' sleep at the Hilton itself. My first *live* hit was at six in the morning and I knew from past experience the importance of being rested on a story that would continue gripping the world for weeks.

I was awakened by Prithwijeet Banerjii at 4:00 a.m. on 27 December. Prithwi, cameraman Sanjiv Talreja and editor Rajesh Mishra had just cleared customs at Colombo International Airport and were calling to inform me they were driving down to the Hilton. I asked them to change plans and head straight to the southern part of the city, where I would rendezvous with them. My crew was equipped with some of the latest lightweight technology in the television business, enabling us to do instant *live* shots. We also had the capacity to file our reports directly from the field using advanced software, designed, built and developed by a team at CNN.

We started work on time and, as the sun came up, the world saw the first *live* images of the carnage and destruction that the tsunami had caused in Sri

Lanka. We regularly panned our *live* camera to show the devastated coast, mourning survivors and miles of damaged railway track. These powerful pictures immediately moved millions around the world and, in the words of one commentator, instantly 'globalized grief'.

In the field, we were fully aware of the power of our pictures and worked hard to be respectful and sensitive towards grieving family members. However, we did want to convey the terrifying ordeal people had been through. Therefore, our cameras captured hundreds of survivors, all still with dazed looks, starting to return home to sift through their destroyed belongings. We took pictures of victims wading through waist-deep water carrying TVs, radios and their belongings out of their shattered homes. The work proceeded for a few hours till I heard some commotion. People started fleeing in every direction, dropping whatever they were doing. Our drivers too deserted their cars and fled in panic. I caught up with one of them and breathlessly asked the reason for the wild panic. 'Tsunami! Tsunami!' he shouted at the top of his voice, gesturing towards the sea.

Our *live* camera was just a few metres from the ocean and we quickly ran towards it. While doing so, I called the International Desk and asked to be put on air immediately. In the meantime, the crew pulled the camera right to the edge of the water, which was rising dangerously fast. The waves were now one-metre high, water was lapping around my feet and there was no telling what the ocean would do next. We captured all this *live*, reporting the fear psychosis that was virtually paralysing this section of the coast.

As our report was aired, Iqbal called, saying that officials were concerned we were spreading fear and panic. I told Iqbal to tell them we had an obligation to report what was happening and how people were responding to the situation. For the next two hours, we continued to closely monitor the ocean, but luckily for thousands of edgy residents nothing untoward happened.

Around noon, we decided to pack our equipment. Our new digital and lightweight gear enabled us to finish a task that normally took thirty minutes in half the time and we made a beeline for the airport, from where we were to take a helicopter to Galle. Disappointment and frustration greeted me at the Ratmalana Air Force Base. Our helicopter flight had been delayed several hours and there was nothing to do but cool my heels.

The first hour of waiting seemed almost intolerable. The death count in Sri Lanka alone had by now risen to more than 10,000 and I was feeling the pressure to establish a *live* presence in Galle, so that the international community not only had a better sense of what was happening there but could also respond to the crisis. My prayers for more information were answered when a plane full of Western tourists arrived at the airport. One man, a German, was badly bruised and clearly distraught. Dressed in just a sarong, he gave his name as Ralph Succo and described what he and his wife, who were in Galle on vacation, had just been through. 'We were in our room when we saw the first waves,' he recalled. 'The first two were not very big but the third wave came into our room. It then pulled me out, and I tried to find something to hold onto but it was impossible.' Seconds later, Succo said that he found himself on a big stone. He went on: 'I saw only water above me, I thought I would die. I had nothing, I was naked and I cried for my wife. She was also in the room and was also pulled right out.' As he finished his story Succo, a photographer by profession, broke down completely, crying and hugging his wife, who had also somehow managed to survive. Other equally traumatized survivors, listening to his story, couldn't contain their tears either. Caught unaware by this spontaneous outpouring of collective grief, I didn't know how to respond and was embarrassed that I couldn't say or do anything meaningful to lessen their sorrow.

As I walked away from this group of tourists, I ran into an Australian backpacker who identified himself only as Michael and told me what had happened to him and other tourists who were standing on a restaurant deck in Galle overlooking the water. 'With an ebbing and swirling motion, the sea just came up and up and...it started washing all the tables and chairs off the restaurant. We just ran back to where the hotel was, behind the restaurant, but by this time the water was waist-deep and there were people screaming everywhere. We then ran up the stairs and tried leaning over a balcony to help two people who were washed off their house and were hanging onto a tree. We failed. And all of a sudden the water just stopped and then the water started draining back. And I think that also caused a lot of problems because buses and trucks and fridges and people were washed out to sea.'

Michael also informed me that Galle needed international medical assistance urgently. He added:

'There's no power and because of that there's no movement and no support is going through to help the injured. There are also bodies that need to be dealt with, identified and transported out of there, I guess, because soon in this heat sanitation problems will arise.'

Doctors by now were sending out warnings that a health crisis or an epidemic could kill even more people than the tsunami itself. Given these circumstances, I decided to send Prithwi straight from the airport on a drive further south from Colombo. If he came across any problems at health camps, his instructions were to use his cell phone and do a *live* beeper. In the meantime, we, the three remaining crew members, finally took off from Colombo in a light drizzle for Galle. The flying time to Galle was about one hour and, just as we were approaching the city, the drizzle turned into a downpour, forcing the pilot to abort the mission and fly back to Colombo. Disappointed that the weather hadn't cooperated with us, I spent most of my time on the journey back, closely viewing a coastline where almost everything had been damaged. The story was bigger than we had all anticipated and for the moment at least, my biggest worry was managing our disappointment. As we offloaded our gear in blinding rain, we decided to continue offering more *live* hits. But from where? I called Prithwi, who, by this time, had located one of the largest relief camps at St Anthony's Church, just outside Colombo. The church was located at a height and was therefore seen as a safe place by more than 1500 people, where they could get food, water, shelter and sanitation facilities. Their plight and living conditions moved us all, and we decided to tell their story through one character: the camp's youngest resident, Baby Rashuda. She was just a few weeks old and was being cradled by her mother in a room that was perhaps four times the size of a standard living room but had 400 people squeezed into it.

The heat and noise were stifling. Sweat, humidity and grief hung in the air. Almost every family here had lost either a home or a loved one. Baby Rashuda's mother, Ashani Ruwangika, was still searching for her younger brother; her mother was dead, swept out to sea by Sunday's tsunami. 'My mother got trapped in a cabinet,' wailed Ashani, adding that the entire cabinet was then sucked into the sea, drowning her in a matter of minutes. Ashani was now making arrangements for the funeral and told me she couldn't imagine life without the support of someone whom she loved so dearly.

As night fell, exhausted families slept as they were – on the floor. I continued filing *live* reports from the church, showcasing the misery of the survivors, who were all united by a sense of loss and fear. One day after the tsunami, it was estimated that more than 200,000 Sri Lankans were displaced and already living in such temporary relief camps. And many believed the sea was preparing to spew more venom.

Sri Lankan officials were at a loss to tell their people what to expect. South Asia, like some other parts of the developed world, has no tsunami-warning system and the entire region was caught unawares as the killer waves thundered towards its shores. The Sri Lankan president, Chandrika Kumaratunga, later told me she was on Christmas holiday in London with her children, when she was woken up at 5:30 in the morning by her security personnel banging on her door.

'In Sinhala, we don't have a word for tidal wave, so I was told that the sea has come to the land. And I was like, so what, why are you waking me up for that? And they said no, no the prime minister has called, your secretary has called, everyone is calling, there is something very serious, so that is how I knew about it.' Like everyone else in her country, the president was at a loss for words. Anyway, she managed to say: 'I was just completely shocked, I didn't know what to feel, because I couldn't understand. Because, I as a person, I loved the sea, I just adore the sea, I'm almost obsessed with the sea, and one of my greatest pleasures is being by the seaside and swimming in the sea and things like that. So it was just a feeling of absolute incredulity that this gorgeous thing which we love so much would just rise up and cause this devastation.'

From London itself, the president began laying the foundation for the single largest relief operation in her country's history. First, she declared a 'state of natural disaster' and appealed immediately for international assistance. She then flew back home at once to raise the spirits of her people. 'I just listened to their stories, some of them were crying and telling me what happened and others were just saying when are we going to get houses to live in, they were just saying what they had lost and things like that. I wasn't even in the mood to ask them how it happened like some foolish people do, you know, when you go ask traumatized people. How did it come, how did the waves come, where were you? That was not a time to ask those things. I just, you know, put my arms around them and reassured them.'

Sri Lankans living on the east coast needed the most reassurance because it was here that the wave killed the most people and wreaked maximum damage. But when nature destroys, it's sometimes humans like Father Dayalan Sanders who can perform the most amazing feats. On early Sunday morning, on Boxing Day, Father Sanders was at the orphanage he runs for children at Navalaji Beach, on the eastern shores of Sri Lanka, when his wife burst into his room.

It was 8:40 a.m. and Father Sanders saw a look of complete horror on her face as she yelled, 'The sea's coming in!' His wife was petrified by what was happening around them. But he reassured her, 'God is with us and nothing will harm us.' Moments later, Father Sanders was out on the beach. This is how he first described what he saw to CNN's chief international correspondent Christiane Amanpour: 'Words defy description. It was a massive 30-foot wall of sea, you know, black in colour, stretching from one end of the beach to the other and the very sight of this mass of water rushing towards us, it was like a thousand freight trains charging at you, that thunderous roar itself petrified you with fear.'

Father Sanders realized speed was critical: 'I was not thinking, only acting. There was no time to think. You had to act on impulse and you had to act instantly.' The only way to save the kids was to get them all into a boat that was kept at the orphanage.

Normally, such an activity would have taken about fifteen minutes, but Father Sanders told Amanpour he got it done in under ten seconds. The motor was on the boat. 'We never leave the outboard motor on the launch. This is the first time we have done this, that this has happened to us.' It was also the first time Stefan, the boatman, was able to get the motor going on the first try. 'He just yanked the starter rope...in one pull, it started. '

With thirty-two people, including twenty-six children, crammed into his small boat, the Catholic missionary felt there was no point in trying to outrun the wave or the massive force it represented. He felt god was asking him to turn the boat, powered by just a 15-horsepower motor, to face the monster wave. As the boat surged towards the tsunami, Father Sanders never felt scared: 'People were crying out for help. Heart-rending cries rent the air. Even with death, helplessness and debris all around, never did I think we were going to perish. God was not going to let us down. I looked up to the sky and I knew god was watching.' Burdened by the responsibility of so many tender lives in his care, Father Sanders recalled a scripture: 'When the enemy comes in like a flood, the spirit of the Lord shall raise up a standard against it.' Seconds later, the priest stood tall in the boat's bow, next to a green fluttering flag that read 'Jesus is Lord', raised his hands towards the heavens and recalled saying: 'I command you in the name of Jesus Christ on the strength of the scriptures, to stand still!'

Father Sanders believes something, perhaps an invisible force, did then hold the wave back, allowing him and his precious human cargo –

dripping wet, but unscathed – to reach the town of Batticaloa. Experienced sailors point out that this was no miracle as Father Sanders claims, but they, nevertheless, praise him for his quick thinking and amazing presence of mind. According to them, the safest place to be when a tsunami hits is on top of the wave, which explains why fishermen and hundreds of boats out at sea did not suffer the same fate as those on, or near, the shore.

Fathers Sanders' orphanage was completely destroyed. Twenty years of his life's work vanished in just a matter of seconds. But he hasn't given up and has promised to 'rise like the phoenix' to defeat what caused so much turmoil in his life: 'It wasn't just a wave. It was a living, fighting and malevolent force. It was out to kill.'

2

The 'Mountain of Water'

The stench of death, soggy debris and rotting vegetation filled my nostrils, almost forcing me to throw up. Animal carcasses still lay on the streets, which were littered with bricks, household items and recognizable pieces of what were once houses...

Dateline: Galle, 28 December 2004

THE WEATHER GODS FINALLY ANSWERED MY PRAYERS on the morning of 28 December. The forecast predicted a clear day, allowing us to resume our second attempt to fly into Galle, so that we could report from the heart of the disaster. We reached Colombo's Ratmalana Air Force Base at 7:00 a.m. to meet with the helicopter's pilot, who permitted us to take only 80 kg of gear, about half of what we usually carried. Clothes and personal effects were the first to be discarded; then came food supplies. We were careful, though, to carry at least fifteen bottles of water. The weather was hot and sultry and with the entire water supply contaminated in Galle, I wanted to ensure we were adequately prepared to continuously report the story for at least the next thirty-six hours.

We also unpacked our gear from its normal hard cases, opting to carry our satellite phones, videophone – used for *live* shots – computers, two cameras, cables and batteries in soft bags instead. After considerable fretting and fussing, the pilot agreed we could fit all our equipment in a small hold in the side of his helicopter and we took off.

We flew south from Colombo, hugging the coast. It was a perfect day – clear and tranquil – allowing me to view the intense and immense damage all along Sri Lanka's coastline, where entire communities and neighbourhoods had been wiped out. From the air, I noticed the sea had advanced almost 1 km inland, demolishing everything – homes, hospitals, government buildings and jetties – that stood in its way.

Only coastal trees – coconut, palm and mangroves – escaped the tsunami's fury, and from my vantage point in the sky, this seemed very odd. I could spot the complete annihilation of massive buildings and concrete structures, but standing right next to their remains, the tiniest palm or coconut tree stood intact, swaying gently in the breeze, as if nothing had really happened. This phenomenon surprised me as I compared it with an earlier experience of covering another coastal tragedy – the 2001 supercyclone that had ripped out almost every tree along India's eastern coast.

So how did the trees survive the tsunami? According to marine biologists, mangroves withstood the might of the powerful waves because of their thick roots that spread almost 10 metres around the trees. The coconut and palm trees survived because their thin trunks offered minimum resistance to the water and their flexibility ensured that they didn't snap. Thousands of Sri Lankans survived by clinging onto coconut trees, whose fruit then provided them both water and nourishment for the first few days following the tsunami.

'We're approaching Galle.' My thoughts were interrupted by cameraman Sanjiv. I braced myself as the pilot lowered altitude and then banked the helicopter, which gave us our first look of the ravaged city. My immediate reaction was that the area had been hit by an atom bomb. Everything I saw on the coast had been virtually flattened or wiped out. It was truly eerie because the sea surrounding the damaged areas was calm and blue, with the occasional splash of white as a breaker rolled in towards the shore.

Hundreds of fishing boats were strewn across beaches: some had snapped clean in half, others had turned turtle, entrapped and smothered by their own fishing nets. I tried to count the number of smashed boats, but gave up, realizing that all I had to really report was that the entire fishing industry – a major source of livelihood in the south – had been destroyed. I wondered how people would cope with the tragedy, without their homes, loved ones and jobs. Everything just seemed so hopeless and empty.

As we descended, I caught a glimpse of Galle's internationally renowned cricket stadium. Over the years, rival teams had enjoyed playing at this breezy venue, situated almost on the beach. The ground was considered Sri Lanka's 'lucky' stadium, with the home team winning seven out of the eleven matches played here since the first test match in 1998. But when the tsunami struck Galle, the stadium's location ensured it bore the brunt of the raging water. Within minutes, the sea entered the pavilion, the stands and the beautiful grounds, snuffing out a proud cricketing tradition and culture. From the air, I could see the stadium's ripped out bleachers, apart from many ruined cars and buses as well as piles of debris everywhere.

Just a short distance away, Galle's bus stand was also a complete mess, with water surging into the bays where passengers boarded buses. The force of the sea carried away almost everything in sight – telephone and electricity poles, cables, and small tin and wood shacks that sold snacks to travellers. Most of the buses at the stand had toppled over; others had been dragged along by the power of the water and had got wedged into shops and buildings. I also noticed a small mountain of cars. The water had piled them on top of each other in what appeared to be a grotesque display of its might and malevolence.

Very few cars were on the road. The main city resembled a ghost town and the harbour area was just as deserted. Only demolished fishing boats, yachts and trawlers were cluttered together. I could also clearly make out the contours of a large Sri Lankan naval missile boat that had capsized, entombing several Sri Lankan sailors in the process. It would be a while, I guessed, before any large ships would be able to dock here.

As we circled the harbour, I was glad that we had decided to pay the extra money to hire a helicopter. Not only were we getting the best aerial video shots possible, but I also now knew exactly where to get the most compelling pictures once we were on the ground. I held my breath as I noticed that a huge 1500-tonne ship – almost as big as an entire city block – had been lifted 15 feet above the water level onto a jetty. When the wave receded the ship remained stuck on the ground and from the air, it looked like a giant, helpless, beached whale.

It was a searing image, one that captured the stupendous power of the tsunami and also clearly indicated the enormity of the reconstruction job facing Sri Lanka.

When the pilot set the helicopter down on a patch of green just by the side of the stadium, I became a bit nervous. The city looked like a wasteland. We had no transport, virtually no food, very limited supplies of water and no secure place to spend the night. But it was time to move, not think. We offloaded our gear and I ran in the direction of a few waiting police officers. I persuaded them to give us a ride to the city's bus station, which from the air seemed to have suffered the worst damage, and I wanted to set up my equipment there as soon as possible.

After dropping off our gear and two crew members at the bus station, I asked the police to help me procure a car. They merely shrugged their shoulders, and seemed to be irritated that I was making such a demand when they clearly had other priorities. But I was desperate: we weren't carrying a generator and I needed a vehicle battery to power up my equipment. If I couldn't find a car, our operation in Galle was destined to collapse even before we got started.

I eventually convinced the police into driving me to the closest big hotel – the Lighthouse – at a distance of about 3 km. As we drove along, I rolled down my window for a closer look and immediately regretted it. The stench of death, soggy debris and rotting vegetation filled my nostrils, almost forcing me to throw up. Animal carcasses still lay on the streets, which were littered with bricks, household items and recognizable pieces of what were once houses, such as beams, doors and windows. It took us almost twenty minutes to reach the hotel, during which time I took the opportunity to grill the police, who were clearly my most reliable source of information. 'Huge numbers have been killed in this town alone,' they said mournfully, adding that more than 1000 people had been killed just outside the city near the town of Hikkaduwa, when an entire train had been washed away by the tsunami. The police also told me that there was no heavy machinery available in that area to lift the train's battered coaches. Hence, they had given up hope of finding any survivors.

I absorbed the information quickly, making mental notes that we should begin our *live* broadcast from Galle with the story of the train. Before I could fish for any more details, our jeep screeched to a halt in the foyer of the Lighthouse Hotel. My attention shifted to the smashed cars blocking the entrance to what many considered the city's finest beachside hotel. As I made my way through the cars, I noticed a large curving wooden staircase leading to the lobby of the hotel. The staircase was decorated with life-size metal images of mermaids and other deep-sea creatures. The entire atmosphere felt surreal.

As I entered the lobby, gentle waves were breaking on large rocks just a few hundred metres away, but there were no tourists or guests to enjoy the breathtaking view. There were no staff members either and it took me fifteen minutes of wandering through deserted halls to locate the hotel manager, who told me I was in the wrong place if I needed a car. He also made it clear that he wasn't booking in any guests that night.

Disappointed to have failed in my mission, I ran out of the hotel to hitch a ride back to the centre of the city with the police. But much to my dismay, the police had left, leaving me stranded and enraged. Not only did I have no transport, but I was also separated from my crew. I felt I had let them down and ran out onto the street to try to flag down any vehicle. No one stopped; no one even bothered to give me a second glance. In a town that had lost so much, in a place where entire families had been wiped out, giving a stranded stranger a ride must have been a very low priority.

But desperate times called for equally desperate measures. I stepped right into the middle of the road and began flapping my arms, praying someone would stop. I knew I must have looked quite a sight to the passengers of an old van labouring up the hill, but I was beyond caring. As the van got closer to me, I noticed a look of alarm on the bespectacled driver's face as he virtually stood on his brakes. Without speaking a word, I opened the van's side door and pushed myself inside. The driver, Wasantha Wijendra, a business executive and long-time Galle resident (these details I came to know later), was in shock, thinking that he and his family were being carjacked. I quickly reassured them that no such thing was happening, digging into my wallet for my CNN identity card. 'Please help me,' I begged. 'I have to borrow your van so I can do my *live* shots,'

I explained with a straight face. I couldn't believe my luck when Wasantha nodded vigorously. 'You have come to help my country and you can keep my van for as long as you want,' he said matter-of-factly. I couldn't believe my luck and was overcome with emotion. The people of Galle had suffered so much, but in typical Sri Lankan fashion, Wasantha, his wife Chanitha and daughter Chatrya were being hospitable and gracious to me, simply because I was a guest in their destroyed city.

We quickly drove past two police checkpoints to the heart of the city where I could team up with the crew. By this time, they had unpacked the equipment. We placed our satellite phone antennas on the top of Wasantha's van, from where we also grabbed our power supply. Minutes later, I started the first of my *live* reports and really didn't feel the need to budge from my location because everything was happening right in front of me.

Every five or ten minutes a fire truck with red lights flashing and sirens blaring would come tearing down Galle's main street. Each truck was a signal that more bodies had been found by municipal workers among the debris. Just a few feet away from where we had set up our equipment, bodies were still being pulled out from the basement of a supermarket. Local storeowners told me the waves had trapped and killed more than 100 shoppers in that one place alone. Just by the side of the supermarket, residents found another bloated body. Someone in the large crowd of onlookers quickly covered it with a cloth and, moments later, municipal workers arrived to load the unclaimed body onto a tractor-trailer and took it away for burial.

Our camera moved to show workers removing ovens and fridges from the Little Lanka Pastry Shop. The store had a proud tradition of serving some of the best ice-cream sundaes, cookies and pastries in town. It was a popular teenage hangout, but on the morning of 26 December, the store hadn't even served its first customer when it was struck by the first of two waves that were to change the city forever. A broken clock, which I found on the floor of the bakery, read 9:32, the time when the first wave hit. Five workers, all girls, were hurled to the back of the store by the force of a furious torrent of water that drowned out their desperate screams. None of them had really stood a chance.

Residents who survived pointed out that they made it only because they saw the water advancing towards them, giving them the few precious extra seconds to be mentally prepared to deal with the deluge – and they didn't panic. One person, who became an icon and a symbol of quick thinking, was nine-year-old Tharesh Liyanage. He was reading in bed that Sunday, when he caught the sound of what seemed like the very loud splashing of waves on rocks. He heard the sound twice, but since he was immersed in his book he left it to his mother and maid to go outside and check. Within seconds, their terrified screams filled the house, forcing Tharesh out of his bed. Even before he could react, however, water entered their living room. It came in so fast and with such awesome intensity that it knocked down their ancestral home's main wall. 'We were trapped and couldn't move,' recalled Tharesh. 'We couldn't find the keys to open the door and get to the safety of the first floor.'

The Liyanage home was built about seventy years earlier by Tharesh's grandfather. Located about 100 metres from the shore, it was lavishly decorated, showcasing the family's wealth and prosperity that had been earned from decades of building and renting property. The Liyanages also owned a large part of the town's main commercial district as well as a factory in the harbour that manufactured and sold ice to Galle's fishermen for preserving their catch.

On the morning of 26 December, Tharesh's father, Udyoga Liyanage, kept to his routine, leaving for work at 7:30 a.m. His wife Ishwarie, two maids, son Tharesh and the family's cat stayed at home. At about 9:30 a.m., Udyoga heard some commotion and rushed outside his office. 'I saw the sea coming into the harbour,' he exclaimed. 'It wasn't a wave. It was a mountain of water.'

Udyoga held his nerve and yelled at his workers to get inside the building. Everybody heeded his advice, except tractor driver Gunapala Mabotuwana, who opted to drive his vehicle away from the advancing wave. Udyoga knew Gunapala's life was in grave danger because the waves had, by this time, advanced right up to his factory, hurling a fishing boat through the front of his own office. But before trying to rescue his employee, Udyoga had to somehow warn his family members, who were directly in the path of the waves. Sweating profusely, he rushed to the phone and dialled home. 'The phone rang ten times,' he recalled. But no one picked it up. In that time, the water had raced upwards from Udyoga's ankles, to his waist and then to his neck.

As he looked around, Udyoga realized he himself could die. He didn't know how to swim, so he rushed inside the factory into a room that had a 20-foot-high ceiling to accommodate generators and other machinery. Sloshing about in the water here were two large wooden boards that were once fitted with meters and the electrical circuits of his factory. He clambered onto these boards and then, mustering every ounce of strength in his body, he pushed himself towards a narrow opening. 'There was only about a foot of space left between the rising water and the ceiling, but I managed to drag myself to the other room, where I clung onto a piece of machinery.'

Back at the Liyanage home, it took just about fifteen seconds for the water to cover Tharesh up to his neck. (His mother was holding onto him in an attempt to save his life.) Like his father, he too couldn't swim and was having difficulty breathing. 'The water was pushing me up and down, but every time just before I went down I always took a deep breath,' he said, stressing that it was getting harder with every passing second to clasp onto his mother's hand: 'My mother was pulling one way and the water the other. But the water was so powerful that my mother could not hold onto me.'

Seconds later, there was the sound of a huge crack. An iron grill in the living room snapped and all the water trapped inside the house, with Tharesh in it, surged out onto the road, towards the front of the Liyanage home. Once on the road, Tharesh was dragged down thrice by the tremendous force of the water. 'It was as if some invisible arms were pulling me down by my legs. Every time I went down I tried not to drink that black stuff. But the last time I went under, I stayed there for a very long time and swallowed water.'

When he came back to the surface, Tharesh could clearly see the mango tree in his front yard. His mother was floating next to it in a state of complete disarray. The last time he saw her, she had fainted. In the meantime, the water continued destroying everything in its way, this time tearing down the steel door to a warehouse about 100 metres from the Liyanage home.

As the water roared into the warehouse, Tharesh too was hurled inside. The warehouse was dark, but the nine-year-old didn't panic and when his eyes had adjusted to the light he noticed that tonnes of stored chemicals had leaked into the water. 'I knew that if I swallowed some of the stuff in the water I would die,' he remembered, 'so I climbed up onto some sacks and reached a metal grill, which I clung onto.' Then he shouted at the top of his voice for as long as he could. 'People saw me but no one could come and rescue me. It was as if I was at one end of a big lake and they were at the other.'

While he was stuck in the inky darkness of the building, Tharesh found that he had a calf for company. (We found out later that the calf somehow managed to survive.) 'He floated for a while and then he too clambered onto some sacks for safety.' As he held on for dear life, Tharesh heard his thirty-five-year-old maid, Neelanti, cry out to him: 'Are you okay, are you okay, my baby?' she asked repeatedly, weeping all the time. Ten minutes later, there were no more questions. The sea had claimed yet another victim.

At work, Udyoga had by now started to worry about tractor driver Gunapala, who was caught in the swirling, churning waters. From the safety provided by the height of the factory, other workers tried hurling ropes to him, but to no avail. He just couldn't latch on. Udyoga then asked him to cling onto a tree and he managed to do so for a while. But the strong current soon toppled the tree. All Udyoga could do was watch helplessly: 'I saw his face then and just can't describe it. It will stay with me forever. He knew he was going to die.' Seconds later, a screaming Gunapala was swept out of the compound. Workers later found his body crushed by a telephone pole that had crashed onto him.

It took the sea just about one minute to tear past the Liyanages' factory, flood their home and then sweep Tharesh out onto the street and into the warehouse. As he clung onto the metal grill, waiting to be rescued, Tharesh had a moment to pause and think about his torment. 'I first thought this wave would be the end of me,' he felt. 'But I then said to myself: "I have to survive, I have to manage myself. I want to see my other family members and be happy. I want to see that moment."'

But to see that moment, Tharesh had to put up with a lot more trauma. Several tourists went by his house and he was sure they had heard him. 'They didn't help me and I wanted to shout out at them: "You jerks".' Forty-five minutes later, two locals heard him and transported him into the waiting arms of his father. As they embraced, both realized that Ishwarie was probably dead. But there was no time to mourn or look for her body. They had to immediately move to a safer building away from the water, just in case the sea moved in again.

'We jumped over dead bodies to get to that building,' said Tharesh. 'I could feel flesh under my feet.' As they walked through waist-deep water they saw people hanging and screaming from windows. By the time they reached the fourth floor of a building, almost half a kilometre from their house, Tharesh noticed that the water was rising again. 'From the balcony I could see many elderly women climbing up trees and people running everywhere – they were running like deer. Then I saw the water catch one running man. A second later, he was gone.'

For the next few hours, till almost 2:00 p.m., father and son stayed on in the building. By that time, Tharesh had developed a fever and was also throwing up. His father kept vigil, staring all the time at the harbour. He observed: 'Large ships were moving in and out of the harbour as if they were being controlled by some force.' By watching the landmarks he was familiar with, Udyoga realized that the water level had receded and it was time to make a final dash for the centre of town. As they raced out of the building, they found that both weren't wearing any shoes and suffered lacerations when they stepped over the scattered debris, which contained sharp objects such as nails and glass. Seeing their plight, a young man stepped forward and carried a semi-delirious Tharesh for the last 2 km into town.

As he made that journey, Tharesh thought about his 'miraculous escape', which he attributed to his presence of mind. 'I didn't know how to swim, but I knew it was important to hold my breath,' he later stated. He also acknowledged that he was lucky to have survived because he could just as easily have been swept out by the sea into a drain, instead of the safety of a warehouse. His father was more philosophical. 'Tharesh survived because of all his good deeds or karma. If you do good, then good happens to you. For us Buddhists it's a tit-for-tat principle. Tharesh's karma gave him the luck and strength he needed to survive. It's what we call *karmashakti*.'

Once they reached the centre of town, the Liyanages – one of the town's most prominent families – were immediately recognized and swarmed by a small crowd of well-wishers. All offered emotional support. Someone ran to get them water and just as quickly a scooter taxi was located to transport them to Udyoga's eldest brother's house in Galle. 'As I reached the house, I was shouting: "The maids are dead and my wife's missing".' His three nieces rushed up to him and said: 'So is Dad.'

The turmoil and grief that engulfed the Liyanage household were being replicated in countless other homes across the city. Just a short distance from the bus stand, several residents were standing in small clusters whispering among themselves and reliving the horror of what they had been through. Resident Don Vitarana's eyes were bloodshot when I first saw him listlessly staring out to sea. He still hadn't found the bodies of two members of his family. In all, eight of his loved ones, including his mother, had been killed when their house collapsed on them. 'If my mother was alive, I could do everything,' he sobbed. 'Now that my mother has gone, I can't do anything.'

Those who hadn't lost family members were also traumatized because of all the material damage that they had suffered. Dilipa Charles Silva was visiting Galle from Colombo with his family, when he saw the water racing towards him: 'I just jumped out of my car and saw it going with the water like a rocket,' he told me. Within minutes, the water had taken it hundreds of metres away. Now Silva, assisted by a few friends, had located his car but its body and engine were both smashed beyond repair. Also smashed in the process was Silva's confidence and his outgoing nature. 'I don't think it's possible to celebrate New Year because everyone is in a sad mood and coming here for New Year is like coming to a dead city.'

'Happy New Year' signs splashed across the city now seemed strangely out of place. Sri Lanka had declared five days of mourning and Silva's feelings reflected the national mood. 'I am scared, I am fearful,' he said. 'I had never seen people dying before. Now I have seen a lot of people dying in front of my eyes. I don't think I will go to the sea for a long time. I don't think I will drive in that area again.'

By now the interest in the CNN system for what had happened (and was happening) in Galle was growing by the minute. My next *live* shot was for our Europe show, beamed out from London and anchored by Richard Quest – whom I regard as one of CNN's best. 'Why are you in Galle?' asked Richard as he 'tossed' to me. I explained that the country's second-largest city was now representative of what Sri Lankans in general were going through. As we talked, cameraman Sanjiv continued to pan his camera to show the hectic activity all around us.

At the bus stand, there were scenes of utter confusion. Government engineers, who were arriving to take stock of the situation, didn't know where to begin deploying their heavy machinery. But small-time efforts at recovery continued, with a solitary crane pulling out buses smashed by tonnes of rubble. Dozens of residents also attached cables to cars and vans, heaving and groaning in their struggle to pull them out.

As all these activities continued, Wasantha and his family patiently stood by the bus stand in the blazing sun with nothing to eat and drink. I felt terrible and offered them the only food we had – bananas. I also pleaded with Wasantha to find us any form of transport so that he and his family could go home. Half an hour later, a huge bus pulled up beside us. It was owned by professional photographer Nalaka Karunarathna who had heard that CNN was looking for a vehicle and offered us the bus for $100 a day. I grabbed the opportunity, but even before we could start loading our gear on board, Nalaka briefly excused himself. Attaching a thick steel cable to a hook at the rear of his bus, he pulled out two other buses tangled among the damage and debris of the bus stand. I was upset at first, but then realized business was only a secondary concern for the people of Galle. They first felt that they had to help each other.

Once our equipment was loaded onto the bus, we prepared for another *live* shot and bade goodbye to Wasantha and his wonderful family. Their compassion and kindness had moved all of us and we had become good friends in just a matter of hours. As he left with a cheery wave, I knew we would be running into Wasantha again.

With transport on hand, I could finally breathe easier. We even had airconditioning on board and in temperatures that were now about 35 degrees centigrade, it was a welcome relief. I felt even better when I checked the fuel meter. We had enough diesel to last us the full day, even if we kept the engine and airconditioning running.

I also had to keep building the momentum on the story. And to do that, I needed more eyewitness accounts of what had happened. Just across the bus stand, I noticed Galle's railway station, where I sought out the stationmaster. 'I can never forget that moment,' he recounted. 'The tsunami was like a black snake coming towards us at a height of about 20 feet through the bus stand.' As he spoke, he pointed to the bus depot, just a stone's throw away. 'The black water that came at us wasn't a wave, but it was like a river,' he said.

Luckily for him and other train commuters, there was a huge drain in between the bus stand and the train station. The drain acted as a barrier, marginally slowing down the force of the water. Still, when the water washed into the station, it carried such a punch that entire trains, weighing thousands of tonnes, started floating and bobbing around almost 4 feet above the platform.

The stationmaster's first concern was for the safety of about twenty people milling around the ticket counter: 'I took them upstairs and then over a bridge and then ran over to the hill there,' he said, pointing towards it. No one was killed at the railway station, but the entire railway network was destroyed. It would be months before a vital lifeline for the people in southern Sri Lanka could be put back in place and trains could run again.

It was now just past 3:00 p.m. and recognizing the pace at which we had been working, my 'minder' at the International Desk informed me we had two hours before the next *live* shot. We decided to keep the bus with all our equipment parked at the bus depot and to make our way to the local hospital to find out how doctors there were coping. Once again, our trouble was transport. And once again, Wasantha 'rode in' to our rescue. After a few hours of rest and a shower at home, he was back to see if we needed any help and volunteered to drive us to the hospital a few kilometres away.

Nothing, not even all my prior experience of reporting wars in Kashmir, Iraq, Kosovo and Afghanistan, and also natural disasters and riots, prepared me for the horror of what I saw at the hospital. Hundreds of coffins were littered everywhere. The smell of disinfectant hung in the air. A man wailed, beating his chest, and others stood by with tears in their eyes and handkerchiefs around their noses and mouths. A truck was parked just metres from the entrance packed with what I estimated must have been more than 100 bodies.

Masked hospital workers were loading dozens more onto the truck and were quite obviously in a rush. Many bodies had bloated to almost four times their normal size and had to be buried quickly. Cameraman Sanjiv volunteered to find some other shots elsewhere in the hospital. I stopped him. I strongly felt that there was just no point in putting such pictures on our network.

Instead, I decided to observe the scene so that I could talk about it in my *live* reports. Vans and trucks continued to bring in fresh coffins to the hospital. Almost as soon as they arrived, they were filled up with bodies, and mourning and wailing family members were left to take their loved ones home. My concentration was interrupted by Wasantha tugging at my arm. At his side was his childhood friend, the forensic pathologist at the hospital, Dr Rohan Rowanapura, and he wanted to make an introduction.

Dr Rowanapura managed a weak smile as we shook hands. The Russian-educated pathologist had been working non-stop for the past two days photographing, fingerprinting and taking DNA samples of seven hundred bodies that had been brought to the hospital within hours of the tragedy. 'I couldn't believe it. I didn't expect to see that many dead bodies at once,' he said. 'And when I saw children, ladies and males all dead, for some time I couldn't get myself organized; I didn't know what to do.' What was even more disturbing for the father of three girls was that a majority of the dead were children. 'Most children died of drowning,' he pointed out to me, basically because the water level took some time to recede. Even with so many dead children, though, no one had stepped forward to claim their bodies. 'This wave killed not only the children, but entire families,' lamented Dr Rowanapura. 'Mothers, fathers, grandfathers, the whole lot, were killed in some cases, and there was no one to come and identify [the bodies]. It's a very sad experience but you have to cope with it.'

Despite his initial hesitation, Galle's leading forensic pathologist quickly organized his staff so that bodies which had been identified could be released to family members, even without postmortems. His biggest challenge, however, was dealing with more than four hundred unclaimed bodies. There were no refrigerated trucks and his hospital's own refrigeration unit had broken down. He could have stored all the bodies on ice slabs, but every single ice factory in and around Galle had been damaged. Embalming was another option he considered, but every undertaker in the city was extremely busy. Finally, he decided on partially embalming the bodies with formalin, a chemical that prevents decomposition and also minimizes odour.

Once this process was complete, Dr Rowanapura and his staff photographed the four hundred unidentified bodies and took DNA samples from each of them. He then logged, sealed and stored all personal belongings found on the bodies, such as watches, keys and jewellery, because he believed they would later help families identify their relatives. Also, by this time he had heard widespread reports of bodies being looted and he wanted to put an end to that: 'It is utter disrespect for the dead if you take their jewellery and money. And if you do that you can't be recognized as a member of society.'

With the forensic formalities completed, Dr Rowanapura took one of the most painful decisions of his life, and ordered a mass burial. All the unidentified bodies were trucked to a rubber plantation (about a thirty-minute drive out of town), where Sri Lankan soldiers had dug a 50-metre-long ditch. Standing beside tonnes of freshly dug earth, a group of Buddhist, Christian and Muslim priests read the last rites for those who had perished without any warning and in the flicker of an eye. As he watched, Dr Rowanapura felt himself caught on the horns of a dilemma. As a deeply sympathetic and caring individual, he strongly felt the need to hand over all the bodies to relatives. He believed such an action would have given thousands closure and reduced their stress and suffering. On the other hand, when he put on his scientist's hat, Dr Rowanapura knew the bodies had to be buried quickly, otherwise the island faced the risk of an epidemic.

Before he had ordered the mass burial, Dr Rowanapura was extra careful, and had even told his staff not to keep men and women together because that could offend some Sri Lankans. 'I did everything possible to give dignity to the dead,' he said, pausing to let his thoughts sink in. 'When people are alive they can talk and defend themselves,' he said, 'but when they are dead there is nobody to speak for them so you should respect them. You should work for them and you should speak for them. So I took a human and professional responsibility to do that and tried to give the maximum for people who are dead.'

Dr Rowanapura's diligence ensured that no dead body was dumped into a mass grave as an unknown.

Amidst all the grief and suffering, Dr Rowanapura just kept going. For many Sri Lankans he was a true hero – a man who did a tough job quietly and with an understated style that often belied his strength as a wonderful and caring human being.

As I drove away from the hospital, I knew our paths would cross again. But for the time being, I had to concentrate on the story. I had to tell the world what I had seen at the hospital. Minutes before my *live* shot, I was overcome with nausea and a splitting headache. I immediately doused myself with cold water and tried to come to grips with my emotions. I had just seen too much and, as a father of two young girls, the death of so many children had affected me deeply. What added to my anxiety was the fact that I was now entering my third straight day without any sleep or proper food.

But I had to wait for hours before these needs could be met. Both CNN International and CNN USA were still asking for *live* shots, but with no power or street lighting, working conditions were truly ghastly. We were being 'eaten' alive by swarms of mosquitoes that had bred in the unhygienic environment caused by debris strewn all around. And each time we turned on our battery-operated lights for a *live* shot, they attracted thousands of winged insects that got into my mouth, nose and eyes. What added to my sense of discomfort in these dreary conditions was that I still didn't know if we had a place to spend the night, so I started forewarning the crew – which had by now been strengthened by the arrival of assignment editor Prithwi by road from Colombo – to be fully prepared to sleep in the bus.

It wasn't a bad idea. The bus was fairly large and we could easily stretch out on the seats to catch a nap. There were also enough lights inside to make it a functional office and it was here that I started writing my script. I hadn't written more than a few sentences when yet again I was interrupted by the arrival of Wasantha. He had a funny habit of disappearing on us, but each time he came back, he had some piece of news or information that helped me tell the story better. I smiled as Wasantha walked into the bus and introduced me to a local photographer.

Ajanta Samarawickrama had the presence of mind to keep his video camera rolling as the tsunami swept into the city and we quickly set up our equipment to transfer his footage. There was hushed silence as we recorded the first frame of the video. It showed a scooter taxi being propelled along by a raging torrent of water. The taxi knocked over a man as it raced along at tremendous speed. As the video had been shot from one of the tall buildings at the bus stand itself, it was easy for all of us to identify landmarks and locations. (Our current *live* shot location was, till just recently, under 20 feet of angry water that carried everything with it: scooters, cars, vans and small wooden shacks.) Ajanta's video had captured many more scenes: People struggling to get away from the torrent and able-bodied males quickly clambering onto buildings and overturned buses.

Hundreds of women and children weren't as fortunate. The footage showed a group of about twenty trying to seek shelter behind a concrete wall. Within seconds the water came roaring at them and for a nanosecond it appeared that they would be able to withstand its awesome power. But then the water won the battle, dragging screaming children and women out to sea. These were clearly some of the most powerful eyewitness video clips of the tsunami from anywhere in the world and they would soon be on our network. I decided I didn't need to use too many words or a lengthy script to describe such self-explanatory and incredibly emotive images. My script that night would be short and punchy.

The tape continued to roll. It showed waves demolishing almost everything and pushing tonnes of debris made up of smashed cars, buses, neon signs and pillars towards several stores on the side of the bus station. Almost everything in sight had been destroyed except for two large Buddha statues. The water had smashed the glass case enclosing the figures, but they suffered no major damage. One shot, in fact, captured three children clambering to safety on top of the concrete structure that housed one of the Buddhas.

Fifteen to twenty minutes after the tsunami shattered Galle, the water started retreating and photographer Ajanta now focused on family members looking for their loved ones. Some found them quickly and began dragging them through waist-deep water. Others who had sought shelter on high ground also started clambering down. Except for one woman. When the water rushed in she had somehow managed to climb or had been helped onto the roof of a store adjacent to the bus stand. Now she was sprawled on the roof, her head thrown back in a sure sign of death. I could only guess that she had suffered a heart attack brought about by the suddenness with which the tsunami had struck.

As I raced through the video I saw a tall man fighting with a younger, shorter person who was carrying a woman in his arms. It was hard to tell if the woman was dead or alive, but the taller man was agitated enough to rain blows on the shorter fellow, who had by this time dropped the woman he was carrying on the ground. A heated argument then ensued, ending only when the shorter man picked up the woman and retreated out of the frame. The video was disturbing, but since I couldn't provide any context or background to what was happening, I decided not to air it, at least for the moment.

Some 20,000 people were by now confirmed dead in Sri Lanka and this video explained how many met their end. Without wasting a moment we started to transmit these pictures to Atlanta and I began writing a script to augment our footage. It didn't take long. I had seen so much, the script literally poured out of me in a matter of minutes. The time now was well past 2:00 a.m. We were all emotionally drained, but by this time we had managed to find a hotel with enough rooms to take us all. I felt a wave of relief wash over me. In the midst of so much human trauma, small things did matter and it was important that the crew slept well. We still had a lot of work to do.

Just before we left for our hotel, the phone rang. It was Chris Cramer, my boss and managing director of CNN International. He told us that he had been deeply moved by our coverage, which he described as evocative and human. His words meant a lot to me and I quickly passed on his message to the crew.

As professionals, we all felt we had done our best. We also recognized that our coverage would bring much-needed relief and assistance to Sri Lanka, but we still couldn't come to terms with what was still happening around us.

I decided to sort out my feelings the next day. All that mattered to me now was to get some sleep. My body needed it.

3

Another Killer Wave

'I managed to hold him for a while, but I just couldn't hold on...
I could only see my son's face as he was being swept away.'

Dateline: Galle Harbour, 29–30 December 2004

I WOKE UP ON THE MORNING OF 29 DECEMBER FEELING refreshed and ready. Sleep had become a rare luxury since the tsunami, but there was a certain rush of energy that kept us all going. My 7:00 a.m. *live* shot was set up outside Galle's main police station, which, as seemed to be the case everywhere, hardly had anything worthwhile left behind. Inside, hundreds of files, communication equipment and furniture had been destroyed and, outside, in the courtyard, several smashed police cars and a huge fishing boat lay in disarray. But perhaps the single most stirring image here was a car planted half way up a tree, perfectly defining the chaos and shock throughout the city. With even the police and government infrastructure destroyed or rendered ineffective, I thought the day's top story ought to be the struggle involved and the effort needed to provide relief to hundreds and thousands of homeless Sri Lankans.

As the possibility of finding survivors became increasingly remote, many CNN anchors, including the legendary Larry King, wanted to know how those who had managed to escape were coping. Before the tsunami, many Americans knew little about Sri Lanka, but now they had been so deeply touched by the tragedy, they wanted to know more and find out how they could help. Their deep sympathy was reflected in our numbers. Since CNN started reporting the story on Sunday, 26 December, our prime-time numbers in the United States were 26 per cent higher than the previous three-week average. On Monday, our numbers soared 69 per cent over their normal average. And on Tuesday, CNN's prime-time audience had grown to almost 1.5 million or 81 per cent greater than the same day last year.

The interest in the story was unprecedented because of the sheer scale and geographical expanse of the disaster. Twelve countries had been hit in a matter of seven hours. Nations such as Sri Lanka and Thailand, both popular holiday destinations, were struck at the peak of the tourist season when coastal hotels were jampacked with visitors from all over the world. Almost 2000 Swedes alone were killed, making it that country's worst-ever national tragedy. People across the world were drawn to the story because all humans everywhere have an intrinsic relationship with their natural environment. What happened across Asia was now redefining that relationship and what struck hundreds of millions across several countries was a sense of mutual vulnerability. The overwhelming feeling was that this could have happened anywhere, to anyone.

In spite of the huge losses and my pangs of guilt and remorse that I couldn't do more to help, I realized we had to continue with our journalism and professional mission. My team was tired, jittery and anxious, but in remembrance of those who had died and to support those still grieving, we had to stretch ourselves beyond our presumed physical and mental capabilities. I started to think of the assignment as a marathon, but one which we were running at the pace of a 400-metre race. I knew such an approach could lead to a quick burnout, but for the sake of the story, which was being so closely followed across the world, I knew this was a risk we just had to take.

With Galle more or less covered, we decided to travel further south towards the nearby town of Matara, which was under Portuguese and Dutch rule at different points of time. The narrow road to Matara winds along the coastline and the windswept beaches along the way are a sight to behold. But that's not what caught my eye that morning. I was more interested in a unique display of local ingenuity. Frustrated with the delayed arrival of recovery teams, residents had deployed some elephants to salvage their precious belongings. One elephant was trying to drag out a car from the collapsed porch of a house. A rope attached to the back of the car was wound around the elephant's trunk and, after a series of tugs, the tusker managed to pull it clear of fallen beams and shattered tiles. Cheers and hoops of joy greeted the elephant's effort, and he returned to his task of pulling out yet another car with gusto.

With the road from Colombo now cleared, more and more heavy-lifting equipment, bulldozers and other vehicles were being driven south to help remove debris. As we continued our journey, we came across several trucks carrying drinking water in bottles and large plastic tanks for distribution. We also noticed small clusters of people lining up by vans, distributing a wide range of items – clothes, candy, cookies and tea. Many complained that the supplies were insufficient, but the good news was that relief was finally arriving.

With thousands of bodies yet to be cremated or buried, officials understandably remained concerned about the outbreak of an epidemic. The overwhelming stench of decaying bodies lingered all along the coast, forcing residents to take cover behind masks and towels. Many doctors had warned of an epidemic that could eventually claim more victims than the tsunami itself. Such fears never materialized, fortunately, but it was clear that another health crisis was looming. With relatives and friends dead, millions of Sri Lankans were emotionally traumatized and needed help far beyond the capabilities of the state. Graveyards by the highway were still full of mourners levelling the earth after burying their loved ones. Our cameras caught forty-year-old Anura Aparekkage shovelling mud into his father's grave. 'He was pushed by the water, out onto the street and then swept away to sea,' he told us, lamenting that it was the last time he saw him alive. Aparekkage and most others in this neighbourhood had, by that time, given up all hope of finding any survivors. It was more important for them to conclude religious rites of lighting lamps and placing flowers by the graves of those they had lost so suddenly.

Just a few kilometres down the road, hotelier Gamini Sumitnanaykar was rummaging through what remained of the restaurant and hotel he had constructed with his life savings. Sumitnanaykar had been forewarned by a guest that huge waves were coming towards them, but his first thought was to find his family and rush them to safety. When he returned to his property, all that was left was rubble. His dream of coming to Sri Lanka and providing adequately for his family after several years of waiting tables in the Gulf had been swept away by the tsunami. 'I feel very very alone,' he sobbed. 'None of us know if we have a future.'

Sumitnanaykar's story underscored the intense damage to one of Sri Lanka's major industries – tourism – which brings in a large majority of the country's foreign exchange. Several hotels along the coast had been demolished and with thousands of tourists cancelling their bookings, it was unclear how the country would ever get back on its feet. Sumitnanaykar's uncertainties were mirrored in dozens of towns and across thousands of homes in the country. Some even estimated that 400,000 jobs in the country had been wiped out.

Our next stop was the town of Matara, where many lives had been lost in a small Catholic church, named 'Our Lady of Matara'. The church was just a short distance away from the sea and, on 26 December 2004, the Reverend Charles

Hewawasam was at the altar giving communion to about 100 parishioners when the sea poured in. The force was such that a van was carried by the water towards the church's front door. After the water receded, and ensuring that most of the worshippers had escaped to the safety of a taller building next door, Reverend Charles himself rushed back to the altar. He was deeply concerned about the safety of a 500-year-old relic, the famous idol of Mary and Baby Jesus, which had given both the church and city its name. He looked everywhere and was crestfallen to find that it had simply disappeared. There was more bad news. Twenty of his parishioners were dead, including the nun who had been giving communion with him. For the next three days, a despondent Reverend Charles buried the dead but continued praying for the idol's safe return. On Wednesday, the priest went to the water's edge and later described his mood at that moment to CNN's Anderson Cooper: 'As I was watching the sea, I said, my goodness you have to come today. That was the only thing I said. You have to come today. I have a great mission. I have to console my people.'

A few hours later, the idol was found in a pile of debris about one-and-a-half kilometres from the church. Remarkably, the crown on Baby Jesus's head had suffered no major damage. Reverend Charles's prayers had been answered and he told CNN it was one of the most poignant moments in his career as a clergyman: 'So what I [felt] is that she was with the people, with her children. She didn't want to escape and she didn't want anyone to take her and hide her somewhere. She went with the people and she carried Jesus. For her to come back is a miracle.'

According to local legend, the relic first came from the sea when it was found 500 years ago by fishermen. It was then lost twice, first on its way to Europe and then on the way back. But miraculously on both occasions the image was relocated. Now after being found a third time, the affection and religious sentiment surrounding Our Lady of Matara had multiplied.

Just a short distance away from the church, we were surprised to find heavy traffic and shoppers going about their business. After surviving for several days on just bananas and coconuts, this was an opportunity we were not willing to miss. We stacked water, cookies and tinned food, relieved that our palates were finally going to get a taste of something different. What we forgot in the midst of our shopping frenzy was how low we were on fuel: we didn't even have enough to drive back to Galle for more *live* shots.

We tried our luck at a few gas stations, only to realize the hopelessness of the situation. Tempers were flaring in the long line-up and, even if we did get our chance after waiting for hours, the best we could hope for was a few litres of diesel. Realizing we were sunk, I decided to meet the senior most police official in town, who was remarkably receptive. Within moments, we had an escort and the requisite paperwork that would provide us enough fuel to get back to Galle.

On the drive back, I received an important call from New Delhi informing me we had received clearance from the Indian Navy to cover its largest-ever humanitarian relief operation outside its territorial waters. What was even more encouraging was that we had been cleared to fly in their helicopters; permission Indian authorities are normally very reluctant to give to international news teams. Within moments of receiving the message, I called my old friend Nirupama Rao, the Indian high commissioner in Colombo. Formerly a spokesperson for India's Ministry of External Affairs, the high commissioner was well respected in media circles and quickly understood that we wanted to report *live* from the ships. She promised to help us get on board the naval vessels as soon as possible.

Indian ships had by now arrived and anchored off the coast of Galle in an operation that was launched with incredible speed and efficiency. Within half an hour of the first wave lashing the east coast, India's military advisor attached to the High Commission in Colombo received a phone call. Captain Suraj Berry was on a picnic with his children in Pinnewala, an hour's drive from Colombo and home to an orphanage for baby elephants, when he was told that huge waves had lashed the east coast. The next call was from Nirupama Rao. She was holidaying in India and wanted Captain Berry to check into calls she had received that said Sri Lanka had been 'lashed by tidal waves'.

Realizing something serious was afoot, Captain Berry contacted a senior officer at Sri Lanka's Naval Headquarters. The official told the Indian defence advisor that they had been hit by a tsunami and Sri

Lanka immediately needed boats and helicopters to deal with intense flooding and widespread casualties on the coast. By 10:30 a.m., Captain Berry had abandoned his picnic and was driving back at full speed towards Colombo. On his way, he called India's Naval Headquarters in New Delhi to inform the concerned officials that Colombo had requested air evacuation facilities as soon as possible.

By 2:00 p.m., Sri Lanka formally made a request to the Indians for helicopters, boats, rations and medical teams. By 3:00 p.m., New Delhi had readied a Dornier aircraft with a doctor, two paramedics and 750 kg of medical supplies to be flown into Sri Lanka. Shortly thereafter, the Sri Lankan prime minister, Mahinda Rajapakse, spoke with his Indian counterpart, Dr Manmohan Singh, and by 4:30 p.m. the aircraft was cleared to fly. When this aircraft landed at Colombo's Ratmalana Air Force base at 7:30 p.m. the same day, it signalled the beginning of what would be the world's largest relief operation; one in which the Indians – whose own coastline had also been smothered by the tsunami, killing more than 10,000 people – were to play a sterling role.

The first Indian doctor to arrive in Sri Lanka on board the Dornier was surgeon Lieutenant Commander Gopalan Parthasarathy, from the state of Tamil Nadu – India's worst affected area. While he was preparing to deploy, his own home had been swept away and his mother and grandmother were missing. Just hours before he boarded the plane, the Indian medical officer learnt his mother had been located. As he left for Sri Lanka, his grandmother was still missing and wouldn't be found for another day.

Meanwhile, frantic preparations were being made by the Indians in the coastal city of Cochin in Kerala. India's chief of naval staff had given the green signal to send the offshore patrol vessel, the INS *Sharda*, with medical teams, divers, inflatable craft and 2500 kg of medical supplies to Galle. The *Sharda* sailed on 26 December itself, arriving in Galle the next day. Another Indian ship, the INS *Sutlej*, with nine doctors, eighteen paramedics, medical supplies, blankets and a diving team also set sail, reaching Galle on the evening of 27 December.

The lightning speed with which the Indian relief operations were deployed was facilitated by some intense training conducted just before the outbreak of the Iraq war in 2003, when New Delhi feared it may have to evacuate more than three million of its citizens from the Middle East. The need for a mass evacuation never materialized, but when Captain Berry called Naval Headquarters to inform senior officers of a humanitarian catastrophe in Sri Lanka, they quickly seized the opportunity to put that training to good use. Besides, as Captain Berry explained, it was time the world learnt of the 'Indian Navy's capabilities and its intention to be a blue-water force'.

On 27 December, Captain Berry himself flew to Galle to make an on-the-spot assessment. 'I saw two buses on top of each other. There were boats and bodies on the road and a car was stuck on the first floor of a building. The general public looked dazed.' As he toured the area, the Indian defence advisor took dozens of pictures. In a few hours, he had emailed the pictures back to New Delhi. By 11:00 a.m., Indian naval officers steaming towards Galle

Photograph taken at Campbell Bay, Andaman and Nicobar Islands.
(*Courtesy*: Associated Press/Manish Swarup.)

Photograph taken at Nagapattinam, southern Tamil Nadu.
(*Courtesy*: Associated Press/Gautam Singh.)

An entire fishing fleet destroyed in a coastal area of Tamil Nadu.
(*Courtesy*: *India Today*/Gireesh G.V.)

People searching for their belongings amidst the devastation
at Nochikuppam, near Chennai, Tamil Nadu.
(*Courtesy*: Associated Press/M. Lakshman.)

Photograph taken at Nagapattinam, southern Tamil Nadu.
(*Courtesy*: Associated Press/Gurinder Osan.)

A tsunami survivor being carried to the only doctor for the entire population of Teressa, Andaman and Nicobar Islands. (*Courtesy*: *India Today*/Soumitra Ghosh.)

The last rites: Sri Lankan soldiers carrying away bodies from the wreckage of a train, Peraliya, southern Sri Lanka. (*Courtesy*: *The Sunday Times*, Colombo, Sri Lanka.)

started bombarding him with questions. 'They wanted to know the state of the harbour and if power was available,' recounted Captain Berry. 'I told them they would have to do everything themselves using the resources available on the ships.'

Captain Berry's advice was based on what he saw within Galle harbour itself – perhaps one of the most important naval bases in Sri Lanka. A large part of the base had been wiped out, many naval personnel had been killed and the survivors were in a state of shock. The Navy had been caught completely off guard and none of its ships on the seas had even radioed-in a warning. On that morning, base commander Captain Suddhararan Silva was in his bungalow where he had planned to celebrate his younger son Karishka's eighth birthday. Suddenly, his wife rushed into the room screaming: 'The water's coming.' Captain Silva's initial response was to stay put in his room. 'Being a naval guy you don't panic when you see water.'

But in a few seconds, the water came up to their necks and the base commander quickly put his wife and children on a high window ledge. 'There were just six inches left between us and the ceiling and that's how we managed to breathe.' The entire family then clung onto a ceiling fan and tried breaking the ceiling to get onto the roof, but failed. 'We couldn't do anything,' remembered Captain Silva. 'You couldn't even swim with so much stuff floating around in the room. You sort of had to be upright. It was very difficult.'

When the water level receded, the Silva family jumped out of a window and made a dash for the nearby two-storeyed Officers' Mess. Here, he managed to break the roof and lodge both his sons there. 'I grabbed two cushions from some chairs and told the children to use them if they needed to float. I then took my wife to the bar counter and asked her to stand on it.' With his family safe, the captain tried to take stock of the situation from a professional angle, but there was nothing he could do as the waves had lifted a Sri Lankan naval craft from one side of the jetty to the other, toppling it on its side in the process.

Aware of these circumstances, Captain Berry instructed his naval high command to throw everything into this effort. Accordingly, the Indians brought in six Russian-built helicopters, which commenced relief missions immediately. Their Dornier aircraft had already flown four sorties by 28 December and another Indian transport plane, a Russian-built Ilyushin 76, arrived that same night, ferrying in more supplies. By 29 December, the Indian relief operation was in full swing with two Indian ships in Galle and another two in Trincomalee.

With so much happening, I felt we had to stay on top of the story. I called the desk and briefed staffers that India had done all this despite suffering so much itself. We all agreed this was a rare story of international warmth and good neighbourliness that deserved a major play on CNN.

Early on 30 December, I planned to meet an Indian Navy liaison officer just outside the Sri Lankan naval base in Galle. Our escort was to arrive by boat from one of the ships and then take us back on board. As we waited for him, we gathered video shots of citizens cleaning up their streets. Some had brooms; others used their bare hands to clean out debris and shards of glass. After their mind-numbing experience, this was the first sign that the people of Galle had started their struggle to get on with their lives.

We entered the harbour only after our naval escort had managed to convince the Sri Lankans that we were not a security risk. Harbour guards were understandably quite concerned and sensitive to cameras because any pictures taken in here could reveal to rebel forces – which had been fighting the government for years – that the Navy's capabilities had been severely curtailed. As we walked into this high-security zone, I noticed that dozens of once proud ships that sailed the sea were now all on land. Those that were still in the harbour were so badly damaged that they weren't going anywhere soon. Almost everything – roads, huge bridges and pillars – had been ripped out of the ground. I got the feeling that they were mere toothpicks in the face of the tsunami.

Apart from thinking about what had happened, I also had to plan our current mission. We wanted to go *live* from the ships and, to do so, I first had to get all my gear on board. My heart sank when I saw our assigned transport, a small inflatable rubber dinghy, rigged to an outboard motor. It took 15 minutes to get the crew in and load the gear on board and our discomfort was heightened by the swell in the harbour that washed into the boat, soaking all of us and our precious cargo. A few moments later, our escort, Lieutenant A.H. Naqvi, gunned the outboard motor to life. As he opened the throttle, the boat's bow rose alarmingly, drenching us with another spray of salt water. The good part, I thought, was that we were moving at last, but we came to a lurching halt when our escort's radio crackled to life.

'Get off the water, get off the water,' screamed the anxious voice from the other end of the transmitter located aboard one of the Indian ships. 'A tsunami is hitting the coast in twenty minutes. '

I've covered wars and cyclones, but never had a sentence caused me more fear and panic. My legs froze, my normal quick thinking – honed after years of experience as a war correspondent – deserted me. I didn't know what to do and was overcome with a spell of dizziness and disorientation. 'I'm going to die in a few moments,' was all I was thinking about. Images of my wife and children flashed in my mind. And then I found hands pushing me out of the boat. Lieutenant Naqvi was yelling in my ear. 'Run,' he screamed, pumped full of adrenaline. 'Get to high ground.' After what seemed like an eternity, I managed to clamber across a six-foot harbour wall and back onto the jetty.

Here I was hit by another panic attack. Wherever I looked in the harbour, I saw death and destruction. There were overturned boats and smashed trawlers. Hundreds had died and drowned at this very spot and we could be next. There wasn't a tall building or anything resembling high ground in this area and I was quite inclined to leave our gear in the boat and just run for our lives. I was hyperventilating by now, but despite all that panic, I decided to take all our gear with us. It was very bulky and would slow us down, but I just couldn't bear the thought of telling my bosses – that is, if we survived – that we had lost a few hundred thousand dollars of equipment.

Weighed down by more than 30 kg of gear, I ran past a destroyed bridge and a few overturned boats. Behind me I could hear the heavy breathing of the rest of the crew, who were also burdened with heavy equipment. I stumbled over a rock and screamed in pain, wondering why no one from the desk had called to warn us. As we ran, the fog slowly lifted from my mind and I fumbled for my phone to call the desk. Luckily, we still had phone coverage in the harbour and I got through to desker Tess Eastment on my second attempt. She confirmed that Indian authorities had now put out a tsunami warning. The desk was getting its information from New Delhi-based correspondent Ram Ramgopal, who had been deployed off India's eastern coast in the small village of Pattinachery Nagore, about 250 km south of Chennai.

Ram and his crew, consisting of cameraman Vijay Bedi and producer Maya Garg, had started their day at about 10:00 a.m. They had been filming bulldozers that were clearing debris for over an hour when they noticed officials rounding up residents and telling them to leave. Minutes later, the CNN crew was also asked to run for safety: 'This is serious and you must leave immediately,' a government official told Ram, warning him they were expecting another tsunami. Ram, who hadn't seen the first tsunami strike the coast, didn't take the warning seriously, but by this time villagers in the area were in a state of frenzied panic. Some 3000 people rushed onto the road about 100 metres from the shore and made a dash for the railway station, where hundreds started boarding a train. Those who couldn't get inside started clambering onto the roof. No one wanted to be in the area if another tsunami was headed their way.

. Alarmed by the local reaction to the warning, Ram and crew decided to pull out. What they didn't anticipate was several people clinging onto the CNN van as it slowly moved away from the shore, where policemen were making announcements for everyone to leave. 'Within seconds, shops closed their shutters and I could sense the fear in people's eyes.' Others, recalled Ram, were very angry: 'Many people came up to me and complained that because of the warning all government officials had fled the camps and the entire relief effort and the plan to recover bodies had collapsed.' Faced with so much uncertainty and panic, Ram decided to check the story with New Delhi and called senior officials at the Home Ministry. 'I was told by an overzealous bureaucrat that a tsunami was imminent. He said they had received their information from a foreign source and they were taking it very seriously.'

Armed with this information, Ram called the International Desk to pitch for a *live* beeper: 'I felt we had to report the reaction to the warning,' he said, 'but was advised by senior deskers that a CNN report would only add to the chaos and mayhem. Besides, deskers argued, they had checked on all seismological activity in the area within the past 24 hours and were told that there was just one routine aftershock, but nothing large enough to cause a tsunami. Even though the desk had a rock-solid scientific case, I still felt we had to report the story on the ground.'

Ram's observations were mirrored by my own and, shortly after that radio warning from one of the Indian ships, the news had spread around the dock area like wildfire. Within seconds, people had started to flee in panic. The Indian ships too were not taking safety for granted and set sail at top speed for the high seas, where they would be safer. Watching these developments and the drama unfold right in front of my eyes, I felt we should be on air immediately, but I understood the desk's position to be careful, not cause any panic and emphasize to viewers that experts consulted by CNN didn't see the need for any alarm.

With a consensus finally thrashed out, Ram was the first to go on air. I listened in on my cell phone and, just seconds before I was to go *live*, Colombo stringer Iqbal Athas called to say Sri Lankan officials had also heard of the warning and they would be putting out their own advisory very shortly. Unknown to me, senior Sri Lankan officials had by this time contacted the US ambassador in Sri Lanka and asked him to call the Pacific Tsunami Warning Center in Hawaii. While these checks were going on, I reported what I was seeing. The sea was calm, the wind appeared normal, but all clearing-up operations in Galle harbour had been suspended and there wasn't a soul in sight.

By this time, my earlier sense of dread had vanished and I was composed, thanks mainly to the fact that we had found high ground and reached the Closenburg Hotel. Built by an English sea captain in the 1860s as a residence for his wife, the hotel was located on top of a small hill and provided a panoramic view of the harbour. This stunning colonial property was crowded with Indian soldiers, none of whom had panicked. The Indians have a reputation for being a disciplined force and naval doctors were calm and collected as they crowded around a radio, trying to listen to a Sri Lankan news broadcast.

I continued to report all these developments *live* through my cell phone and the crew used the opportunity to quickly set up a *live* shot. If a tsunami was on the way, we would want *live* pictures from the best vantage point, which, at the Closenburg, was a large observation post that jutted out like a peninsula into the sea. This position was also about 30 feet above sea level and I felt fairly confident that we would be safe here and not be swept away by the first wave. Adding to my confidence was the fact that the last time the tsunami had wrecked the harbour, this entire area had been left unscathed.

What I didn't factor into my risk or safety assessment was the reaction of an Indian naval helicopter pilot who had been tasked to get people as far away from shore as possible. For ten minutes, he had been flying just a few hundred feet above the coast and aggressively manoeuvring his helicopter inland. His posture highlighted his goal of getting everyone as far away from the water as possible. Trouble was, his mission clashed with our intention to be prepared to broadcast *live* at a moment's notice.

Even with the noisy and low-swooping helicopter, the crew continued to set up our *live* equipment. But the chopper pilot was in no mood to brook any interference. He made a couple of passes, one of which was so low the crew almost got haircuts. Remaining where we were was by now fraught with risk. Surviving the tsunami suddenly seemed far away; we first had to get away from a pilot who had no intention of letting us stand by the water's edge. Reluctantly, I asked the crew to dismantle the equipment and I quickly figured out a worst-case scenario plan. If the tsunami did reach here, the safest place I felt was the roof of the hotel. I had spotted several large wooden desks that were being used by Indian doctors and I made a mental note to use these to climb to the roof if we had to.

By this time, the US ambassador had called Hawaii and subsequently told Sri Lankan officials there was no reason to panic. Armed with the latest information, officials in Colombo backed down from earlier plans to issue an alert. Within minutes, Iqbal had relayed this information to me and I was back on air again, reporting the latest turn of events. Ram was in a more awkward position because the Indians never officially withdrew their warning. 'After a few hours people just started meandering home,' he reported. There was so much confusion that the Indian prime minister even had to cancel his planned trip to the area. But on the ground, Ram saw a silver lining in the entire episode: 'It showed that there was a system in place, no matter how crude or unsophisticated, and if there really had been a threat, it [the warning] would have saved a lot of lives.'

Later that day, India's science and technology minister, Kapil Sibal, was highly critical of the Home Ministry for issuing the alert. It was also then revealed that a private US-based research group had predicted the tsunami. Admitting the goof-up, India's home minister, Shivraj Patil, declared: 'If we committed the mistake, we made it for the sake of safety.'

As the tsunami scare died down, I stayed on in the harbour and talked about the day's developments in my next few *live* shots, which we, to make a point, shot at the same location from where we were forced to move by the helicopter pilot. This position also offered us a perfect shot of the 1500-tonne ship that had been lifted out of the water and was stuck on the jetty. Producers in Atlanta were amazed by the pictures and the day's high-adrenaline developments, but I still didn't have enough material to file a story that evening.

With daylight quickly fading, I ran back to the Closenburg Hotel where I witnessed something truly heart-warming. The owner of the hotel, Kumar Abhayawardene, had collected a small mountain of clothes from across the country to distribute to those who had lost everything. The clothes were piled up in the lobby of the hotel, a place where once the city's well-heeled enjoyed their high tea. This time around, rather than the rich and famous, it was the city's displaced and needy who were coming to one of Galle's swankiest hotels to pick up the bare essentials of life. In addition to allowing his hotel to serve as a base camp for Indian medical teams, Abhayawardene was also offering free meals: 'Profit is not everything in life,' he stated simply. He was also motivated by a sense of putting the past, and all the country's sorrows, behind him: 'We've got to move on from here. We can't remain and wallow in melancholy and despair, and things like that. We've got to move on.'

Abhayawardene's work marked him out as a strong character in my story and to get my remaining 'elements', I went down to the Galle harbour, where Indian sailors were surveying the area where most of the boats had sunk. Indian divers had plunged into the sea to locate the wrecks and manually pulled out three boats that day itself. The harbour channel also had to be marked, and cranes pulled up sunken buoys, enabling the first Indian ships, the INS *Sutlej* and INS *Sarvekshak*, to dock on 4 January 2005.

Cameraman Sanjiv Talreja and editor Rajesh Mishra also took some close-up pictures of the beached 1500-tonne ship that I had first spotted from the air. As I ventured right up to it, I noticed it was undamaged but the only thought that came to me repeatedly was how on earth this city-block-size ship was going to be put back into the water. More than anything else I had seen across the country, this ship symbolized the enormous challenges facing all Sri Lankans.

It was now almost dark and I pleaded with our escort to give us one final quick round of the harbour. We had all been through a lot and I was keen to file my story as soon as possible so that we could get some rest, but the day still had more in store for us. While taking pictures of several damaged fishing boats, I came across the *Norfolk Virginia*, a 40-foot sailboat gently bobbing on the now calm waters. I detected a tiny light inside so I banged on the side and, to my utter surprise, I was greeted by two weary looking Americans, Walter and Jane

Lecompte. They were on a sailing trip around the world and had docked in Galle for a few days when the tsunami had roared into the harbour.

I found it almost miraculous that they had escaped without a scratch and that their boat was still afloat. But as Walter Lecompte explained, they were lucky to be out on the water: 'The advantage we had is that boats float. The wave, when it came, washed us out of the bay. It broke all the mooring lines and ripped us loose and we floated clear. People on land, when the water came up, they were trapped and they couldn't swim fast enough. The currents were unbelievable. The force of the water was tremendous. You can't believe how ferocious it was.'

In fact, it was so powerful that the *Invincible*, a huge tanker and the largest ship in the harbour, broke free of its moorings and headed towards the *Norfolk*: 'It was coming straight down on us, but we managed to turn a little bit,' recalled Jane Lecompte. 'We got away but found that our rudder didn't work because the force had broken the cabling from the steering wheel so we got washed out of bay and we managed to stay off the rocks with Walt using another steering and me at the controls.'

A few minutes later, both the *Norfolk* and the *Invincible* were washed back into the bay. They were both pulled out and then sucked back again into the bay at least three to four times. Not once did the two collide, until, finally, the American sailors managed to drop anchor. 'We did fine for a while,' said Jane Lecompte, but then, one of the fishing boats, which had broken in half, caught their anchor chain and dragged them onto one of the harbour's piers.

It was at this pier that I found them. Their story was very similar to that of Father Sanders in eastern Sri Lanka. Just like the Catholic priest, the Americans had no time to think; they could only act. Two days after the scariest day of their lives, Walter told me they felt almost guilty they had survived while so many around them didn't make it: 'We feel very sad for the so many people that got trapped up in this event. It's hard to come to grips with how many people have lost their lives and livelihoods, lost their houses. Lost everything.'

The Lecomptes were keen to talk to me because they wanted to put out a message through CNN to their president and all Americans that Sri Lanka needed their help. 'I think Americans are pretty generous and I think they will respond with open hearts,' observed Jane Lecompte, stressing that, 'Sri Lankans deserve help; they need so much help. We've had good experiences here, please reach out to them because so many people here are so desperate.'

The desperation the Lecomptes talked about was most evident at Galle's hospital. On New Year's eve, I took a quick tour of the wards to check on the injured and it was here I came across Sunil Vithanagame and his wife, Chana Atanayake. Both were crying loudly and uncontrollably. I couldn't understand a word of what they said, but didn't really need to. It was evident their grief and sorrow were unbearable.

Mustering up all my emotional strength, I approached the couple with the help of interpreter Nalaka and, within minutes, they were pouring their hearts out. Sunil was at his carpentry workshop and his wife was at home looking after their two young children when the tsunami struck. Chana instinctively grabbed both the kids, but remained guilt-ridden that she couldn't save her elder four-year-old son: 'I managed to hold him for a while, but I just couldn't hold on,' she said remorsefully. 'I could only see my son's face as he was being swept away.'

Sunil's leg was in a cast all the way up to his hip, causing him to moan in pain. Again, without speaking his language, it was evident that his physical pain paled in comparison to his emotional discomfort. He was distraught that he had let his family down and couldn't come to their aid fast enough because the water had forced him to seek shelter on a tree. It was while he was clambering down in a tearing rush to reach his family that he fell, breaking his leg.

The only thing Sunil had to look forward to was being discharged from the hospital. One of life's few mercies was that the tsunami had spared their home and the couple was keen to get back there as soon as possible, so that they could be reunited with their younger two-and-a-half-year-old son.

Just a few feet away from Sunil, I witnessed more emotional trauma. Eight-year-old Gayan Sandakelum was screaming in pain and trying to comfort him was his mother, Ranjani Samanthala. Both of them had been knocked unconscious and separated by the tsunami. Hours later, Gayan was found by strangers who brought him to the hospital. Meanwhile, his distressed mother had spent five agonizing days searching for him, till she had been reunited with him just a few hours earlier. Even with his mother around him, Gayan repeatedly screamed for his father. 'I want my dad,' he wailed. As she caressed his bandaged head, I noticed tears streaming down Ranjani's face. She just couldn't muster the courage to tell her son that his elder sister and father were still missing and presumed dead.

Both these stories were powerful, riveting and so human that anyone who watched them would be moved to tears. And I had just scratched the surface of misery in these wards. In the past twenty-four hours, hundreds of other patients, mainly children, had been admitted here after they'd been injured fleeing in panic from a tsunami that eventually never came. In the bed next to Gayan, eleven-year-old Kasala Madusani was covered in welts and bruises. She had been wounded when her scooter taxi ploughed into a pole, as the driver scrambled to rush away from what he and many other Sri Lankans were convinced was going to be another killer wave.

Given that it was still just 4:00 p.m., we decided to drive back towards Colombo to team up with a large contingent of CNN staffers, who had by now arrived to bolster our presence on the story. Our headquarters in Atlanta had by this time also flown in a satellite dish, which, after being initially set up in Colombo, had now been moved to a Buddhist temple converted into a relief camp, about 50 km south of the capital. Heading our operations here was London-based Phil Turner, an old Asia hand, whose father had served as a missionary in South Asia for decades. After greeting him and other CNN correspondents, I sat down to write my script, but was interrupted by loud singing.

The camp's residents were heralding the New Year, hoping it would bring them better luck. I said a silent prayer and went back to my script, which took me less than ten minutes to write. Such stories told themselves and would have a major impact across the world. I was also planning to release the story when millions in the US and other parts of the world were beginning New Year festivities and it would certainly deepen the intensity of their feelings for Sri Lankans. Over the next few days, as millions watched our coverage, they would soon put enough pressure on their governments to launch what many in Sri Lanka were to describe as another 'wave', laden this time with compassion and kindness.

4

The Queen of the Sea

'The train had rolled over, coaches were hurled everywhere and most of the passengers were dead in and outside the train. I started calling my wife's name. No one answered my call.'

Dateline: Peraliya, 26 December 2004

IT WAS A BUSY SUNDAY MORNING AT COLOMBO'S railway station. In addition to the usual weekend travellers, hundreds of holiday-makers had packed the platform from which the *Queen of the Sea* – with its eight coaches and Canadian-built diesel engine – was to leave for the southern town of Matara. One thousand tickets had been sold for the 112-km journey, which normally takes just under three hours.

The train pulled out of the station at 7:10 a.m. On board with those going to the coast to meet family members or enjoy the golden, sun-soaked beaches were Chandrasiri Liyanage, his wife, daughter, two sisters and brother-in-law. The Liyanages had just spent Christmas with relatives in northern Sri Lanka and were now returning home to Galle.

At Moratua, the next station south of Colombo, fifty-four-year-old nurse Anushka, her thirteen-year-old daughter Yasapali and husband Temiyaratne Kongalagame, waited for the *Queen of the Sea* to arrive. The train had a reputation for running late so they were pleasantly surprised to see it pulling in at 7:30 a.m. – bang on schedule. Like the Liyanages, Temiyaratne and his family were also heading home to Galle after spending a fun-filled Christmas weekend with relatives. As the train stopped at the station, the Kongalagames boarded coach no. 15059. It was the second wagon from the engine and one of the two second-class coaches on the train. Four of the carriages were third class and two of the compartments carried the luggage and the train crew.

Most of the coaches on the train were weather-beaten relics. The seats were ripped apart and tattered and almost everything could do with a fresh lick of paint. With no airconditioning, fans within grills attached to the roof of the coaches, helped keep passengers cool in the sultry tropical heat. But the Kongalagame family didn't mind. Like thousands of other middle-class Sri Lankans, they considered the train to be a lifeline. A one-way train ride cost just under one US dollar and, for that price, they were quite happy to put up with the noisy and overcrowded conditions.

At 7:34 a.m., the train pulled out of Moratua, swaying sideways and clattering over a single railway track that had been laid out decades ago. From their second-class seats, the Kongalagame family watched women in the backyards of their homes putting out their laundry to dry. Hundreds of temple trees along the track were in full bloom. The sweet smell of their creamy white flowers wafted into the coach and a refreshing morning sea breeze ensured that the entire family, tired from the weekend's festivities, dozed off fitfully.

It was the sound of squealing brakes that woke them up from their slumber. It was about 9:30 a.m.

and the train had stopped near a school in the village of Peraliya, about an hour's ride from Galle. A fellow passenger told them that the ancient signalling system on the line wasn't working, but curious to find out more, Temiyaratne, a tall, strapping man weighing more than 100 kg, stretched and got up from his seat. That was when he noticed several nervous local residents had crowded around the train. One of the men on the track outside was talking about inky, black water hurtling towards them like a 'a herd of thundering black elephants'.

Just a few coaches away, forty-two-year-old accountant Chandrasiri was seated on the left of the train, the side that faced inland. Unaware of what Temiyaratne had heard, he got the shock of his life when the entire train was jolted by a powerful surge of water. The sea smashed the train with such intensity that it unhooked many of the coaches. 'Within thirty seconds my entire coach was filled with sea water,' remembered Chandrasiri. 'I had no time to think of what to do. Instantly, I jumped out of the window and into the water, which was above my head.'

Meanwhile, Temiyaratne's coach had tilted under the impact of the water, which gushed in with so much force that it knocked both him and his wife unconscious. They recovered a few minutes later, dazed and completely confused. Within a matter of a few seconds, their tranquil holiday weekend had turned into a nightmare. People inside the coach were screaming in terror and all they could see and sense around them was panic. Hearing all the commotion, some people from nearby villages rushed to the train and screamed at them to jump outside. But realizing they faced almost chest-high water outside, the family decided to hold its position. 'We had to save ourselves from being washed away,' reasoned Anushka, 'so we held onto the overhead luggage racks. Our feet were resting on the seats under us.'

When Temiyaratne looked outside, he almost passed out again with fear. Coach 15059, weighing a few tonnes, was leaning against a tree, which appeared as if it could snap any second under the burden. If it did, the family along with all the others in the coach faced certain death. They also realized that if they lost their grip, they could be swept out to sea within seconds by the swirling waters.

As they pondered their fate, the family's attention was yet again diverted by excited and animated voices outside. For the second time in ten minutes, hundreds of local fishermen began to swarm the train. This time, they were not on a rescue mission. As they watched the first wave retract, their instincts told them it would roar back again and the train was a safer bet than their ramshackle homes.

When the first wave slammed onto the shore, it swept away hundreds of homes. Like others, fisherman Kaluarchi Chandasa's shack was reduced to rubble in the blink of an eye. On that day, Kaluarchi himself was visiting his sister in a nearby town. But his small home was crowded with his wife and three children who were hosting his visiting brother and his three kids. Worried about the safety of all the children, none of whom could swim, Kaluarchi's brother made a decision that would haunt the family forever. He put them on board the *Queen of the Sea*. Eight members of the family were killed.

In the train itself there was utter chaos. Accountant Chandrasiri, who had jumped from the train into the water and was holding onto a tree, began yelling at those still on board to hand over his three-year-old daughter to him. They refused, scared perhaps for the safety of the child, so he clambered back onto the coach where people had started to chant and pray. Ignoring the prayer session he chose, instead, to run towards one of the doors of the coach from where he noticed the water level had dropped. He also saw all sorts of furniture, utensils, tables and debris awash in the water.

A few coaches away, Temiyaratne too observed that the water level had receded. So he convinced his daughter and wife to jump out of the wagon and cling onto a coconut tree for dear life. 'In one hand I was holding my daughter and with the other hand I was clutching the tree. I knew if I lost my grip we would be dead for sure. At this time, my big worry was a second wave because if that came there was no telling what would happen.' As he looked around, the burly fifty-four-year-old Temiyaratne, who worked in a government office as a typist, noticed there were about twenty-five people with them. Another 125 were still on the train and those who had fled the coach were pleading with the ones inside to keep still or else they warned that the precariously perched wagon would tilt over and fall into the ditch killing them all.

Both Chandrasiri and Temiyaratne now noticed the train guard screaming at passengers trying to leave the train. 'The guard yelled at the crowd, accusing them of being suicidal and warned them to get back into the train,' recalled Chandrasiri. 'There was a man half way up a coconut tree. He was crying hysterically and asked the guard if he should come down to the train. The guard scolded him and asked him to get in.'

Seconds later, all hell broke loose. Full-throated screams filled the air as another monster wave hurtled inland, forcing Chandrasiri and his family to grab the bag containing their money, jewellery and clothes from the overhead rack and jump out. 'I was struggling because I had my baby in one hand and the bag in the other. But as soon as we were out of the train, we ran as fast as possible. In our hurry, the heavy bag slipped away from me and one of my sisters caught it. While we were running for our lives, I heard a huge noise.'

It was the sound of the second 20-foot wave hitting the train. It made contact with the intensity of a thunderclap, instantly hurling several coaches into the air. The water was packed with such ferocious energy that it almost effortlessly ripped the steel wheels off several wagons. The coaches and the massive diesel engine itself were hurled hundreds of metres away by the sea, which advanced almost half a kilometre inland. Even the steel track was twisted like a straw and large sections were torn apart and swept off their foundations.

When he first saw the wave rush into the coach, nine-year-old Basura Weerakon tried running down the aisles away from the water. 'But then the train toppled over and the water quickly reached the roof of the coach which was completely underwater,' Basura recollected. He managed to clutch onto the window. His father wasn't so lucky and, as he fell, he tried to grab onto his son's legs, but couldn't. Basura too was soon sucked in by the water. 'When I fell I thought I was drowning. But then I saw a light and I floated up towards it.' Moments later, he clambered onto the roof of the train, where the safe hands of other adults kept him away from the monster wave.

With no idea of what was happening on board the train, Chandrasiri and his family continued running till they reached a small house. As they paused to catch their breath, the waves caught up with them: 'A 15-foot wave flowed in towards me and I shouted to my wife. She wasn't there. When I turned back I collided with something and fell down. Both me and my daughter were dragged down by the water and we came up again. Close to us there were some people on the roof of a house. I tried to hand over my child to those people. But my daughter refused and clung onto my body. Instantly, another big wave came in. Both of us were flung far away and got stuck in between two houses. At that moment, I found a small papaya tree close by and grabbed it. The waves were so huge that they were flowing over my head several times. At this moment some people on a nearby roof saw us holding onto the papaya tree and began shouting to try to save us.'

The people on the roof were the Kongalagame family. Just seconds before the second wave had slammed into the train, they had climbed down from the safety of their perch on the tree and had moved into the toilet of a nearby home. But they were far from safe. The water followed them into the toilet, forcing them onto the roof, from where they noticed Chandrasiri and his daughter clinging on desperately to the slender papaya tree, which they knew would either collapse under their weight or be swept away by the raging tide.

Realizing he had just a few seconds to try to save his daughter, Chandrasiri looked around for something stronger than the papaya tree to latch onto. His eyes fell on a wire trailing from a TV antenna and he screamed at Temiyaratne and his family to hand it over to them. According to Chandrasiri: 'They tried to untie it but couldn't. I saw another roll of wire from a downed electricity pole and shoved it to them. They took it and threw one end of the wire towards me. There were about eight feet between us, but this time around I managed to catch it.'

Seconds later, the papaya tree was consumed by the waves. Chandrasiri and his daughter had managed to escape in the nick of time with the help provided by another traumatized family. Both families stayed on the roof for the next two hours watching the fury of the water flatten homes, electric poles and trees, which were crashing down around them with alarming regularity. As she watched bodies and vehicles float past them, thirteen-year-old Yasapali Kongalagame broke down and pleaded with her parents to come together for one last farewell hug.

But fate had better things in store for the survivors. Once again, the water level was coming down and Chandrasiri was heartened to see his elder sister clinging onto two rafters of a roof close by. She soon joined her brother and with three members of the family still missing, they began walking towards a temple located on higher ground. They had barely gone a few metres, when they both fell into a well and managed to extricate themselves with the greatest difficulty. A few minutes later – exhausted and emotionally drained – they reached high ground where another surprise awaited them. Chandrasiri's younger sister too had escaped and, along with 700 other survivors, welcomed the two latest entrants into the camp where they had found shelter.

Tears streamed down Chandrasiri's cheeks as he hugged his sisters. But there was little time for lengthy reunions. He was still worried sick about his missing wife and brother-in-law. So, leaving his sisters within the safe confines of the temple, he wearily trudged back to the train. When he got there he could hardly believe what he saw. He described the scene thus: 'The train had rolled over, coaches were hurled everywhere and most of the passengers were dead in and outside the train. I started calling my wife's name. No one answered my call.'

Dejected and disappointed, he walked back to the temple where the rumour mill was working overtime and people were already talking about fleeing from what they feared would be yet another killer wave. The survivors had identified two safe locations, but to get there they had to cross a river. However, with so much water everywhere, all that they could see was the top of electric poles. As they watched some children being put in an old bathtub for the journey across, both Temiyaratane and Chandrasiri made a bold decision: they too would go. Clutching onto ropes which local residents had stretched across trees, both families began yet another treacherous journey. Chandrasiri's daughter clung onto his back and, within a few minutes (the time was then 5:30 p.m.), they reached dry land, about one-and-a-half kilometres away from the wreck of the train.

Chandrasiri's harrowing experience, however, was far from over. He still had to find the bodies of his wife and brother-in-law. The next day he checked out all relief camps and hospitals in the area without any luck. Eventually, he came back to the train with some friends to continue his search: 'Here I saw dead bodies everywhere. I looked at about 800 bodies but couldn't recognize any. My brother-in-law and wife were not there. I felt like dying myself and only came back home because I wanted to be with my daughter.'

On 28 December, Chandrasiri was back at the hospital where he examined more than 1200 bodies, one by one. He narrated his experience: 'All the dead bodies were swollen and it was hard to recognize them. Others were being transported by trucks. At the same time, the place was smelling badly. I couldn't find the bodies of my wife and brother-in-law, so my friends brought me home. They all pressed me to live on for the sake of my daughter, but I questioned such an existence. What was the point? Why did this happen to me when I had harmed no one in my life?'

Thousands of other Sri Lankans were in similarly despondent states of mind as they rushed to the train to search for the bodies of their loved ones. More than 1000 people, including the train driver and his assistant, were killed here, marking it out as the single largest loss of life in one location alone. Among the survivors were the train's guard and nine-year-old Basura Weerakon, but like all others who made it, Basura would carry the scars of that train ride for the rest of his life.

As word got around of what had happened to the *Queen of the Sea*, there was not much anyone could do. The closest city to where the train had been pulverized by the water was Galle, which itself was reeling from the aftermath of the tsunami. The road from Galle to the train was inaccessible. Only when it was cleared the next day could officials dispatch 100 sailors from Galle's heavily damaged naval base to try to help.

Lieutentant Manjula Alahakoon was the officer in charge of the naval rescue team. Within seconds of reaching the scene, he noticed five policemen listlessly standing by the wreckage and knew they'd already given up hope of finding any survivors. So, he quickly refocused his mission and began the grisly task of removing bodies from inside the overturned coaches. 'When I arrived, I couldn't understand what had happened. It was the first time I saw something like this. After that, I settled down and so did my sailors. They worked so hard they didn't even stop to eat. I can't say how we did our job. Ultimately, we just completed it.'

On the first day, the sailors began their gruesome assignment at 2:00 p.m. and, by the time they had finished, at 9:00 p.m., they had recovered 300 bodies. On 28 December, another 200 bodies, many of which were in an advanced state of decay, were recovered. Since they were in no condition to be transferred to the hospital, they were buried in a mass grave that the sailors dug under the shade of some palm trees. In all, Lieutenant Alahakoon and his men found more than 850 bodies, pulling many out, as he recalled, with their bare hands: 'My sailors really wanted to help. We wanted to help the civilians. They were like our brothers, fathers, sisters and mothers. That's why we all wanted to do this job.'

Most of the dead were women and children who, Lieutenant Alahakoon believed, just didn't have the physical endurance or stamina to either get away from, or swim in, those swirling waters. Over the next few days, an entire nation would agonize over what had happened in Peraliya, with the media questioning if this was a tragedy that could have been avoided. Many Sri Lankans speculated that if the train had followed its usual pattern of running late, more than 1000 lives could have been saved.

More importantly, as reporters scrutinized what had happened in closer detail, they exposed a shocking failure in communication. The train's last stop before it ran into the tsunami was the station of Ambalangoda, from which the *Queen of the Sea* departed at 9:28 a.m. Seconds later, staffers at that station received word that the train was heading straight towards the tsunami. They could have ordered the train to stop, but the ancient signalling system on the track had broken down. Since none of the train's staff carried cell phones, the *Queen of the Sea* continued for another 9 km with hundreds on board unaware that they were rushing to a watery death. Reacting to the media criticism that followed, Galle's stationmaster could only throw up his hands and exclaim: 'That's the problem, it is a big fault that we have no communication system between trains, railways stations, railway guards and the train drivers. What can I say, we do live in a poor country.' Another senior railway official, Gunapala Vithanage, recounted how his own wife, father and mother had been killed in the tragedy, which was of such an immense scale, that there was no point in indulging in a blame game. He added: 'This is the first time anything like this has happened in Sri Lanka. No one knew how to react, what to do – we had no experience.'

With all the human drama and emotion surrounding it, the story of the train was by now one of the most widely reported events in the world. As one of the first correspondents to arrive in Galle, I informed CNN viewers about what had happened here. However, with so much happening in Galle itself, I continued to remain there and other CNN staffers including chief international correspondent Christiane Amanpour, the US-based Anderson Cooper and medical correspondent Dr Sanjay Gupta quickly arrived on the scene to report on happenings, which, by now, had international viewers deeply concerned by the scale of the tragedy.

Over the next few days, the story would only get bigger, forcing CNN to deploy even more resources and the skills of the newly recruited Hong Kong anchor and correspondent, Hugh Riminton, who arrived on location as Lieutenant Alahakoon and his men were still pulling out bodies. As he tellingly put it: 'There was a sense of overwhelming waste and loss. This tragedy wiped out so much, so quickly, that survivors were clearly in the minority. It was hard to imagine that water – something many of us think of as a benign force – had done this. All the survivors were bridged together by an indescribable grief and the only mild comfort I could take from here was that there was no malice. No one had meant them to die like in Darfur [in Sudan] and Rwanda. [Both regions witnessed gruesome civil wars.] That sense of evil is much harder to deal with.'

One of Australia's most distinguished international correspondents, Riminton had recently been hired by CNN. He had covered many wars and disasters during his career. But just like me, he was personally struggling to cope with the scale and scope of the disaster: 'With every minute, more bodies were being pulled out and laid on the sand underneath the palm trees. There was an awful smell everywhere. Bodies had swollen up and they were stiff with rigor mortis. On some, the skin had peeled off. It was pretty unpleasant.'

Inside the train that had entombed hundreds, CNN correspondents found it harder to contain their emotions. This is how CNN's Anderson Cooper captured the sense of emptiness and loss he felt when he boarded one of the *Queen of the Sea*'s mangled carriages:

You don't have to use your imagination to figure out what people were doing the second the water hit. Here's a plate of food someone was eating, surrounded by flies. There's a woman's purse. There's another one down here. Over here is a baby's diaper.

This looks like a child's purse. There's no way to know whether the people in this car survived, whether they got out, whether all of them were killed. Look at this wall, too. I mean, the water – clearly, the water just came up, just left this residue here, left all the silt that it brought with it, even up here – the fans are filled with sea grasses, seaweed.

By 29 December, the authorities had moved excavators to the site and Riminton and his crew filmed them digging mass graves to bury the bodies, mainly those of children: 'There was no ceremony, but it was not ghoulish either. There, watching all this, were 2000 people still looking for their relatives. There was one man who had lost fifteen members of his family and he had to look everybody in the face and at all the bodies to check for family members. He claimed that he had seen hundreds of corpses as he searched for his relatives. He was a shattered man.'

None of the survivors had any physical afflictions. But their suffering was intense and there was nothing, Hugh reported, that anyone in the area could do to relieve that or console them: 'What do you say anyway? It's beyond human capacity, to try to say something reassuring to someone who's lost fifteen members of his family.' Others turned to religion to try to make sense of what happened. 'Why has god done this?' they repeatedly asked Hugh, who noticed them struggling to come up with anything that was remotely convincing. 'It was a terrible natural event that creates waste; you feel the suffering but you can't relieve it.'

While he was there, Hugh noticed a sailor lose his footing and slip into one of the mass graves. The loose sand in the pit made it difficult for him to scramble back up so Hugh decided to help: 'I dropped down to my stomach to help him up. He grabbed my hand to hoist himself back up and raced back to work to pull out more bodies.'

For all the hard work of the sailors, many relatives did not find the bodies of their loved ones and they had to settle for a visit to a nearby police station, where rescuers had laid out driving licences, bank books, credit cards and pictures. As they pored through this motley collection, some family members found closure. Others returned home crestfallen, not knowing how and where their loved ones had been killed. In the coming weeks, Peraliya would continue to symbolize the collective agony of a nation. And tens of thousands, would converge on the site to pay homage to those who perished in the path of a destructive wave.

5

'CNN Full Force'

For journalists it was 'like camping in the world's largest graveyard'.

Dateline: Atlanta, 25 December 2004

IT WAS 8:00 P.M. ON CHRISTMAS DAY WHEN THIRTY-five-year-old supervising editor, Eli Flournoy, walked into CNN's football-field size newsroom in Atlanta and headed towards the International Desk. It consists of about twenty work stations, operates 24/7 and is a beehive of activity, even on holidays, because it's tasked with the critical responsibility of checking events across the world and staying in constant touch with twenty-seven international bureaus. Eli's role as supervising editor that night was to flag the show producers on CNN's international and domestic networks about the latest news developments, bring in news stories and deploy correspondents as warranted. He also had to ensure the smoothest possible communication between show producers and correspondents, conveying programming needs to us in the field as soon as possible. It was a critical role, but after fourteen years with the company, Eli knew CNN's internal functioning like the back of his hand and, with an intricate knowledge of international affairs, he was up to the task of dealing with the momentous events that were about to unfold.

As he made his way to his work station, Eli paused to say hello to two other deskers and check if there was any major news he should be concerned about. 'No, it's quiet,' was the response. But they did inform him there had been an earthquake off the coast of Indonesia and CNN's Jakarta stringer, John Aglionby, was checking into developments. Eli then spoke with John, who told him initial assessments of the quake appeared to indicate it was quite low on the Richter scale. The desk also checked with the US Geological Survey, which at that point was still trying to determine the magnitude of the earthquake.

With these initial reports, it was a routine start for Eli. But as the hours passed he quickly realized the gravity of unfolding events. By 10:00 p.m., the desk received word from Indonesia that the undersea earthquake was fairly large and parts of Aceh on the northernmost tip of Sumatra island had suffered extensive damage. Given the situation, Eli asked John in Jakarta to do two 'beepers' or *live* phone interviews. By midnight, the desk started receiving reports of a tsunami. The first of the reports came in from Thailand, which made perfect sense to Eli because of the country's proximity to the epicentre of the quake. Shortly thereafter, news wires indicated large waves rolling onto the coasts of Sri Lanka and India.

In New Delhi, producer/correspondent Suhasini Haidar was fast asleep on Sunday morning when the piercing ring of her phone jolted her out of her slumber. It was just about 8:00 a.m. and it was Suhasini's father calling from Chennai on India's southeastern coast to inform her that there were strange things happening at his beach-side home. 'There's water everywhere,' he said, completely baffled and mystified. 'It must be your sewer line that has burst,' retorted Suhasini, before promptly going back to sleep.

Back in Atlanta, as Eli continued to get more reports from India about massive waves, he called producer/correspondent Ram Ramgopal, who was filling in for me while I was vacationing in Sri Lanka. Ram immediately began monitoring the half-a-dozen Indian news channels. When he realized they were not reporting anything significant, he widened his search, switching to a Tamil-language station where a reporter was talking excitedly about the sea roaring onto land. Intrigued by these developments and the call from the desk, Ram checked in with Suhasini, who relayed to him what she had just heard from her father. As they took stock of the situation, both figured that what could have occurred was a tidal wave, which was not itself a major news development and Ram decided to continue with his lunch appointment.

No one had yet used the term 'tsunami' in India, but, by 10:30 a.m., India's mainstream channels were talking of a gigantic wave in southern India and shortly thereafter Eli called Suhasini to tell her that a bus full of orphans had been swept away in Tamil Nadu. Worried about the latest turn of events, Suhasini called her father, who subsequently confirmed from Indian intelligence sources that twenty-five people across South India had already been killed. As she heard of these casualties, Suhasini quickly packed a bag and drove at top speed to the New Delhi Bureau.

Our news machinery was by this time also gearing up in Sri Lanka, where Colombo stringer Iqbal Athas and I had reached the conclusion that we were in the midst of a major story that would last for weeks. Minutes later I called Eli to inform him I was cancelling my vacation. My next call was to New Delhi assignment editor, Prithwi, to forewarn him that the death count in Sri Lanka was mounting steadily and he should be fully prepared to deploy all crew members and staffers from our South Asian base – New Delhi. Just hours after the earthquake, CNN's giant network was building steam and getting ready to send its news-gathering teams to all the affected areas.

Certain changes that I had slowly been implementing in the New Delhi Bureau over the past few years would also serve us well on what I had already realized would be the biggest story of my career. Since arriving from Vancouver, Canada, as the bureau chief in New Delhi in 1999, I had spent months training the team and acquiring the latest lightweight gear that would enable us to work more effectively. In 2002, I had also started an experiment in multiskilling – encouraging staffers to be proficient in more than one job function. Everyone had responded valiantly to my call and, within months, all our producers could shoot and edit. All the cameramen too had learnt to edit and very soon, multiskilling had become not just a bureau mantra but an effective force multiplier.

With such a wide array of resources and with a confident team that had bonded well through the rigours of Afghanistan, Iraq, Kashmir and numerous other challenging assignments in the subcontinent, it was time to put their well-honed skills to the test. Eli bought my plans to deploy three news teams from New Delhi, and assignment editor Prithwi was assigned to pull all staffers off their annual break and put them on standby to travel.

As she drove into work, Suhasini's mind was ticking furiously. She needed to get more reliable information quickly and the first call she placed after arriving in the bureau was to Sanjay Baru, the Indian prime minister's media advisor, who gave her the grim news that more than 100 Indians had already been killed. The next call was to India's Union petroleum minister, Mani Shankar Aiyar, whose constituency in South India was one of India's worst-affected areas. Seconds into their conversation, Aiyar asked her to hold on for a few seconds as he grabbed another call from the prime minister's office. As he commenced talking, Suhasini could hear him asking for a special Air Force plane to fly him to South India as soon as possible. Her ears perked up at the mention of a flight and, minutes later, when the minister was back on the phone, she implored to be taken along. Unsure whether there would be enough room for her and a CNN crew, the minister was noncommittal. 'Just reach the airport in forty-five minutes,' he said to her before hanging up.

It took quite some effort on the part of Suhasini, cameraman Mahadev Rao and producer Maurya Gautam to gear up and reach the airport so quickly, and, when they arrived there, they learnt that another Union minister, Dayanidhi Maran, also from the south, would be travelling with them. They also received confirmation that the entire CNN crew had been cleared to fly because other news organizations that had been invited to come along had decided the story at that point didn't warrant the addition of extra staffers to beef up their existing operations in Chennai.

Seconds before the plane's scheduled lift-off, Ram called Suhasini to inform her that I was reporting that the number of casualties in Sri Lanka had crossed the 1000 mark. Suhasini's worst fears were now confirmed even though she had by this time checked out that all the orphans on board the bus in Tamil Nadu state were safe and had not been swept away as originally feared. Three-and-a-half hours into the long flight, the ministers on board received word from the ground that the casualty count in South India had grown substantially. As the plane landed and rolled to a stop at Chennai's airport, Maran made a chilling remark: 'What we know now is just the tip of the iceberg. This is a very big tragedy.'

Suhasini promptly picked up the phone and conveyed the latest information to Eli, who was by now swamped with news. Apart from huge waves lashing Thailand, Sri Lanka, India and Indonesia, he was also hearing that Bangladesh had been inundated; this information later proved to be incorrect. The death toll was also rising so rapidly in different countries that it was hard to judge which area was the worst affected. I was reporting that Sri Lanka appeared to have suffered the most, but Eli was also receiving reports that an entire island in the Andaman and Nicobar archipelago, just off India's eastern coast, had been wiped out, and thousands had perished.

Even before he could turn the system's radar towards the Andaman and Nicobar Islands, Eli had to deal with another pressing priority. He estimated that the damage to property and loss of life would have been most severe in heavily populated Aceh, the closest to the epicentre of the earthquake, but since there was very little official information at all from this remote region, Eli decided to seek the advice of our Tokyo correspondent, Atika Schubert. Atika had grown up in Indonesia and was, by coincidence, holidaying in Bali when Eli called. Aware that Indonesian authorities liked to block information from an area where they had been battling separatist insurgents, Atika informed Eli it was vital to deploy a news team there. Agreeing with her assessment, Eli dispatched her to Banda Aceh immediately.

It would be another two days before CNN teams actually hit the ground in Aceh. And with little information filtering out from heavily damaged parts of Sumatra, our initial reporting focused mainly on Sri Lanka. Thailand too figured prominently, where coverage responsibilities fell on our recently appointed Bangkok correspondent, twenty-five-year-old Aneesh Raman. On the morning of 26 December, Aneesh had woken up early and, while brushing his teeth, he had felt a tremor. Ignoring the incident he continued with his plans to take some visiting family members sightseeing to the Museum of Natural History. It was here at about 9:30 a.m. that Aneesh received his first call from the desk informing him many people at a hotel were missing after it had been struck by a huge tidal wave. 'I thought we would file a news wire on the incident and continued to explore the museum,' recalled Aneesh, but seconds later, when he received another call informing him there were hundreds missing across Thailand, Sri Lanka and Indonesia, it became clear to Aneesh that he was not just handling a story but a 'disaster beyond comprehension'. For the next few hours the Bangkok bureau staffers worked in close tandem with the desk, which provided them with telephone numbers of the Western tourists calling our headquarters in Atlanta in complete panic from the resort town of Phuket. CNN was now everywhere, with correspondents providing the very latest information from all the four main affected countries: India, Sri Lanka, Thailand and Indonesia.

'We responded so quickly,' remarked CNN's senior vice-president of international operations, Tony Maddox, 'because we were in an unusual situation with Satinder on vacation in Sri Lanka and Atika holidaying in Bali.' This, according to Tony, enabled us to be 'very aggressive, very early on'. That sentiment, he pointed out, was picked up by the German *Bild* magazine, which reported: 'When CNN turns up the volume, all the others can go home.' 'It was CNN full force,' emphasized Tony. 'We piled everything into it.'

Managing director Chris Cramer had this explanation for our headstart: 'Our biggest advantage was we didn't have to deploy, but with so many Asian bureaus we were self-deploying. This story was a culmination of [founder] Ted Turner's brilliance and his realization twenty-five years ago that the world was being poorly covered. Ted then visualized that you really shouldn't have to deploy – you shouldn't have to put planes in places, instead you should have people in places.'

Back in New Delhi, Ram had decided to go to the bureau by about 3:00 p.m., but midway through his lunch, an Associated Press photographer told him that he had received a call from his office and was being deployed to the south. Taking this as his cue, Ram sped off to the bureau. With Suhasini in transit, Ram handled all the *live* requests out of India and also took on the added responsibility of regional coordinator, scanning at least ten TV sets so that he could pass on all the relevant information to myself and Suhasini in the field.

It was late in the evening when Suhasini reached the beach in Chennai and the first thing she said aloud to herself was: 'There's nothing here but rocks and stones.' Thoroughly confused, Suhasini wondered if she was even in the right area till she walked around a bit more. Then the horror of what had happened at that spot stopped her dead in her tracks. The beach where she stood had till just a few hours earlier been inhabited by people who had built some 200 houses there. Now all that remained of an entire neighbourhood were a few scattered bricks and stones.

A short while later she visited Chennai's mortuary, where she got her first glimpse of the tsunami's human toll. Bodies had literally been piled up on either side of a narrow corridor. Small children were stacked on the left and women and men on the other side, to make identification for grieving relatives easier. The next day, hospitals and morgues gave up such organizational functions because there were so many bodies that they had to be buried in mass graves on the beach. Some of these images were truly gut-wrenching and hard to shoot, forcing the crew members to become almost 'mechanical' in their functioning. They also had to perform the delicate and sensitive task of showcasing the scale of the disaster in a manner that was not gruesome and could be aired.

The scale of what she had witnessed shook even a seasoned TV journalist like Suhasini, who recorded the following entry of her first day's experience in her journal:

We didn't sleep much that night – editing, then preparing to hit the road and travelling down the southern coastline to take a look at more areas hit by the tsunami's fury. But I was beginning to get quite anxious – this story was becoming bigger by the minute – on television, the numbers were rising – first hundreds were dead, then a thousand, then thousands worldwide. I knew that search operations would be abandoned at night, and the next morning would bring more dead bodies. How many more? I could literally feel the ground slipping from below my feet as I crashed out for the night.

Early next morning Suhasini and her crew motored down the east coast to the worst-affected area in Tamil Nadu, Nagapattinam, from where CNN had received reports that entire beaches had been converted into funeral grounds. Fishermen living on the coast had suffered the most, and all that the crew got in these once thriving communities were grieving relatives, mass graves and funeral pyres. With thousands of homes destroyed, many families were taking shelter in temples and schools, where teachers busied themselves preparing lunch. 'There was a feeling that everyone was in this together,' observed Suhasini, 'and I am sure it was appreciated by those who came into the relief camps that day.' Most of the camp's residents had a hollow and exhausted look on their faces. One shot in Suhasini's story that night showed three children huddled together in sleep. It didn't take Suhasini more than a second to imagine the fear, horror and magnitude of what they had witnessed.

Days later, Suhasini returned to the comfort of her journal to record her shattered emotions of that day:

Why was this story beginning to affect me? I had seen dead bodies before, I had covered tragedies so many times – death, disaster, destruction are the staple ingredients for any news organization, and these are commonplace in South Asia. I guess the answer is the numbers involved – but there's more. For those first few days we visited so many families, attended so many funerals, spoke to so many people made homeless overnight, so many parents and mourning children that, after a while, our own reality seemed to fade away. I can speak for myself – as we uncovered more and more areas hit by the tsunami, I forgot that there was much of a world outside the tsunami. It seemed like the whole world had been swallowed up by this whirling wave – and we were somehow still travelling inside the storm.

That night, Ram informed Suhasini that Mallika Kapur, a London-based producer/correspondent of Indian origin, was also being dispatched to the area to help out. Since CNN had yet to report the story from the Andaman and Nicobar Islands, it was decided that Suhasini and Mallika would be deployed at the archipelago's capital, Port Blair, leaving Ram to replace them in South India.

Suhasini and Mallika arrived in Port Blair on 28 December. The city was on high ground and had not suffered any major damage. Further south, however, in the lower lying Car Nicobar Island, many thousands were missing or feared dead. Some southern islands were reported to have been completely wiped out; many were inundated and, in a few, the Indian military had evacuated all the remaining survivors. Just like in Sri Lanka, the Indian armed forces in the Andaman and Nicobar

Islands performed heroically. At the Port Blair air base, pilots put in twenty hours a day, as they flew in relief supplies to many of the surrounding islands, and flew out hundreds of evacuees.

It took Suhasini almost a whole day to convince the Indian authorities to fly her to the island of Car Nicobar, where she was stunned to see what had happened to the Indian Air Force base. More than a hundred people had died on the base – most of them officers and their families – and practically every building had been destroyed. Suhasini was driven to the base by the station commandant, Group Captain Vivek Bandhopadhyay, who had been working non-stop, organizing first aid all over the air field, sending out search parties for survivors and coordinating evacuation flights.

Captain Bandhopadhyay was performing all these tasks despite the fact that he had barely recovered from a harrowing experience himself. On Christmas night, the station commandant had attended a party and returned home early in the morning. He had barely gone to sleep when he was woken up by a massive earthquake. The pyjama-clad Captain Bandhopadhyay drove to the airfield, located a few kilometres inland, and was relieved to find out that there had been no loss of life or damage to his planes.

While driving back he noticed hundreds of people running towards him – shouting something about a massive wave. Once the wave retreated to the sea Bandhopadhyay, felt sick to his stomach. He knew all his fellow officers on the beach front were probably dead. He himself had a miraculous escape and would also have been dead if he hadn't driven to the airfield. Responding to Suhasini's question about what remained of his own home and belongings, he replied in his starchy stiff-upper-lip military style – 'Not a sausage.'

Not prone to being emotional, Bandhopadhyay refused to be drawn into questions about how the death of his men had affected him. But he did talk with a catch in his voice about the relief operations that he was heading. 'I'm doing it for my men. If I leave now I would not be able to forgive myself. Every man I save today helps me deal with the losses we've suffered.' The courage of men like Bandhopadhyay was one of Suhasini's most treasured memories in an assignment overladen with grief and sorrow. Two weeks later, the air base commandant and what remained of his force were flown off the islands but not before they had saved hundreds of other lives.

By the time New Year's eve came along, both Suhasini and cameraman/producer Maurya Gautam had reached the end of their emotional tether. They were tired and were wandering aimlessly through a relief camp in Port Blair when a little girl caught Suhasini's eye. She spoke to her distraught father, Rustom Khan. It was a poignant and moving conversation, one which Suhasini jotted down for posterity in her journal:

Rustom told me the little girl was the only one of his kids with him – two other daughters, aged three and one, who had been staying with their grandparents when the tsunami struck, were missing. When he spoke of the two girls, it was like someone had punched me in the gut – I had tried, so far, not to relate the stories I had covered to my own family, basically by being numb to what I had seen. But there it was – 2000 km away from my own home – a man telling me how he had left his girls to stay the night with their grandparents – exactly what I would do on a Saturday night – and his story quite literally came home to me.

I could easily imagine the panic he was feeling – as he scoured other relief camps in Port Blair, looking for any member of his family. And then, there in front of us – and Maurya's camera – Rustom saw his sister-in-law. The Nicobarese are very dignified, reserved people, and so far Rustom had been fairly controlled as he told me his story. But now nothing could stop his tears as he hugged his wife's sister, asking, begging her for some news of his precious little ones. She told him that his girls had survived the tsunami, and the last she had heard, they were stuck in a forest on one end of their island with some relatives, but had not been able to walk the ten-odd kilometres to the airfield where the military was evacuating people by plane. Rustom's dilemma was all too visible – relief that his little ones were alive quickly turned to worry about whether they had enough food, and agony about how frightened they must be.

A crowd had gathered around us at this point, and as I explained the story to one man – I am afraid I started to cry as well. We stayed on an extra day – to see if Rustom's girls would somehow turn up, but they didn't.

I guess it was just as well that we were asked to pull out the day after we met Rustom. I could see that I was crossing some line in journalistic objectivity – and however hard it may be – I think it's necessary not to do that. I remember calling my children that evening – and finding it very difficult to sound normal. Kids are so intuitive, I am sure that mine knew something was up – if for no other reason, but that I actually asked about their school homework, and worked my younger one through some addition sums over the telephone (I hadn't so far had the time to do more than ask how they were). On the flight back to Delhi I was happy to be going home – but my heart was very heavy. I knew I would return to the tsunami region pretty soon – and it was a tough tragedy to cover, even so, it was also a very tough story to leave. [Rustom has now returned to his own island – more than a month after the tsunami, he and his wife were reunited with all their daughters, and in my last telephone conversation with Rustom, he said he was trying to rebuild his small grocery business.]

Aneesh and his crew arrived in Phuket by plane at 7:00 p.m. on 26 December. It was completely dark there and, with no way to power up their *live* equipment, they decided to rest and resume work early next morning. The destruction was so total, that, for the first few days, the team members were overwhelmed by the scale of it. For Aneesh, the goal was to put a human face to the story. 'The news,' as he put it, 'was so huge, the destruction so bad and… there was nothing more tragic.' From Phuket Aneesh brought to the world the story of the 'Wall of Hope'. This was the spot where family members put up posters of their missing children and other relatives. Just a few feet away was the 'Wall of Despair' on which officials had stuck pictures of the dead so that they could be identified by their loved ones. There were so many dead bodies that the government could barely cope and even monasteries and temples had to be converted into temporary morgues.

A few days later, the Bangkok crew travelled to the completely destroyed coastal area of Khao Lak, just north of Phuket. While they were doing *live* shots from the beach, Aneesh noticed a woman silently staring at a crater left by the wave. As people milled about, the woman continued to just sit there, prompting Aneesh to go up to her and strike up a conversation. 'She told me her daughter, who was in her mid-twenties, had last been seen working in the area, so every day, she just sat there hour after hour looking into emptiness, hoping that if her daughter was alive she would somehow come there. It was the most dignified form of grief – she wasn't crying, just silently staring.'

A week later Aneesh relayed the highly moving experiences of Chinese-Americans Rong Shi and Yan Sun. For a week, the couple had scoured every hospital and morgue across southern Thailand looking for their twenty-five-year-old missing daughter Hannah. The young investment banker had left for Thailand just a few days earlier to celebrate her first Christmas away from home and her father tearfully recalled his last conversation with her at 11:00 a.m. on 25 December. 'She called me and asked: "Dad did you open your present?" I said no, we didn't have a Christmas tree this year, because you (Hannah) weren't there.'

After failing to find Hannah in the country's makeshift morgues, her parents had to endure the agony of trying to identify her by poring over some 650 pictures. For Rong Shi the pain of that experience was more than she could cope with: 'You know, from these pictures...you can recognize someone's face, shape and then after that you cannot see anything. We have to study them. You have to spend the whole day looking and thinking about which one is my daughter, that's the most difficult thing to do for parents...'

The Chinese-American couple eventually recognized their daughter from a picture of a body that showed two piercings on the left ear. With the first part of their mission now over it was time to take their daughter home, to the city she was so fond of: 'She loves New York, she told us many times she missed us, missed the family, missed New York,' sobbed Rong Shi. 'She grew up in New York. She had a lot of friends in New York. We should bring her back to New York. That's her wish.'

As he reported the anguish of the family, Aneesh, like Suhasini, felt that he was living the story himself and had become part of it: 'Hannah was my age and I saw so much of my parents in Rong Shi and

Yan Sun. They were quintessentially Asian-American – the way my parents are. As I watched them I got a sense that my parents too would react this way if they faced a similar situation. That is when it really hit me, seeing parents like my own in such grief.' For the Bangkok crew, Hannah's family had become more than a subject. They were a connection, linking two continents, and by telling their poignant tale, Aneesh felt he had conveyed to CNN's viewers a true picture of what had happened in Thailand: 'What we did well was to really give a face to a story that was incomprehensible. We had to build a purely human connection between people; otherwise they could have felt distant from what happened.'

Also reporting from Thailand, a country he had once lived in, was veteran CNN correspondent Matthew Chance, who had covered the Kosovo, Iraq and Afghanistan wars. Matthew's first impression, when he got to southern Thailand, was that it looked even worse than many of the war zones he had been in: 'In a war zone at least you have buildings and landscape, but here, as far as you could see down the coastline, five-star tourist resorts had been completely flattened. These weren't straw huts, but were big brand-name hotels, where people from Europe and the US spend a lot of money to come on their honeymoons and things like that. This whole area was devastated.'

More than the devastation though, it was the emotional turmoil of the survivors that Matthew realized he had to chronicle. Among the first people he met was Swiss tourist Thomas Zumbuhl, who had come to Thailand for a vacation with his pregnant wife Bertie. They were inside their room when the water rushed to the hotel's first floor, carrying Bertie out to sea. 'I feel empty,' Thomas later confided to Matthew. 'I don't know what to do now when I go home. I have to begin a new job but I can't do that now. I feel that I have lost all these things, like clothes and cameras and jewellery. But all these things are nothing. They have no value, finally, when so many have died.'

Thomas's story had a profound impact on Matthew: 'I felt terrible because here was Thomas on a high with the woman he loved and was going to have a child with. They were so happy together and then everything got swept away. Thomas lost his wife and unborn child.' Affected by Thomas's plight, Matthew pledged he would focus more on 'people' stories. 'In the end what all journalism is about is people. It's not about politics, economics, war or strategy; we have to focus on the human condition, which everyone in the world relates to.'

On 28 December 2004, Matthew introduced CNN audiences to a twenty-month-old blond and blue-eyed baby, whom doctors at the Phuket International Hospital called Boo-Boo. Badly bruised and his face full of mosquito bites, Boo-Boo was found just hours after the tsunami by an American couple, Ron Robbin and Rebecca Beddal. They had no idea of his nationality or the whereabouts of his parents, but since he had swallowed a lot of water and was swimming in and out of consciousness, they went out of their way to get him to hospital. Almost three days after he was admitted, the world learnt that the 'miracle' boy's name was Hannes Bergstrom. He had been through a terrifying ordeal and his story was so touching and remarkable he soon became a symbol of hope the world over.

Hannes's story began early on the morning of 26 December on Khao Lak beach, just north of Phuket, where he was in the care of his grandparents while his parents were out on the beach. Just a few minutes after 10:00 a.m., when the tsunami crashed into their hotel, Hannes was swept out of the arms of his grandparents. A short distance from the Swedish family, Americans Ron Robbin and Rebecca Beddal were sleeping in their second floor hotel room, when Rebecca heard what sounded like an earthquake and a plane crash happening at the same time: 'We were woken by what sounded like an explosion,' Rebecca later told CNN's Larry King. 'The first floor of our hotel [was] being wiped out from underneath us and we managed to climb to the roof. Ron grabbed me, pulled me to the roof and we just – we sat on the roof and watched the rest of the hotels and everything around us collapse.'

From their vantage point, Ron and Rebecca could see the water rising as it does in a bathtub. Cars that had moments ago been swept out to sea were now crashing back into buildings with awesome force. Twenty of the twenty-five staff members on duty at the hotel and 5000 tourists in either direction of their hotel were killed within minutes. After sitting on the roof and watching the deaths around them there for about one-and-a-half hours, the couple made a dash for higher ground in the mountains, where Rebecca, recounting her story to Larry King, first saw Hannes: 'We found him in this construction site of a bungalow, and he was lying with a group of Thai people who were watching him at that point. He was all wrapped in blankets [so] I went over and sat with him and tried to figure out if his parents were around...It seemed like he was going in and out of consciousness. So I was just trying to keep him cool, give him water, wake him up a little bit, trying to talk to him, seeing what language he spoke, just trying to figure out anything that we could at that point. But basically, I just – I just held him and cuddled him for the day. It was probably about five hours before we could actually get him to a hospital.'

Once stable, the Swedish toddler was transferred to a larger hospital, where Matthew first saw him with scratches and mosquito bites on his face. The hospital too took his picture and splashed it on the Internet. Within an hour of the story going online, family members in Sweden recognized him and he was reunited with his father, who was in a Phuket hospital with tsunami-related injuries. The boy's grandparents too had survived the ordeal, but Hannes will have to grow up without the love and care of his mother, who's still missing and now presumed dead.

Tokyo correspondent Atika Schubert touched down in Aceh's capital, Banda Aceh, on 28 December, the same day President Susilo Bambang Yudhoyono was visiting the province. Airport authorities were told to expect just one crew member but they didn't seem to mind the large CNN contingent that had arrived at the airport. Besides Atika's crew, our Hong Kong desk had also dispatched senior Asia correspondent Mike Chinoy and his team to Aceh. After a quick meeting at the airport, Atika veered off to follow the president, while Mike and his crew stayed on at the airport with their interpreter to establish a *live* CNN presence. At that time, hundreds of shell-shocked people were camped outside the barely functioning airport and were desperate to get out of Banda Aceh. Many of these people had lost homes and loved ones and were also having to get by with no power. In such conditions, it was a tough task to find transport, but after some hard bargaining, the crew managed to hire a van and set off to see a mass grave, which locals said was just a ten-minute drive away.

Even before they reached the graveyard located on the side of a small divided highway, the smell of decomposing bodies wafted into their van. After twenty-three years of reporting experience with CNN, Mike knew what death smelt like, but this stench was overwhelming. So too was the graveyard itself, where Mike saw four or five earth diggers operating in an area roughly the size of three football fields: 'They were scooping big chunks of earth from this area and we saw piles of bodies, stacked one on top of the other. Most of them were not even in bags and were just lying there in a pile that was as high as I was. As we walked across, these digging machines would shovel bodies into these big pits and cover them with dirt. There was no ceremony, no attempt at identification; they were just getting rid of these bodies before they became a health hazard. It was one of the most shocking sights I had ever seen.' Mike estimated that 1000 bodies were hurled into the mass grave in the short time he was there. Later, he found out that the Indonesian authorities had buried 14,000 bodies at that site.

As the earth diggers went about their business, Mike noticed Yus Niati, a pretty young woman, just sitting there. Mindful of how horribly intrusive it could be to point a camera in someone's face in such a delicate situation, Mike asked their interpreter to approach her and ask if she was willing to share her story. She willingly agreed, and told the stunned crew that all her four children and husband had vanished. A few hours earlier, as she was wandering around the street, she had come across the body of her four-year-old, whom she picked up and brought down to the mass grave to be dumped in with the other bodies. As cameraman Neil Bennett filmed the site, Mike noticed that the woman just sat there. 'She was watching all these bodies that were in a grotesque stage of decomposition being shovelled into the earth. She was weeping throughout and I couldn't imagine a more horrible experience.'

The experience was equally traumatic for cameraman Neil, who, till just recently, was on a beach in Hong Kong in the company of his family, and was playing with his younger son, who was scooping up sand in small a yellow plastic front-end loader. Twenty-four hours later, Neil wondered about the irony of being in Aceh, where he was filming another large yellow front-end loader scooping up the dead and dropping them into a large freshly dug grave. As he took pictures of grieving relatives at the site, Neil was deeply troubled that he couldn't be more sympathetic to all those who were in mourning: 'One of the problems is how to express your sadness for the people you are interviewing and filming, especially as you don't speak their language. I would regularly take my camera off my shoulder, shrug my shoulders and sometimes put my hand to my heart, hoping they would appreciate that I did sincerely feel for them. It felt bad to be constantly focusing on people's suffering, but nearly everyone seemed really pleased we were there, letting the world know what had happened to them. Many times I was thanked; some even shook my hand.'

Neil had no time to marshal his thoughts and had to quickly spring into action when he saw a truck containing more bodies arriving at the graveyard. The scene was just too much for a grieving relative who passed out in shock right in front of CNN's camera. Seconds later, Neil was recording a brief on-camera report from Mike in which he explained that the number of bodies at this one site was probably just a fraction of all those killed in Aceh. Within hours of arriving in Banda Aceh, Mike and his team had obtained an extraordinarily powerful story, one which they titled 'Field of Death'.

Atika and her team were watching similarly catastrophic images on their drive with President Yudhoyono. Almost one third of the city was flooded and covered in mud. At their first stop, Atika counted more than a hundred bodies before the president's entourage moved on to the great mosque of Aceh, which was awash in a sea of debris and bodies. There were so many bodies that the president himself almost tripped over one. As they proceeded with the trip and moved to the hospital, Atika was surprised to see that the army had not been called in and not much help was being given to the people. Relief workers were also bitterly complaining that many parts of Aceh had still not received any assistance. Angry and emotional at what she had seen, Atika prodded the president for answers, forcing him to testily respond: 'The system is working. The system is working. The system is working. I think what we were facing in the initial stage of this quake was lack of communication, lack of information.' Overwhelmed by the tragedy and annoyed by the questions, the president, who had barely completed a hundred days in office, didn't wait for the interview to conclude. Instead, he walked away in a huff. No one, it seemed, was left unaffected by the tragedy that was still unfolding in Aceh.

That first night in Aceh, both CNN crews decided to camp out at the governor's office, which was the only building in town that had electricity. On their drive in, lit up by their car's headlights, were the silhouettes of hundreds of bodies lying by the side of the road. Inside the building, Atika's and Mike's crews set up their sleeping bags along with the only other TV journalists from the UK-based ITN and the Australian Broadcasting Corporation (ABC). As they crept into their sleeping bags at 2:30 a.m., one reporter loudly remarked: 'This is like camping in the world's largest graveyard.'

Mike had barely been asleep for about forty-five minutes when he was awakened by some commotion and a huge banging noise: 'I looked up and saw that thirty to forty people were running outside and I realized we were having a very powerful aftershock. There was nothing more stressful than to be sleeping like the dead and then be woken up with the fear that the whole building was going to fall on you. My heart was pounding away, but I dozed off and about and hour later we had another aftershock. After that I just couldn't could go back to sleep and I was awake when the third aftershock came rolling along. Then it was time to just get up and start working.'

On their second morning in Aceh, Mike accompanied by Neil and producer Tim Swartz decided to drive to the centre of the town and into the main commercial area, where they came across a bridge. What Mike saw there was just as haunting as the images they had recorded at the mass grave barely twenty-fours hours ago: 'There were bodies everywhere on the bridge. Untouched, they were just out there. I counted at least fifty. Some were lying there and others had been bagged. On one side of the bridge was a green-and-brown 70-foot long fishing boat. Its prow was up in the air and it had obviously been hurled onto the bridge with a great force by the tsunami.'

As Mike glanced around, he was astounded by the huge number of damaged boats driven right onto the land. Many were smashed into so many bits and pieces of wood that it was hard to imagine they were once boats. As he looked around some more, Mike's mind could only conjure up one thought: 'It looked like an atom bomb had flattened the downtown core of Banda Aceh. People were walking about in a daze with no help from the army or police. Acres and acres of what had been densely packed teeming residential neighbourhoods had nothing left. There were stunned residents trying to find the remains of their homes and they were walking around bodies as if they were trees blown over by a storm, obviously completely traumatized. The sight was absolutely overwhelming.'

Over the next few hours Mike set up his videophone at the bridge to offer up a series of *live* shots. The stench was so powerful that all crew members had to wear masks. Mike took his mask off for his on-air appearances and then put it back on again. Later in the week, one of CNN's satellite engineers told Mike he should try rubbing 'Vicks Vaporub' on his face protector. One of CNN's most experienced correspondents would later learn this was an effective technique in combating the nauseating smell of rotting bodies.

Three days had now passed since the tsunami first rolled ashore, but both Mike and Atika were yet to see any sign of relief or help. While Mike was at the bridge, Atika visited a military hospital, which was packed with patients . 'Many people were dead and others were dying,' observed Atika, who also noticed that 'people were just milling around in front of the hospital, waiting for help. I didn't know what to do, so I sat around for a few minutes thinking about options. That's when I noticed an eight-year-old boy, who was whimpering in pain and just holding his injured eye. He could barely tell me what had happened to him and just said there was water everywhere.' Atika later came to know that the boy's name was Yudha and that his parents and his entire family had been swept away by the tsunami. When Atika first saw him, Yudha was clinging onto two women – both sisters – who had lost their homes and thirteen members of their families. The sisters had found Yudha weeping near the hospital morgue and instantly adopted him. The grief and loss of these individuals had instantly bonded them into a family.

Later, as Atika walked through the wards, she met doctors who told her that there was no water, sanitation or food. Some of the patients in the hospital had not eaten for three days and CNN's team was soon surrounded by a crowd that wanted answers: 'People were asking me "who are you, what are you doing here, how can you help?" It was really overwhelming, everyone had lost families. While I was there I met a grieving twenty-year-old woman and she was trying hard to be a leader; she was trying to take charge. But she really couldn't and started to cry. That's when Yudha who could barely speak himself put his arm around the crying woman's arm and she stopped crying. It was a touching moment. It was a sad and a heartening moment. All these people were complete strangers but they were connecting and becoming family.'

Soon Atika noticed that the small crowd around her had swelled to about fifty people. 'They all were screaming: "Where's the government, where are the doctors, where is the international aid?" One woman was yelling: "Where are all the white people?" I told them we'll help you get your story out and one woman came up to me and said "that's not what I want, I need help". And then this woman took out a picture of a girl and asked me: "Can you help me find my daughter?" I saw my producer Kathy Quiano break down and I couldn't hold back my tears. That was really so hard, I didn't know how to respond.'

◆

Over the next few days, concern mounted over the conditions prevailing on the western coast of Sumatra, the area closest to the epicentre of the earthquake. Like everyone else, Mike too had no idea how people here were coping. So, he hooked up with a British conservationist who had hired a plane to enable him to take the first aerial pictures of the ravaged coastline. As Mike looked at the grainy images, it was clear that there was almost nothing left along 100 km of Sumatra's coastline. Realizing the news value of these pictures, Mike's crew quickly transmitted them to Atlanta, just in time to be aired on one of CNN's most highly rated programmes, 'Larry King Live'.

Back in Atlanta, the latest aerial video reinforced the senior management's commitment to shore up the ongoing operation in Aceh and, shortly thereafter, a satellite dish, along with two engineers and additional staff were flown in on a chartered plane to Banda Aceh. Within hours of the dish's arrival, it was attached onto the back of a pick-up truck, enabling CNN crews on the ground to travel almost anywhere and set up *live* shots. Pleased as he was with these developments, Mike knew his top news priority remained the western coast of Sumatra. An opportunity to get there soon presented itself when a young American soldier approached Mike and told him he was under orders from his government to locate him. This meeting took place the same day the US carrier *Abraham Lincoln* had arrived in the region. Aware of the goodwill that their massive humanitarian operation could generate, US officials were keen to have Mike and his crew on board the helicopters that were carrying relief for thousands of Indonesians.

The helicopter carrying Mike and Neil was stacked with liquid food enhancements, water and packets of instant noodles. Its destination was Kuede Teunom, a coastal community area that had been completely wiped out. As they flew from Banda Aceh down the coast, the CNN crew pulled back the door of the helicopter and the images Mike saw were by far the most disturbing of his entire career: 'All you could see from the chopper was the outline of the foundation of the buildings. You could see what looked like four lines, squares and rectangles of where the buildings had been, but there was no sign of any structures. It looked like somebody had taken a big long stick and swept it across the landscape. It was absolutely levelled. We passed not just one or two such areas; it went on for mile after mile after mile. Occasionally we would see an intact building – almost always a well-built mosque – but everything else was gone. It was shocking to see such images for the better part of an hour or over 100 miles. We flew over a bridge that had been cut in half, you could see big, high trees had snapped like matchsticks, and I wondered how could anyone survive this? At that point I was so tired and numbed by what I had seen that you just kind of gasp in amazement and the other feelings that haunt you don't come back till later.'

As the helicopter approached its destination, Mike could see what appeared to be stick-like figures chasing them. In a place where everything was destroyed, survivors emerged from ruins and from under the shelter of trees, waving frantically at them.

Minutes later, when the helicopter settled down in a cloud of dust, Neil and Mike jumped off and got the shock off their lives. A large crowd of survivors, who Mike guessed had not had any food, water, medicine or communication with the outside world since the disaster, started running towards Neil, who didn't know how to react: 'I will never forget the look in those people's eyes as they ran towards me. A couple of guys started pulling things out of my camera bag and couldn't hide their disappointment when they pulled out a microphone and found no water or food.' It was an act of sheer desperation and made for very compelling video as did the images of Marines throwing out boxes of food and nutritional drinks to people almost crazed with hunger and thirst.

Next, it was time for Mike to record a quick on-camera segment: 'I said we were the first people these survivors had seen. One guy just kept saying: "Aceh is drowned, Aceh is finished." Another guy just grabbed our microphone and said: "Thank you, thank you, thank you." Then we hurriedly got back on the chopper and prepared for takeoff because we were worried that the crowd which was rocking the chopper back and forth would topple it over.' As he watched the crowd, this time from inside the helicopter, Mike noticed that, despite their hunger and desperation, people weren't fighting each other. 'They weren't hostile and all of them appeared to be getting along well. But there was just this incredible desperation and incredible gratitude. The Marine who had been handing out food said he had never seen anything like this in over twenty years of aviation rescue. When we lifted off, everybody just sat there stunned and silent.'

More than an hour later, Mike's helicopter made a refuelling stop at the aircraft carrier and since they didn't have prior clearance to disembark, the crew had to wait on-board, where they were served lunch consisting of a soft drink and peanut butter sandwiches. But even before they could start eating, the helicopter took off again for Banda Aceh airport. As they disembarked, the reality of what they had experienced hit Mike and Neil in the face. It had been a gut-wrenching mission and everything that the CNN crew had seen and filmed was tough to absorb, but Mike knew he had the story that everyone was dying to get. As he jumped into his van, Mike immediately started writing his narrative, which held CNN viewers spellbound for almost fifteen hours of our coverage cycle.

With both Suhasini Haidar and Mallika Kapur reporting from the Andaman and Nicobar Islands, Ram Ramgopal moved in to take their place in South India. Like all the other correspondents, Ram too was struggling to make sense of the big picture. 'It was hard,' as he put it, 'to get your head around the losses and the statistics.' So he decided to focus on fisherman Sampath Kumar, who, even after having lost five members of his family, was a picture of dignity and calm. Other than his demeanour, Ram was also taken in by the fisherman's poetic touch: 'The sea is like our mother, the land our father,' he remarked philosophically. 'We love the sea and respect it like God. But now we are weary.'

As Sampath continued talking, Ram was overcome with emotion: 'Sometimes you just wanted to put your arms around these people.' While reporting from South India over the next few days, Ram concluded that many of the generalizations made about television as a medium were just plain wrong: 'Sometimes TV is accused of being very shallow, that it just scratches the surface, but in this particular instance we were able to capture the emotion and many people remembered the stories we did.'

One of Ram's most memorable stories was about another fisherman Mahesh (he used only his first name) who lost his home, but also gained something very precious the day the tsunami invaded his straw hut. Flung around like a doll by the force of the water, Mahesh's only thought then was to save his pregnant wife. He managed, but only barely. Seconds after he dragged her out their hut collapsed: 'I didn't know what I was doing. I saw the wave, I acted. I wanted to save my wife's life.' Moments later Mahesh pulled his wife onto two planks from a fishing raft and managed to keep them floating till she could be taken ashore to the safety of a hospital. Nine hours after her rescue, Mahesh's wife gave birth to a boy, whom the couple named Monish. His father has great aspirations for him and hopes he will grow up to become not a fisherman, but a police official. 'In any family, only one generation needs to struggle', pronounced Mahesh. 'My son should have a better life.'

Further south of India's coastal villages, CNN operations were proceeding at a blistering pace in Sri Lanka as well. On 28 December, London-based producer Phil Turner arrived in Colombo to manage both our coverage and the large team of correspondents based there. As he approached the immigration line-up at the airport, one of the officials asked Phil if he was carrying any medicine and supplies for his countrymen. Embarrassed and taken aback by the question, Phil responded: 'I'm just bringing cameras to take pictures, but if we do our work properly then the medicines will follow.' Little did Phil realize how prophetic his words would be.

Hours after he arrived, Phil had to help set up a satellite dish in Colombo itself. For the next two days he coordinated dozens of *live* shots from here, but feeling uneasy that he wasn't closer to the heart of the story, he asked the desk for permission to move the dish further south to a place called Beruwala. The desk agreed on the condition that Phil set up the next *live* shot from the new location within eight hours. It was a tall task, but Phil – whose father had served as a missionary in South Asia for many years – knew the local culture well enough to make things happen. He soon convinced two reluctant van drivers to load forty cases of oversized gear and drove with haste to the south. Within a few hours CNN's satellite engineers had managed to get a signal from a satellite that allowed us to broadcast *live* from the heart of the tragedy.

Even with an operational dish, Phil's next big worry was to get a correspondent into Tamil Tiger rebel-held areas in the north of the island from where we had been receiving reports of heavy damage and loss of life. It was a difficult task fraught with danger and uncertainty, but it had to be done and the assignment went to CNN's China correspondent Stan Grant, who had arrived in Colombo in the early morning hours of 29 December. That same morning itself and with no rest at all, Stan and crew took off on a ten-hour drive to the north and managed to convince the rebels to take them to the hardest hit area of Mullaitivu. When they got there, a visibly shaken Stan noted: 'Nothing could prepare me for what I would see. I've been to Hiroshima and seen the museum, the complete demolition; it reminded me of that. All the trees had vanished and buildings and roads had been washed away. The rebel forces were collecting bodies everywhere, there were bodies in bushes, in trees, and they were dredging bodies out of the flood water, getting as many as they could for cremation.' In comparison to the chaos of the south, Stan noticed rebel forces were disciplined and organized. 'After having gone through years of war, the Tamil Tigers knew how to dispose off bodies. And were fairly unsentimental about it.'

Everywhere that Stan looked he noticed a complete absence of life. 'There were no birds singing. There was stillness, emptiness, and eeriness. Things had been just obliterated. I saw nothing but bodies.' What was particularly difficult to deal with was the number of dead children and babies. 'They were completely helpless against the waves and were scattered across the landscape. To see them lifeless on such a scale was quite something. I imagined what life must have been like before the tsunami and visualized children playing in a church, which had had a service on the morning of 26 December. To have seen that area once full of life and then in its current state was astounding.'

As Stan tried to come to terms with what was happening around him, he saw three dead children, aged perhaps between one and three. 'From a distance, it just really didn't look real. They looked almost like mannequins or dolls. But as we got closer, I saw that their arms were locked around each other. They were clinging onto each other. Their bodies had been tossed in the torrent as it came through. Somehow, these three little kids had stuck together and died together. In those moments, you stop being a reporter. The tools of our trade, the objectivity and the distance that we need to be able to do our job effectively in most cases desert you. Being a reporter just isn't enough anymore. I remember standing there, looking, and I couldn't help thinking about my own children. I have three little boys of my own. And I know I look in on them sometimes before they are about to go to bed, and they are often lying there and they have their arms around each other. Looking at these three little children, with their arms around each other, reminded me so much of my own kids. And I started thinking about the little things that matter. I wondered: Where were the parents? Who was there to grieve for these kids? Who was going to remember them? What were their names?

'As I stood there, I actually started to broadcast *live* on my phone into one of the programmes and Richard Quest, one of our London anchors, was on the other end of the line. As I was speaking to him, a bulldozer came through and lifted up those three bodies. Tamil relief workers stacked the wood about a metre or so high and placed these bodies on the funeral pyre. I remember standing there, live on air, describing this scene, and realized I had to reach for something more intimate to show what I was dealing with. That required something more than just journalism. I had to expose my own frailties. I dropped the veil of professionalism; I had to connect the stories of these kids with the people of other nations. I felt the need to be human. These kids had names, they laughed and played just like mine. I related them to my own kids, to give dignity and humanity to them. It wasn't something that came easily because we were trained to hide our own feelings. But I realized there was no way to tell such a story with distance and detachment; I had to be personal and real. I had to feel this as a father, a son, a husband, not just as a journalist.'

Later, Stan visited a child-care centre where about sixty children had perished. 'This was the only place I saw anything alive. A pack of dogs, half-starved and hungry had come back to the place. They were missing those children who had played with them, who had fed them. I heard the most mournful howls and the dogs refused to leave the place. Where were the children? Their forlorn howling was the only sound we heard. And then there was emptiness. A total absence of life.'

Like it did all of us – Suhasini, Ram, Matthew, Aneesh, Neil, Atika and Mike – the story really changed Stan: 'I think it changed me as a journalist. It also changed how I related to people I loved in my life. I've gotten to be more vulnerable and human. In the past I had been to the Middle East and Northern Ireland, which served me well. There I was dealing with death and destruction and human conflict of a kind, something you can strangely make sense of. You can rationalize man's inhumanity. But this wasn't like that. It was so much bigger and it reminded me of our place in the scheme of things. As a man, what mattered most to me now was family and kids. I also thought about going home and getting angry with the kids if they had dropped milk on the table and hadn't done their homework. At the same time I also thought about those parents who weren't in a position to get angry with their children and what they would have given just to be feeling this way.'

Stan doubts he will ever cover a story as big as this again in his career: 'A little piece of this story will stay with you forever. This wasn't about an army or a conflict. It was something far bigger than that. Here was a portion of Sri Lanka carved out through war. The whole place is a homage to the gun. The gun has given them power and suddenly they realized there was something bigger then the gun. What they had could not withstand this so they suddenly reached out to their enemies in the south; they suddenly realized there was a bigger enemy. They no longer felt they were a minority. They were a part of the majority in Sri Lanka, the majority of sufferers.'

6

'Competitive Compassion'

'It was mind-boggling to see. Some people didn't know Sri Lanka on the map and the way they responded was amazing. To see the amount of cargo coming day and night was amazing.'

Dateline: Cochin, South India, 26 December 2004

INDIAN NAVY DOCTOR, COMMANDER GOPALAN Parthasarathy, was spending a relaxing weekend at home when the phone rang. It was 10:30 a.m. and on the line was his breathless older brother informing him that a tsunami had lashed parts of the southern Indian city of Chennai. The conversation immediately brought Commander Parthasarathy to his feet. His hands turned clammy and he could barely speak. Then, he slowly enquired about the whereabouts of his mother and grandmother who lived on a beach-front property. There was no good news there either. His brother had not been able to contact them.

Seconds after concluding his conversation, Commander Parthasarathy turned on the television set to catch the latest news. He then picked up the phone, silently praying he wouldn't have any problems contacting Chennai. After more than two hours of continuous dialling, he got through to his mother, who told him she was safe but his eighty-two-year-old grandmother had been evacuated to an unknown destination. As the Indian naval pathologist sat down to lunch, the phone rang again. This time the call was from naval officials at the hospital asking him to prepare immediately for deployment to Colombo.

As he packed his bags, Commander Parthasarathy was still unaware of both the condition and the whereabouts of his grandmother. It was only four days after his arrival in Sri Lanka that he got to speak to his emotional grandmother on the phone. Anyone in his situation would have been alarmed and would have thought twice about his impending trip. But not Commander Parthasarathy. He was all set to go. This is what he had trained for and he felt duty-bound to help the people of Sri Lanka. By 2:00 p.m., he had packed almost 750 kg of medication and, shortly thereafter, reached the airport with two paramedics who helped in loading his gear onto an Indian Navy plane. At 7:30 that same evening, Commander Parthasarathy and his team arrived in Colombo, heralding the onset of the world's largest-ever relief operation.

The next morning, Commander Parthasarathy was deployed with the Sri Lankan Army at Hambantota in the south of the island. Relief workers there were finding it hard to cope with hundreds of bodies that had been deposited at the local hospital and morgue. Heavy rains in the area had further compounded their difficulties as it was now impossible to cremate the bodies. Left with no choice, Commander Parthasarathy and his team prepared for mass burials. Army bulldozers were pressed into action to dig huge pits near the beach. These graves were then lined with lime and bleach to slow down the decomposition of bodies so that they wouldn't contaminate the local water supply.

For the next few days, the small Indian medical contingent teamed up with a group of Sri Lankan medical students who acted as their interpreters and they drove to all the relief camps in the area. They often travelled 250 km a day, saw almost 150 patients and worked long hours, but for Commander Parthasarathy, the intense effort was certainly worth it: 'There was a lot of appreciation for what we did and people in the district were deeply thankful.' Parthasarathy was also heartened to see how the people came together. 'Such disasters always bring out the best in humanity. For example, there was a group of people in Hambantota. Most had lost their entire families but when they heard the Army was pulling out bodies from the muddy and swampy waters, forty of them volunteered to help. They actually helped us pull out bodies, line them up and photograph them before they were buried. They didn't expect a single penny for what they did and it was phenomenal.' A lot of people from Colombo also drove down to help. Among them were large batches of students who loaded vans with hundreds of coconuts and plied relief workers with sweet coconut water. 'What I saw reinforced my belief in humanity. It taught me people are not always bad and there is always a helping hand when we face these kinds of troubles.'

Commander Parthasarathy's experience also reinforced his faith in god. 'Everywhere I went mosques and shrines were often the only structures standing. And it made me wonder why they were still intact when every other building around them had been destroyed.' He also never felt guilty about leaving India, which itself had been ravaged by the tsunami: 'I could trust that there would be somebody in India doing what I was doing in Sri Lanka. You have got to have that faith. That's what you've got to think. If my country can send people abroad, of course they can look after their own.' Commander Parthasarathy's spirit, his magnanimity and his selflessness were soon to become a shining example for millions across the world who showed unprecedented generosity in helping the people of Sri Lanka.

Over the next few days, Colombo residents barely managed to get any sleep as dozens of the world's largest transport planes – many of whose pilots didn't even inform the Sri Lankan aviation authorities that they were arriving – began landing at the city's international airport. The planes were laden with relief supplies from every imaginable corner of the world, but perplexed Sri Lankan officials had never anticipated such missions of mercy and barely had the resources to cope with the influx of flights.

Thousands of kilometres away, in Brussels, forty-four-year-old DHL manager and father of two, Chris Weeks, was watching the events unfold on his TV screen with great interest and could almost predict what would happen next. Chris had spent a lifetime with the international courier company and a few years earlier had signed up as a volunteer in a relief team set up by DHL to coordinate the efficient arrival of international relief wherever disaster struck. Chris's last assignment was the 2003 earthquake in Bam, Iran, where the world had responded with tonnes of aid, but because of infrastructure problems, huge amounts of this largesse just couldn't get through.

Smarter after his experience in Iran, Chris recognized that he needed more manpower and better organization to fulfil the vision of international business leaders, who had pledged, at the World Economic Forum in 2001, to finance such a disaster network. So, a few months later, Chris recruited sixty volunteers from seven different companies such as TNT and Emirates Airlines to form an *airport emergency team*. The next eight months were spent in rigorous training, with each company being responsible for one aspect of getting the volunteers ready. Chris got around his limited budget by encouraging companies to put their own expertise to work. For instance, DHL staff, who normally trained company insiders on security matters in Iraq, took on the task of teaching first aid, offloading planes safely and informing them of what to expect in a disaster situation. Pleased with his efforts and the enthusiasm shown by his volunteers, Chris planned to hold a 'graduation' ceremony in February 2005. This ceremony had to be postponed, however, when he received an email from the UN on 27 December 2004 asking him to put his expertise to use in Colombo.

Accompanied by a few of his volunteers, Chris arrived in Sri Lanka on 28 December. Within hours of landing, he met with Sri Lankan authorities and told them that if the international response was similar to what he had witnessed in Bam, they should expect to get 'deluged'. The officials listened attentively, surprising Chris, who realized that they perhaps trusted his neutrality: 'We were the private sector coming from professional companies and the Sri Lankans liked that independence.'

Hours after the first meeting, the Sri Lankan Government signed a memorandum of understanding with Chris's airport emergency team, giving them the authority to offload and clear aircraft on the runway. They were also provided with 200 personnel from the Air Force and a huge warehouse was put at their disposal, which could accommodate 17 tonnes of goods to help them in their mission. Their operation formally began on 29 December at 8:00 a.m. and what happened in the coming days was truly momentous; an event that Chris calculated saved tens of thousands of lives. 'I was surprised by the global reaction; we had flights from Cuba, Romania, the Russian Federation and tonnes of stuff from the Middle East, South America and Brazil. In the early days, we even received a shipment of tomatoes, bread and oranges from Austria.'

International media coverage had generated such a surge of worldwide sympathy, that it was becoming increasingly difficult to manage the traffic at the airport. On 30 December, fourteen relief flights landed in Colombo carrying a total load of 270 tonnes. In the following two days, twenty-three more flights touched down with 500 more tonnes of material. Providing logistical support to Chris and his team was Ramzeen Aziz, a senior Sri Lankan airport manager who was touched by the world's generosity: 'It was mind-boggling to see. Some people didn't know Sri Lanka on the map and the way they responded was amazing. To see the amount of cargo coming day and night was amazing.'

Along with relief, nations were also competing with each other to up the ante in pledges of aid money. The US soon increased its contribution to $950 million; Germany pledged $727 million, Australia, $830 million; France, $443 million; Japan, $500 million; Britain, $120 million; and China, $83 million. Individual donors too contributed huge amounts; a phenomenon that donor groups and the international media, including myself, were to describe as 'competitive compassion'.

Receiving pledges of support was what Chris described as the easy part. The more taxing part for him was dealing with the complete lack of communication from countries sending plane-loads of relief: 'Sixty per cent of the time we had no idea a plane was coming until it hit the runway outside. The Sri Lankans had a board up at the airport supposedly announcing what was coming. But most of the time flights never turned up, or were late, or were never announced. So what we did was keep our people ready all the time to offload planes.' Some countries also filled up planes with what they wanted to send rather than what was needed. For instance, there was a shipment of six large packs of Viagra, the sex-drive enhancing drug, from Australia. A lot of Asian countries sent noodles, without realizing that this was a dish to which Sri Lankans were not accustomed. Some donors sent winter clothing such as woollen jackets and Mickey Mouse pyjamas for a country well known for its sunny, but mostly sultry, climate. Then there were heavily embroidered curtains, black-and-pink thong panties and a large batch of used oversized shoes from Italy. 'What these donors forgot,' complained airport official Ramzeen Aziz, 'was that Sri Lankans have small feet.' He also gently reminded those sending used clothing that his compatriots 'had lost a lot but weren't prepared to lose their dignity'.

With so much activity going on and with so many pilots exceeding their flying hours, Chris feared a crash or pile-up at the airport. His worries were further compounded by two events. The first had occurred at Banda Aceh airport, which had to be closed for several hours after a buffalo ran into an airplane. The second incident had occurred in Colombo itself when the pilot of a jet suddenly switched on its engine on the tarmac and the blast sent a wooden crate lying close by streaking across the runway. Realizing that the large number of untrained people at the airport posed another safety hazard, Chris played it safe by deciding not to offload planes into trucks directly at the apron. Instead, he chose the slightly slower process of offloading onto dollies that were then brought into the warehouse. From here, relief material was finally transported by trucks or helicopters to other parts of the country.

Helping Chris avoid any bottlenecks at the airport was forty-four-year-old Bahrain-based Sri Lankan expatriate Ajit Pethiyagoda, who also worked with DHL. Having witnessed several deaths in his own family, Ajit felt that a voluntary stint was the best he could do for his country. Since he spoke the language, Ajit began coordinating all critical functions with the Sri Lankan authorities and soon managed to increase the amount of equipment at their disposal. But that wasn't enough to get the job done. Supplies were still coming in without any paperwork and, in many instances, were simply addressed to the prime minister or president of the country. The need of the hour in Colombo was proper organization and streamlining, and Ajit, with his vast experience, quickly rose to the occasion, earmarking specific locations in the cargo terminal for each incoming flight. He also kept a spreadsheet and a master airway bill allowing him to locate shipments within a matter of minutes. His logistical skills soon paid handsome dividends and Sri Lankan soldiers, who earlier took hours to offload planes, now began doing the job in just forty minutes.

For two weeks Ajit put in thirteen-hour stints starting at 8 a.m. 'Normally, the maximum you can work is five to ten days at a stretch. But we ended up working ten to eleven days without a break or a holiday. We had no radio transmitters, so I had to walk everywhere and I walked so much around the warehouse that I got blisters on my feet. Many times Chris kept forcing us to have lunch, but we didn't even have a sandwich; we just said we would have it later. I've never used an energizer drink in my life, but to be very honest there were leftovers of such a drink in a corner of the warehouse that came in very handy for us. Even I was stealing these things.'

By the time its mission was over, the airport emergency team had handled 160 aircraft that brought in 7000 tonnes of freight. As for the entire relief effort, it lasted seventy-six days and when it ended on 14 March 2005, 300 flights carrying an unimaginable 13,000 tonnes of aid had landed in Sri Lanka. The offloading operation cost only $70,000, all paid for by the consortium of companies that had set up the airport emergency team. If the same amount of work had been done on a commercial basis, it would have cost Sri Lanka nearly $2 million – money the country could ill afford at a time of such a serious national crisis. The entire operation proved beyond doubt to Chris Weeks the importance of corporate social responsibility. 'It's not important to throw money around but to do something that's well planned and has a sense, a purpose, and planning,' he declared. 'This brought me immense personal satisfaction knowing that the vision I had eight months ago worked. It's like setting up your own business plan and then when it works you feel a great sense of pride. I had a team of brilliant guys, no one moaned or bitched, everyone just got on with it. There were different companies, different disciplines, different languages and different continents I had to deal with, but it was a pleasure working with them.'

Volunteer Ajit Pethiyagoda too regarded this period as his finest hour. 'What we did is bigger than getting a gold medal at the Olympics; you seriously felt you did something for somebody. You've actually looked after suffering survivors; it was a great feeling. I got very emotional.'

As Washington absorbed the implications of the 26 December tsunami, the US Government offered $15 million in aid for the affected Asian nations. Hours later, the UN's Norwegian-born emergency relief coordinator, Jan Egeland, dismissed the response of the US and other Western Governments to foreign aid in general as 'stingy'. Egeland's comments created a furore and brought a strong riposte from the then secretary of state, Colin Powell, who hinted that the $15 million was only part of what could eventually be a larger aid package. The next day, the Bush Administration announced another $20 million in relief for the victims. Washington also announced that it was dispatching an aircraft carrier and other ships to the Indian Ocean for providing help. Seventy-two hours after the tsunami, President George W. Bush made his first public response to Egeland's comments. 'I felt like the person who made the statement was very misguided and ill informed,' commented the president, but Egeland's words had undoubtedly spurred the US into action. That same day the US president called the leaders of Sri Lanka, Thailand, Indonesia and India to offer his condolences and also his support. By 31 December, the US had pledged a total of $350 million and was aware that the tragedy presented an opportunity to showcase American compassion and repair relations with the rest of the world that had been left in tatters after the Iraq war.

The US response to the crisis was also being closely monitored in New Delhi, which was acutely aware of the geopolitical implications of its own response. By turning down international aid to rebuild its own tsunami-shattered communities, India was clearly signalling that it was well equipped to handle its own problems and was a rising power in the region. Washington recognized that clout by including India along with Australia and Japan to coordinate the first round of relief operations in Asia. But it was in neighbouring Sri Lanka that New Delhi decided to display its soft power by sending a small flotilla of ships to help. Simultaneously, the Indian prime minister also sanctioned $23 million in aid to the island-nation.

By New Year's Day, five Indian ships had docked in Sri Lankan harbours. Given the extent of their deployment and the warm public response they had generated, Indian naval officers readily agreed to fly us by helicopter to one of their ships docked near Galle, in southern Sri Lanka. Also on board was the Indian high commisioner to Colombo, Nirupama Rao, who spoke in emotive terms about her country's long-standing links with its southern neighbour: 'There is a bond that ties ordinary Sri Lankans and ordinary Indians that is most heartening to witness especially in times such as these. People in India have reached out to the people of Sri Lanka – and I'm not talking about government aid. I'm talking about ordinary citizens of India reaching forward across the sea to their brethren in Sri Lanka. So it's been a great emotional outpouring apart from the material outpouring and assistance that has come to this country. It has been truly heartening and encouraging to witness this.' Later that day, Indian authorities also allowed me to broadcast *live* reports from their ships. These dispatches ran at the top of CNN's international news for twelve hours, in recognition of India's efforts and its emergence as a responsible global player.

Pleased with these developments, the Indians agreed to coordinate a trip for CNN to eastern Sri

Lanka, where they were engaged in relief operations. By this time, I was also in touch with US military sources, who confirmed that they too would soon be deploying Marines from their base in Okinawa, Japan, to help the Sri Lankans. The impending arrival of US troops was big news, with some media analysts openly suggesting their presence would upset the 'geopolitical balance' in the area. There was also wider speculation that the regional power – India – would be slighted by the presence of US troops, especially because these analysts believed New Delhi wasn't properly consulted. US and Indian diplomats regularly denied these reports, but I was keenly aware of New Delhi's lingering suspicions.

The Indians were also aware that a large US presence in the area could quickly move the media spotlight away from them in their own sphere of influence. They were quick to organize another trip for us – this time to Batticoloa, in eastern Sri Lanka, where Indian medics were treating almost 800 patients a day at relief camps. At one such camp, an Indian doctor operated on a woman whose earlier neck injury had been aggravated by the tsunami. The delicate procedure lasted five long hours, but, when it was over, the woman could move her once-immobilized neck. The next day, the cured patient brought her daughter with a cleft lip to the doctor with the 'golden touch' and asked him to heal her as well. Further north, Indian ships that had reached the port city of Trincomalee brought hundreds of electricians, plumbers, welders and engineers to assist in reconstruction work. Indian naval teams also went around the countryside to set up pumps to suck seawater out of wells and make them usable again.

India's efforts were hailed not only by the international community but also by Sri Lanka, whose foreign minister Lakshman Kadirgamar specially flew to New Delhi to offer to the entire country his heartfelt thanks: 'In spite of your own disaster, immediately...India came to our aid massively. Ships, planes, doctors came. Field hospitals were set up. It was a frantic but efficient operation which is marvellous. It wasn't unexpected, because our relations with India are very close, very good, so it's expected, but even then the spontaneity, the efficiency, the warm-heartedness with which the [Indian] prime minister phoned our president: it was a very, very fine chapter in this very sad saga.'

US plans to deploy Marines to Sri Lanka started being drawn up on 29 December 2004. In the days that followed, advance contingents began arriving in Colombo to assess logistical support and earmark missions for soldiers assigned to the 'Combined Support Group, Sri Lanka'. On the afternoon of 4 January 2005, one of the world's largest transport planes, a C-5, landed in Colombo, carrying heavy earth-moving equipment and a contingent of Marines including Sergeant Steven Kirsten from Florida. 'I feel sorry...I feel real bad,' he lamented. 'If I lost anybody like that in an earthquake or anything, my family would be really affected by it. I know I would feel hurt.' As they offloaded their gear, I detected an air of impatience among the marine contingent. They were eager to start doing anything at all to help immediately, a feeling best summed up by Sergeant Kirsten: 'We are here to help. We are here to do our best.'

A few hours after the first major contingent of Marines had arrived, a press conference, which was expected to be well attended, had been scheduled at the US Cultural Center in Colombo. We had already set up our *live* equipment there, but two hours before the interaction with the media was to begin, it was cancelled by US officials without an explanation. I didn't press them any further as I was offered an exclusive interview with the commander of the US troops, Brigadier General Frank Panter. General Panter came across as warm and affable, someone who was so touched by the tragedy that he even choked up and had tears in his eyes when I interviewed him: 'We're here, we're focused, we are going to try and help the Sri Lankans as best as we can. We are friends and this is how we help friends.' General Panter's only regret was he couldn't bring with him the thousands of other soldiers who had volunteered to help. By the time our brief meeting was over, I knew I had made a good friend. Over the next few weeks, the US Marines gave us unprecedented access to their operations and General Panter's troops made, as he promised, 'a big difference on the ground'.

For the entire duration of the Marines' stay in Sri Lanka, I continued to hear whispers of India's restlessness. Such concerns were later confirmed to me by Lakshman Kadirgamar: 'The concern is an old mindset, it's really a Cold War mindset, I think, that in this part of the world India is naturally and rightly jealous of its position. It's a major country in this part of the world and anybody else coming in is viewed with a degree of concern, apprehension.' Mindful of these brewing tensions, the foreign minister put in efforts to allay New Delhi's fears: 'We said, "Look, this is what is happening, nothing to get excited about, it's a very simple thing. They [US forces] will be here for a while and then they'll be gone." This is not a permanent presence, these are not armed men, they are really construction people coming in with heavy-lifting equipment and this is what they will do and with that, the whole problem, insofar as it was a problem, was resolved.'

US troops appeared to be the least bit concerned about the controversy surrounding their presence. Most of them felt they had an important job to do and got on with what they called 'Operation Winn-Dixie'. Over the next few days, more than 1600 Marines cleared the rubble from, and cleaned out, several neighbourhoods, removed dangerous debris from schools and set up purification plants that ultimately distributed nearly 340,000 litres of fresh water. US military C-130 cargo planes and helicopters also flew 300 sorties across the country carrying medical personnel and much-needed supplies. Like Mike Chinoy and his crew, we too were invited to fly on board one of the first US helicopter relief flights to take off from Colombo's international airport to Ampara, the country's worst-affected area.

When we arrived at the airport, Sri Lankan airmen and US Marines were loading brown cardboard boxes containing plastic sheeting and jerry cans onto three US Navy Pavehawk helicopters. The work was being carried out at a feverish pace because everyone was aware that even a few hours could make the difference between life and death for those eagerly awaiting such supplies. When the helicopters were loaded, cameraman Sanjiv Talreja and I squeezed into one of them. With no room to sit, I eased myself onto one of the brown boxes, which was marked: 'Gift from the people of the United States'. After an hour and a half of flying in formation with the two other helicopters, we touched down in the soccer field of an Ampara school, where thousands had gathered. The offloading process went smoothly, with residents forming a human chain to offload the precious cargo. But then a large crowd suddenly surged towards the helicopter and helpless policemen and US Marines could only watch the spectacle. Like Mike in Banda Aceh, I was scared the helicopter would topple right over. But luckily it didn't and I realized I had just a few seconds to record a brief on-camera segment. Seconds later, as I was rushing back to board the helicopter, a schoolteacher screamed: 'We are happy, we are happy. But we want more, we want more.'

No one spoke for a long time on the flight back. But I could sense the pride and satisfaction amongst the crew. One of them silently taped the Stars and Stripes to the inside of the helicopter and I tried to strike up a conversation with him. But the din of the helicopter's rotor soon forced me to give up and I decided to conduct my interview by writing a few questions on my notepad for crew member Tiffany Gabbard from Clinton, Utah. In reply, she wrote that it was her birthday. I then asked her what the large crowds on the ground meant to her. She responded: 'It made me feel proud and it was the best birthday present for me ever to see the happy faces.' Tiffany also felt that such humanitarian missions would do wonders for the image of the US Marines that had been sullied in Asia by the Iraq war. She finally stated: 'Hopefully, it will show that America is here to help and we aren't all that bad after all.'

Even before I could write out another question, I felt the helicopter shudder, bank steeply and then steady itself. In front of us was a beautiful waterfall. Its tumbling water glistened in the glowing sun. We all paused to admire the view, relishing this opportunity after seeing only rubble and feeling only despair on the ground. Moments later, we came across a herd of wild elephants. After a successful mission, the pilot felt that we all deserved another breather so he descended lower for an even closer look.

Sri Lankans of all political hues were pleased with what the US Marines had done for their country. But in addition to the international community, it was also ordinary Sri Lankans who magnificently rose to the occasion to help their compatriots. A week after our trip with the Americans to Ampara, I travelled north to Jaffna, once a Tamil Tiger rebel stronghold, but an area now controlled by the government. At the crumbling hospital, I met seventy-one-year-old Dr Sinnathuray Kathiravelpillai. Since the tsunami had struck, he had been working virtually single-handedly to provide care and comfort to those affected among the almost 150,000 people who lived in that area. In that time, the doctor had completed the medical formalities for over 100 dead and had treated almost 150 patients. With only a handful of nurses to help him, he even undertook night duty every other day, but did not complain at all. 'For 15 years I have been running this hospital,' he stated proudly. 'I take it as a pleasure, because I am a man from the local village and I have come here to do a bit of service.' Despite a serious shortage of medical doctors in an area that was the hardest hit by decades of civil war, Dr Kathiravelpillai even served as a back-up psychiatrist and sadly recounted the story of one of his patients, a thirty-nine-year-old labourer: 'He had visited his home and saw that everything was destroyed so he told his wife you might not see me again. Then suddenly his brother-in-law found him hanging from a beam in the house. It was a suicidal hanging.' After weeks of treating his patients with no help at all, Dr Kathiravelpillai was delighted when an American medical contingent armed with the latest technology arrived to support him. 'I think they are good-natured people, it's good they've come,' he graciously remarked, before turning away and walking back to work.

Hundreds of kilometres to the south, another emissary of hope, Buddhist monk Basongoda Rahula, was surveying the damage along Sri Lanka's southern coast. Basongoda was a part-time professor of English and the head of a Buddhist temple in Houston, Texas, which had raised $50,000 to help tsunami survivors. With this amount at his disposal, Basongoda had already counted 139 damaged houses to rebuild and was never short of a sympathetic word for the survivors: 'I am here to help you,' he affirmed repeatedly. 'Out of compassion, we are ready to help you. So you're not alone, we are here to share your grief.' As he mingled with the survivors, Basongoda showed them detailed architectural plans for new houses in the area. The residents, who were amazed by his generosity, thanked him profusely.

After days of just watching endless suffering, I was now chronicling the efforts of highly motivated individuals who, despite the adverse circumstances, were making a difference. Such efforts raised my spirits and, in the words of Sri Lanka's foreign minister, Lakshman Kadirgamar, 'gave the entire country much needed hope'. The minister added: 'The response worldwide from ordinary people, so-called ordinary people, has been truly fantastic. It's very reassuring for everybody to know, givers and receivers, that human compassion is there, feeling is there…it takes a thing like this [the tsunami] to trigger that and release those wonderful emotions.'

Such instances of care and compassion were being repeated across Asia. In Chennai, South India, CNN's Ram Ramgopal met a Malaysian volunteer, insurance executive Thomas Cheng. He was so moved by the images he had seen on TV that he travelled thousands of miles at his own cost to help the victims. 'I saw the people with their hungry faces and the suffering; it was just overwhelming,' he stated, while distributing food to a long line of hungry survivors. 'In this thing we're all brothers and sisters. If one brother suffers, we all feel the pain.'

Other citizens made the ultimate sacrifice – laying down their own lives to help others. In the Indian territory of Andaman and Nicobar Islands,

Ram uncovered the story of Sanjeev (like many Nicobarese he only used his first name), a thirty-two-year-old policeman, who saved four people before he himself disappeared in a towering wave of seawater. Sanjeev was survived by his one-year-old daughter Ishika and wife Deepika, who recounted that her husband was on duty in his tiny police station on the beach when he watched the giant waves roll ashore. Acting quickly, the athletically built policeman first moved his wife and daughter to safety. Then without a thought for his own safety, he ploughed into the water and saved four people in a matter of minutes. He was last seen trying to save an old woman who was struggling amidst the waves. As she reminisced, Deepika remembered frequently telling her husband to be more careful: 'I used to tell him, "I'm afraid for you. What if something happens?" And he'd tell me: "When you're married to a police officer, you should learn to be brave." Only twenty-three years old, Deepika had no idea what she would do later in life. But she was sure she wanted to make her daughter a police officer, just like her father: 'Looking back, I'm happy he so bravely saved so many lives. But I'm sad, too, because if he hadn't done what he did, he'd be here with me.'

In Thailand as well, CNN correspondents chronicled an outpouring of remarkable humanity. After hearing that hundreds of tourists had lost their family members, eighteen-year-old Tan Tai Wongseri travelled to Phuket to help. Wearing a name-tag that listed the several languages he spoke, he tried to assist tourists who faced a language barrier to help them could get by the tragic and difficult days.

Americans Rebecca Beddal and Ron Robbin had certainly taken in their fair share of difficulty and pain, but unlike most others, they also had reason to feel slightly elated after the twenty-month-old Swedish boy (Hannes Bergstrom), whom they had found and looked after, was reunited with his injured father. After witnessing that reunion, the American couple decided to stay on in Thailand. Later Ron explained to Larry King how they helped out as volunteers: 'We went up to one of the temples that was acting as a morgue and Rebecca actually carried bodies. I was so proud of her for doing that. And I carried coffins. And we just helped out any way we could.' Since the time Ron and Rebecca's story was first aired they had become media darlings in the United States and had appeared on virtually all major TV shows. But embarrassed at being the centre of attention, they told reporters who the real heroes were: 'The Thai people were the ones responsible for saving Hannes,' noted Rebecca. 'We ended up getting the credit because we're Americans and the story was the focus of the American media.'

All the media attention soon brought Ron and Rebecca cheques and wire transfers from friends, associates and many others who didn't even know them. It didn't take them long, as Ron yet again explained to Larry King, to decide what to do with that money: 'We just went directly back to the area where we found Hannes and distributed small amounts of money to the people who had lost everything. We owed everything to the people of Thailand. They had been so gracious to us. They gave us clothes. They gave us food and water. When we were in the hospital with Hannes the night we took him there, it was a war zone. You know, there was blood on the ground. I was walking around, and one of the Thai nurses came up to me and offered me her shoes. And we can tell you a thousand stories about how the people of Thailand had been so kind and so gracious to us. Not only us but to all the foreign tourists here. And we wanted to get the message out. In the days and weeks and months to come we want people to come to Thailand and support these people that have, you know, lost their livelihood because they're some of the best people in the world and we just really want to say thank you to Thailand.'

Auto mechanic Andrew Wharam was at home in Auckland, New Zealand, watching television pictures of the tsunami hammering Sri Lanka's coastline and was so moved that he wanted to help. But rather than just write a cheque to an aid agency, Andrew, who was in between jobs, felt the best thing he could do was go to Sri Lanka, where he could use his skills to help in reconstruction. The big question was: how to get there? As he pondered his options, Andrew caught sight of an advertisement in the *New Zealand Herald* saying that there was a tour group looking for people to go over and help revive tourism in Sri Lanka. 'They were looking for carpenters, stone masons and engineers and I felt I've got the time, I should go, I can go and help. I've got the skills to get the fishing boats up and running again which is what they've been asking for, so I wanted to get there, I wanted to go and do something tangible,' he emphasized.

A few days later, after he had managed to shell out almost 2000 US dollars, Andrew was to join a group of twenty-seven other Kiwis en route to Sri Lanka. 'I caught up with them in the western town of Kaluthra, an hour's drive from the capital Colombo, where they were hammering together a shed in blazing heat. It's just a really nice feeling inside that we are able to come here and help people,' chimed Andrew, working away as he talked. 'There's 600 refugees moving into this camp in the next few days, if we hadn't been here to do this they would be living in tents, they would have no cooking spaces at all. We're doing this [so that] they've got somewhere warm and dry to do their cooking. So it's a great feeling.'

The New Zealanders' trip to Kaluthra had been coordinated by the Sri Lankan Navy, but back home, they had to take a lot of flak in the media for trying to do the work that many New Zealanders thought aid agencies were better equipped to handle. The criticism failed to deter the indomitable Kiwis who were moved by the warm reception they had received: 'Three weeks ago there was a tsunami coming through their homes and these people are still smiling and waving at us,' remarked Neil Cairns from Wellington. 'If we had suffered like this we all would be having counselling back home. These people are happy and smiling and welcoming us; it's incredible.'

While we were filming the New Zealanders, one of them got quite agitated. 'I came here to be a volunteer and not a TV star,' he fumed, upset that our camera was distracting him from his life-saving mission. I immediately asked cameraman Sanjiv to pull back and apologized for the inconvenience, completely understanding the dedication of his group, whose work had now also reached the ears of the country's president. 'I have no words to describe this generosity,' noted Chandrika Kumaratunga in an interview with me. 'It's really great and it gives us a lot of encouragement and strength to go on. Not only the government but [also] our people know that they are not alone.'

The success of the first batch of such 'tourists' from New Zealand immediately spawned a mini-industry of sorts. In the coming weeks, more Kiwis arrived, carrying in tow several sewing machines for qualified seamstresses living in camps. The machines encouraged women to go back to their earlier occupations and the clothes they stitched were sold at a tidy profit in New Zealand. Thrilled by their countrymen's efforts at rebuilding Sri Lanka and generating small employment opportunities, many more Kiwis booked additional tours to the island. In fact, space on such mercy tours has now been fully sold out till January 2006.

7

Baby 81

The baby, covered in garbage, had floated onto a pile of brambles on an old tyre. . . . With little time for formalities or detail, a nurse recorded the baby as the eighty-first patient to be admitted to the hospital that day. Without any known parents or a name, staffers from that point onwards began calling the four-month-old boy Baby 81.

Dateline: Kalmunai, eastern Sri Lanka,
26 December 2004

TWENTY-SIX-YEAR OLD JUNITA JEYARAJAH WAS WASHING her baby's clothes outside her home in Kalmunai when her attention was diverted by a huge roar behind her. She turned to look and saw a wall of water, the colour of crude oil, rushing towards her. Throwing down her washing, she let out a blood-curdling yell and shouted at her sister, Vanitha Vadivel, to grab her sleeping four-month-old baby boy, Abhilash.

Vanitha grabbed the baby boy and, just as she clasped him to her bosom, the sea cascaded into their home, knocking down a wall and sweeping both of them up to the ceiling. Outside their house, with nothing to hold onto, Junita was knocked unconscious by the water and swept hundreds of metres away. Junita's sister managed to hold onto a rafter of the roof for a few more minutes. But the next big wave tore Abhilash out of her arms and flung her out of the house like a lifeless rag doll.

Half an hour later she recovered consciousness, but there was no sign of Abhilash.

Meanwhile, one-and-a-half kilometres from the coast, Junita's thirty-one-year-old husband Murugupillai Jeyarajah had just opened his family-owned hairdressing salon in Kalmunai's main shopping district, and was waiting for his customers. Their steady patronage over the years had allowed him some of the trappings of a comfortable middle-class existence. Murugupillai was the proud owner of a shiny red motorcycle and had ploughed most of his savings into constructing a comfortable home on the beach. With no debts and a flourishing business, Murugupillai decided in July 2004 to marry his sweetheart. The birth of his son, Abhilash, shortly thereafter brought him even more joy and happiness. But on 26 December, upon hearing news that the ravaging tsunami had just struck the coast where his house was Murugupillai's heart sank. The only thought in his mind was that his entire life's work had been destroyed and his family had been snatched away from him.

With no word from either his wife or sister-in-law for hours, Murugupillai was forced to reluctantly accept that they were dead. But unknown to him, an hour after the tsunami had struck eastern Sri Lanka, some neighbours had found an unconscious Junita on the beach and rushed her to a nearby hospital. Late in the evening, Vanitha managed to locate Murugupillai and they both arrived at the hospital for a tearful reunion with Junita.

As the family members hugged and kissed each other, life in some of the tsunami-ravaged neighbourhoods slowly started to revive. Survivors who had climbed onto roofs and trees to try to get away from the water, slowly began to step down, still dazed at what had happened and wondering how they'd managed to elude the fury of nature. Later, they returned to their homes to search for their loved ones and their belongings. Among those looking through what remained of their homes was the Jeyarajahs' neighbour, English teacher Sree Skandarajah. All morning, Sree had come across nothing but dead bodies and the search had left him tired, thirsty and hungry. So, when he glanced upon what appeared to be a carton of cookies amidst a pile of rubble, he quickened his pace. As he got closer, he heard some scratching noises coming from the carton. 'I thought it was a chicken,' said Sree. 'But when I bent down I thought I saw god. I saw a crying baby and I thought god had come down to earth in the form of a baby.'

The baby, covered in garbage, had floated onto a pile of brambles on an old tyre. Reaching down, Sree picked up the baby and noticed that he appeared to be in perfectly good health except for some bruises caused by the brambles near one of his eyes. 'I thought it was a miracle,' he declared, and promptly asked a fellow volunteer to rush the baby boy to the local Kalmunai hospital. By this time, the hospital was awash with 1000 bodies and staffers were at their wits' end trying to deal with a catastrophe in which 60 per cent of all the fatalities were children. With little time for formalities or detail, a nurse recorded the baby as the eighty-first patient to be admitted to the hospital that day. Without any known parents or a name, staffers from that point onwards began calling the four-month-old boy Baby 81.

Within an hour of the baby's admission, doctors asked one of the nurses to take the four-month-old home. It was a strange decision, but the hospital's obstetrician explained that there was little they could do for Baby 81 in a facility that was floundering to cope with hundreds of seriously injured residents. 'We had no staff to look after anyone except emergency cases so it was not possible for us to keep the baby in the hospital. There were dead bodies everywhere on the floor and sometimes we even had to walk over them. So with the permission of the administrators we did seek help from a nurse staying close to the hospital.' However, the nurse did not, as ordered, take the baby home. Fearing another monster wave, her family had moved to the safety of a temple and it was in this relief camp that Baby 81 suckled hungrily at his first proper feed since the tsunami struck.

Meanwhile, desperate for any word on his missing baby, Murugupillai left his wife and sister at the hospital to return to his ravaged neighbourhood. However, with no electricity and with so much debris strewn around everywhere, he quickly gave up his search and dejectedly went back to his wife. The next morning, the Jeyarajahs got caught up in a rumour that the town was going to be hit by another bigger tsunami and decided to flee to a relief centre in the nearby city of Ampara.

On 28 December, the head of the camp, a Buddhist monk, told Junita that a baby had been brought to the local Ampara hospital. The family left immediately, but were crestfallen when they saw the child. It wasn't their Abhilash. The next day, after leaving his wife at the relief camp, Murugupillai returned home. What he saw there brought him to his knees. The water had spared nothing. Not a wall was standing; even the brick roof had been swept six houses down the street. All their belongings, including Abhilash's crib and even their clothes, had been carried more than a kilometre away. Numb with shock, Murugupillai tried to find what he thought would be the body of his son. As he searched high and low for any sign of the boy, he ran into schoolteacher Sree Skandarajah, who told him he had found a baby wrapped in a pile of garbage: 'God had been very kind to the Jeyarajahs,' recalled Sree, who advised Murugupillai to rush to the hospital.

Their hearts pounding, the Jeyarajahs reached the hospital only to be met by the vacant stares of the hospital staff, who told them there was no such baby. Angry and confused, the couple once again trudged back to meet their neighbour, Sree. Sensing something was seriously amiss, Sree grabbed the volunteer to whom he had entrusted the job of taking the baby to the hospital and decided to confront the doctors there.

Faced with Sree's angry outburst, doctors immediately asked the nurse to bring back Baby 81 to the hospital and asked Murugupillai and his wife to return the following day. By this time, eastern Sri Lanka had been lashed with torrential rain, creating flash floods in many places. In the midst of a heavy downpour, and tossed about in a narrow boat, Baby 81 was brought back to the hospital. As word got around of the baby's miraculous escape, the local media lapped up the heart-touching story. Baby 81 was catapulted to the status of a local icon, symbolizing the region's grief in general and the immense suffering of children across the country in particular. According to the UN's child care agency, UNICEF, in Sri Lanka, the tsunami had orphaned about 1000 children and more than 3600 of them had lost at least one parent.

It was in such a milieu that the next amazing phase in this saga began. At least eight other couples rushed to the hospital, with some claiming to be the baby's real parents and the others hoping to make a quick adoption. The local media reported scenes of unbelievable emotional outpouring as couples clashed with overburdened staffers and threatened to hurt themselves if the baby wasn't handed over to them. Concerned for the safety of the baby and fearing that he could be kidnapped, the hospital staff began to frequently change his location and remained extra-vigilant at night.

Bearing the brunt of most of the angry outbursts at the hospital was obstetrician Dr Kopalasuntharan Muhunthan, who tried to rationalize the intensity of everyone's feelings for Baby 81: 'Many babies had been killed and in our hospital he was the only baby without a parent. Obviously, anyone who had lost a baby of the same age wanted to come and see this baby. And I don't think all of them were lying because they sincerely felt this was their child.' Parents who had lost children were also burdened by a huge sense of guilt and, for them, Dr Muhunthan felt that Baby 81 could provide a chance to make a new beginning in life as well as help overcome their own sense of helplessness.

Far from feeling helpless, Junita and Jeyarajah were enraged. They felt that the others were getting 'greedy' and eyeing what they were convinced was their beautiful, big-eyed child. `He was found by a teacher, by our neighbour,' announced Jeyarajah, who wondered how others could claim the baby if they lived hundreds of kilometres away. Adding insult to injury was the hospital's insistence that the Jeyarajahs provide the requisite paperwork to prove the baby was, in fact, theirs. With their home and everything in it washed away, the couple felt this was an unreasonable demand and were further incensed when staffers asked them if their baby wore any religious threads or a bangle. When they replied in the negative, doctors told them Baby 81 was actually wearing religious threads and a bangle. 'Just because of this,' remembered Murugupillai, 'the doctors concluded we were not the baby's real parents and asked us to leave.'

The Jeyarajahs held their ground, maintaining the nurse who took Baby 81 home had put the religious threads and a bangle on the child. After hours of waiting, they succeeded in contacting a sympathetic doctor who helped sneak them inside the hospital for a closer look at the baby. The couple broke down as they gazed upon a dozing Baby 81. As they walked out of the baby's ward, Junita pledged to never give up: 'He's a miracle baby,' she stated. 'That's why everyone wants him. I can barely sleep at night and all I think of is breast-feeding my baby.'

To step up their claim, the Jeyarajahs hired a lawyer. But when they still had no luck in convincing the hospital, they registered a complaint with the police and, on 5 January 2005, filed a case in the local magistrate's court seeking custody of the baby. As the only claiming couple to take such steps, the Jeyarajahs were hoping that everyone would now recognize them as the real parents: 'Everyone was claiming the baby, but no one went to the courts. We did, and challenged all those who wanted the baby to come and fight in the courts.'

Baby 81's story had now entered another phase, with the local media, once again, highlighting the country's most bitterly fought custody battle. From being an icon of suffering, Baby 81 now became also a symbol of separation. The infatuation of the local reporters with Baby 81 was annoying Murugupillai, who felt their focus on the numerous other claimants was just making his life a living hell: 'If the media says there are eight other parents why don't they come to meet us? I think I am going to have a heart attack.'

Behind the scenes, however, the Jeyarajahs' lawyer was now making some headway. The meeting with the local magistrate had gone better than expected and he passed an order declaring the Jeyarajahs to be the baby's 'temporary' parents. The magistrate also ruled that in case of any dispute in the matter, he would hold another inquiry. Armed with the order, the couple returned to the hospital, but the doctors felt they couldn't hand over a child on what they considered to be 'a first-come-first-served basis.' Furthermore, the hospital wanted paternity issues to be settled scientifically and also made the point that the baby was in no physical or mental condition to be discharged and taken to a relief camp where he was at risk of picking up various infections.

The Jeyarajahs were inconsolable. 'The doctors are playing a game,' intoned an angry Murugupillai. 'I am going to kill them and then commit suicide.'

For the family this was the last straw. But unknown to them, help was soon going to arrive from an unexpected quarter – the international media. By 14 January, international wires had picked up Baby 81's story, alerting both the CNN desk and myself. It took me barely a few seconds to make up my mind. This was a story tailor-made for television and just had to be aired.

Over the years and through several natural disasters and wars, I had learnt that well-presented stories on children galvanized both our newsroom and audiences, perking up interest in the story. Being an emotional and picture-driven medium, it was also comparatively easy to tell such stories on TV. Finally, a baby's story was also a slice of life that international audiences could both relate to and understand easily.

As I thought about Baby 81, I also recalled the kudos that I'd received for bringing the plight of an injured four-year-old Iraqi boy to the attention of the world in early 2003.

Let me digress a bit here. Days after the last Iraq war in March 2003, four-year-old Bakr Ali Hussein was playing soccer in downtown Baghdad, when a bomb went off nearby. American forces in the area retaliated by firing in the direction of the blast. One of the bullets accidentally hit Bakr in the back of his head. The four-year-old survived, but could barely walk and his vision was badly affected. US forces apologized and offered to help, but failed to follow through on their promise and, months after the incident, the bullet was still lodged in Bakr's head, robbing him of a normal childhood.

It was at this stage that I aired Bakr's story. Two days later, the Greek ambassador in Baghdad offered to airlift Bakr and his entire family to Athens and pay for the expensive and delicate surgery needed to remove the bullet. Our cameras followed the ambassador as he visited Bakr's home to break the news to the family. We captured the melodrama of the moment, but there was more emotional drama in store when Bakr's father allowed us to go inside his house to share the news with his wife, who was in purdah. She broke down in a sea of tears and then reached out to hug and kiss Bakr, realizing that her prayers for her son to lead a normal life had finally been answered. Given the intensity of the feelings we had captured, Bakr's story was aired repeatedly on our international network. A few weeks later, when Bakr was due to return from Greece, CNN cameras and correspondents were present in full force at the airport. When asked how he felt, a completely recovered Bakr hugged and kissed CNN staffers, bringing to an end one of the most meaningful and satisfying episodes of my career.

Bakr's story taught me journalism was about striving to make a difference. And just as I had drawn a large number of people to feel Bakr's pain, I felt I could once again tug at the heartstrings of our audience with Baby 81's story. The only problem was logistics. I was in the capital and Baby 81 was on the east coast in Kalmunai, a bone-crushing ten-hour drive away. With so much news still centred around the capital, I was concerned that I would miss more important news developments if I travelled to eastern Sri Lanka, but the News Desk was by now adamant: we had to cover the story. On 6 January 2005, CNN's chief international correspondent, Christiane Amanpour and New

York-based star anchor, Anderson Cooper, had hosted a one-hour 'special' on children affected by the tsunami and it had created a huge impact. Aware of the feelings and sensitivities of our audience, Baby 81 was by now a top priority for CNN and I was under immense pressure to air this story as soon as possible.

But before I could make any travel plans, there were other important commitments to take care of. After days of relentless phone calls, Sri Lankan President Chandrika Kumaratunga's staff had finally agreed to set up an interview for CNN's Talk Asia programme for 18 January. The meeting was slated for 2:00 p.m. in the ornate and historical presidential mansion but, three hours later, at 5:00 p.m., there was still no sign of the president. As a result of the intense security ring around the president, none of our team members was allowed to carry cell phones, which only deepened my anxiety. If the desk or anyone else was trying to reach me to check on or report any breaking news I would be inaccessible.

To ease the tension and to relieve my feeling of entrapment, I kept myself occupied by walking around and admiring the president's luxurious quarters and the gardens, which had the biggest banyan tree I had ever seen. By 8:00 p.m., I had run out of space to tuck into any more snacks and tea that we were politely and regularly being plied with. It was only at 9:00 p.m. and after some persistent but polite badgering that a presidential aide apologetically whispered: 'Her Excellency has been caught up in more important relief matters and can only see you tomorrow.' Catching the huge look of disappointment on my face, the same staffer tried to raise my spirits. 'Look,' he said, 'I'll let you in on a state secret,' and furtively showed me the president's schedule for the next day. Our meeting had been set for 9:00 a.m., and then at 10:30 a.m. Chandrika Kumaratunga was scheduled to fly to Hambantota in southern Sri Lanka to kickstart a 3.5-billion-dollar reconstruction programme. My eyes lit up when I read about her final destination because it was half way to Baby 81's home town of Kalmunai. I made a mental note to talk the president into taking us along in her helicopter. If I could convince her to do so, my eight-hour wait for the interview would be worth its weight in gold.

The next morning, we were all back in the president's living room, which was decorated with pictures of her two children. After the previous night's experience I was understandably nervous, wondering if I was in for another long wait, but by 9:30 a.m., when the president's staff arrived in full force to fuss over lighting and seating arrangements, I had a strong hunch that our meeting was finally on. I was correct, and moments later, a deeply apologetic president walked into the room. As she settled down and the interview began, Chandrika Kumaratunga herself steered the conversation towards the 12,000 Sri Lankan children who had been killed and hundreds of others who had been orphaned by the tsunami. However, rather than building orphanages, the president stressed that Sri Lanka's deep-rooted family network was best suited to handle the situation: 'We would prefer Sri Lankans to adopt them first because they are going to be in their own country. Then the second system we are thinking of is a foster parents' scheme where they have an uncle or aunt or somebody in their own village or in their areas of habitation, who are willing to take them over.' The foster parent programme, added the president, would also allow Sri Lankans or other interested parties abroad to make donations for the upbringing of the children.

Like all Sri Lankans, Chandrika Kumaratunga too had been so moved by the plight of the children that she had decided to adopt a fourteen-year-old Tamil girl, even though she herself was a Sinhalese: 'I saw her when I went to one of the camps and people who were looking after the camp told me that this girl had lost many members of her family and she looked so cute and lost. This child looked like a lovely person so I decided on the spur of the moment [to adopt her]. I was told that she was a Tamil girl and I said so what! I thought it was a good gesture that I start it off especially with a Tamil because I have been always fighting for ethnic harmony, for understanding between the ethnic communities in Sri Lanka.'

As soon as the hour-long interview was over, I asked the president if we could fly with her to Hambantota. I explained that such a trip would give me an opportunity to showcase the relief effort she was heading and felt reasonably confident that after keeping us waiting for so long she would be hard pressed to say no. The president promised to think about it and, just seconds after she had left the room, an excited aide rushed back to inform me that she had agreed to my request. To make room for cameraman Sanjiv, myself and our gear, the president's media advisor gallantly gave up his seat on one of the helicopters – an offer that we graciously accepted.

The night before the meeting, we had prepared for such a possibility. Both Sanjiv and I had packed small 'go bags', containing a shaving kit and an overnight change of clothes to keep us functioning in the field for a day. Grabbing these bags, we quickly dismantled our gear to meet up with the president's security team members, who would be driving us to the helipad. As I raced down a huge wooden staircase in the president's home, I instructed the bureau's senior editor and producer Rohit Gandhi – he had just joined the team in Colombo after a lengthy illness – to edit and feed out a four-minute interview block with the president for the day's news. The remainder of our conversation would run as a half-hour block on CNN's Talk Asia.

By the time we caught up with the president's bodyguards, they were impatiently stomping their feet. Their boss's motorcade had already roared out of her residence and concerned that we could hold up the flight, her staffers bundled us into a car that drove off at such a speed that I doubted we would ever reach the helipad in one piece. Tearing down one of Colombo's main roads at over 140 km an hour and narrowly evading oncoming rush-hour traffic, we reached the airfield in record time. By this time the president's helicopter had already switched on its rotors; no sooner had we hurled our gear in and scrambled aboard the Russian-built Ml 17, it took off. As I paused to wipe my sweat and catch my breath, Sanjiv and I smiled at each other, pleased to know our planning and, most importantly, patience, had paid off. Years of reporting from Sri

Lanka had taught me an important part of its culture. It was sometimes beneficial not to push the pace in this country. Sri Lankans have their own and unique laid-back style and you win friends by going along with it. The president and her staff had appreciated our composure during our long wait and had rewarded it with a ride that got me closer to a story that meant so much to all of us.

Flying south from Colombo we reached Hambantota in about thirty minutes. Here we filmed Chandrika Kumaratunga inaugurating a housing scheme for thousands whose homes had been destroyed and then we peeled off from the presidential party for the five-hour drive to catch up with Baby 81. I was hoping to reach Kalmunai that night itself, but a thunder shower forced us to end our journey about 30 km short of our destination. In blinding rain, we headed straight for the police station in Ampara so that we could identify a safe place to stay that night.

While we explained to a senior police official why we were in the area, I noticed a man in a white shirt approaching us from the corner of the room. As luck would have it, he was the Jeyarajahs' lawyer and, over the next hour, he gave me a detailed report on Sri Lanka's most famous custody battle. I was also given instructions on how to get to Murugupillai Jeyarajah's hairdressing salon. As I turned in for the night, I marvelled at my good fortune. I had been very lucky to get a ride with the president. And the icing on the cake was my chance meeting with the lawyer – someone so very critical to the story.

Early next morning, we set off on the last leg of our journey, praying our luck would hold. It didn't. We got lost trying to find Jeyarajah's salon so I changed tack and drove to the first English-language school that I could find. The plan was to try to locate Sree, the English teacher who had first found Baby 81 on the beach. But none of the teachers at this school knew Skandarajah or where to find him. However, just as I was leaving, an energetic receptionist said she knew Baby 81's saviour and had just seen him. She said that she would find him.

Five minutes later, a man in his mid-forties with a tousled mop of hair and a goatee, wearing the brightest yellow plastic slippers I had ever seen, breezed into the room. Sree had an air of energetic arrogance about him, but he also came across as intense and highly intelligent. He dealt confidently with all those around him, clearly relishing his status as a hero in this small town. When I asked if he would provide us directions, he readily agreed to guide us to the hospital, where I met with the doctors to get their version of the story. Our conversation lasted over an hour, which suited me fine because I wanted to gain their trust. After we had all warmed up to each other, I asked them for permission to let me take pictures of Baby 81. Reluctantly, they agreed.

Leaving Sanjiv to take pictures of Baby 81, I rushed to meet the Jeyarajahs. Junita struck me as being subdued, but Murugupillai was clearly making heavy weather of his ordeal. His puffy red eyes and restless behaviour indicated his deep anguish and he told me that the situation had affected him so adversely that he had lost the motivation to work: 'I feel hurt that so many people are claiming our baby,' he said bitterly. 'Every time I want to visit my child I have to get a letter from the magistrate. These doctors stand like soldiers over our baby and my wife has not been allowed to breast-feed him.'

The hospital came up with a different version of events. With a raging custody battle over the baby, Dr Muhunthan explained he had adopted a very humane approach, allowing the Jeyarajahs to visit Baby 81, even beyond visiting hours. But with paternity still in doubt, Dr Muhunthan admitted he didn't want anyone to touch, hug or kiss the baby: 'Obviously we don't want the baby bonding with someone before it is proved who the real parents are. Lots of mothers have lost babies of the same age so it could be anyone's.'

Later that day, I accompanied the couple as they visited the hospital. After a lengthy argument, a nurse finally allowed them in, but made the ground rules clear: they were only allowed to look at the baby. We rolled our camera as the Jeyarajahs peered into Baby 81's crib. Then, suddenly, Murugupillai burst into tears and fled the ward. His face contorted in pain, he bounded down the stairs. Ripping his camera off his tripod Sanjiv followed and I raced along to help him. We were filming what was clearly an emotional high point in the story and every tear, every emotion and every gesture was going to be closely followed by millions around the world.

Over lunch, I learnt that Kalmunai was also home to another famous resident. Her name was Kanita

Amphipahan, the girl that President Kumaratunga had decided to adopt. Although she didn't quite fit in with the story that I was filing that night, I decided to visit her at the orphanage that she shared with twenty other children. Kanita was still dazed and confused and trying to make sense of what had happened to her life. I asked her if she was excited that she would soon be living with the president and her answer floored me. 'No,' she replied. 'I prefer to stay here with my brothers and sisters.'

Kanita's pride and dignity left a deep impression on me. She had lost so much, but even at such a tender age, she was calm and content. Her demeanour contrasted sharply with the mood just a few houses away where Murugupillai was exhorting the magistrate to end his anguish: 'All the parents should be called for a DNA test. If the child belongs to them I will commit suicide,' he screamed. A few days later the court finally ordered the procedure and once again it was only the Jeyarajahs among all the claiming couples who agreed to be tested.

The test itself went off without incident. But then the distraught couple, accompanied by a large crowd of cheering supporters, stormed the hospital. Pointing to the tsunami survivor in his crib, the Jeyarajahs implored nurses to hand him over. Murugupillai was by now threatening to swallow a white powder if the baby wasn't handed over, and had to be physically restrained. In the tussle for the child, hospital workers claimed they were roughed up and the police promptly arrested Murugupillai. A few hours later, a more sedate Murugupillai was released on bail.

The intensity of this emotional drama was instrumental in projecting it as one of the best human-interest stories across the world. So, when the DNA test results were declared almost seven weeks after Baby 81 was first found, TV viewers saw an emotional Murugupillai hugging his lawyer, shedding tears of joy. With the story now clearly in its home stretch, newspaper and TV editors also dropped the name Baby 81, and began, much to the delight of the Jeyarajahs, calling him Abhilash. The name symbolized hope, desire and expectation and it was evident that not just for Sri Lankans but also for people around the world his story was all about the resilience of the human spirit.

Adding to the high sense of drama was the magistrate's decision to hand over the baby to his parents in court itself. It was time, I decided, to make another trip to Kalmunai. We arrived in town on 15 February, and, given the huge international interest in the story, I wasn't surprised to find an Associated Press (AP) television team following Abhilash's parents as they shopped for gifts and prepared the room he would be staying in.

With requests for several early morning *live* shots the next day, I decided to go to bed early. Just before turning in, I hooked up my computer to my satellite phone to read the latest news wires. I had barely gone through the first story when the desk called to tell me that NewsNight, which is simulcast on both our US and international channels, wanted me to file a news package. Despite the late hour, I thought it was a good idea because it would draw in viewers for the next day's grand finale. Relying on AP's pictures, my story not only highlighted the parents' joy, but also drew attention to their decision to keep celebrations muted because they didn't want to offend thousands of other Sri Lankans still grieving over the loss of their children.

The next morning, we arrived at a packed courthouse. The international media was well represented and the US network ABC had even flown in a five-member team especially for the occasion. The waiting photographers couldn't believe their luck when the magistrate announced that he would allow cameras into the jampacked courtroom. Fired by a sense of history in the making and enthused by the anticipation all around us, we set up our equipment and waited for the proceedings to begin.

Inside the courtroom, dozens of cameramen jostled for space, elbowing each other in order to obtain the best shot of the exuberant Jeyarajahs. But the real star of the day was clearly Abhilash, whose arrival was marked by a huge roar and an even more energetic scramble by the cameramen to capture his picture for posterity. Flashbulbs exploded everywhere, producers screamed at the photographers not to miss a frame and dozens craned their necks for a better view as a sleeping Abhilash was carried into court by a hospital nurse.

Proceedings began with the magistrate reading out a twenty-one-page statement. Abhilash slept through it all, getting up only once to hungrily suck on his milk bottle. And then it was time for the shot of the day. Court officials picked up Abhilash – still in a fitful sleep – to hand him over to Junita. Carried away by the importance of the moment, dozens of cameramen rushed right into the well of the court.

All the din, the chaos and the mad scramble irritated the magistrate, and his repeated pleas for everyone to stay calm seemingly fell on deaf ears. Concerned by the non-cooperative attitude of the cameramen and feeling the intense heat inside the court, angry policemen began pushing the cameramen back. 'Move out of my shot,' implored CNN cameraman Mahadev Rao. A burly policeman responded by advancing threateningly towards him. Realizing it was time to make a quick intervention, I stepped in and grabbed the policeman's hand, shaking it so vigorously that he wondered if we really were long-lost friends. As the policeman tried to come to terms with the situation, it allowed Mahadev the extra few seconds he needed to explode into action.

Jumping onto one of the court tables and drenched in sweat, Mahedev captured a tearful Junita holding a bewildered Abhilash to her chest. Spectators wiped tears from their eyes, others clapped and Murugupillai's sixty-year-old father, who had arrived in court to witness the handover, passed out, overwhelmed by a sense of relief. Pleased that we had captured the most important video of the day, I dashed outside for a quick *live* hit being shot by freelancer Maurya Gautam. This left Mahadev free to shoot more video with the triumphant Jeyarajah family.

The Jeyarajahs first stopped at the hospital to thank the staff, who told the media that they were proud of the way they had safeguarded the baby's interests and were even happier that the story had such a happy ending. Only too glad to have their son back, the Jeyarajahs too were no longer in the mood to be critical of the hospital. They had other more important things to do and headed off to a temple, where to show their appreciation to the gods, they, as per tradition, broke 101 coconuts. The pictures were powerful and evocative but there was more emotion in store as the family members decided to visit their destroyed home on the beach. With tears streaming down her face, Abhilash's grandmother changed his hospital clothes. Other relatives cried as they hugged and kissed the four-month-old. To try to catch some of this mood, I quickly finished my *live* shots and drove down to the beach in a tearing hurry. I was anxious to talk to the parents and managed to push back a swarm of photographers to ask Junita how she felt. 'I had a very traumatic time,' she responded. 'I went without food and sleep for days, but now we are very happy,' she said, smiling broadly.

Living up to their earlier promise, the Jeyarajahs didn't hold any parties. Instead, they spent their time at a relative's home, cooing at their baby. The couple took turns to caress and kiss him, which gave me opening pictures to file my last story on Baby 81. After eighteen years in the business and after filing thousands of news reports, this was one of my favourite human-interest stories and I too had reason to feel satisfied that the world had responded so warmly to Baby 81 and his family's struggle.

Despite the jubilation surrounding these events, I also had to keep things in perspective and not lose sight of the fact that Abhilash had been incredibly lucky. Thousands of Sri Lankan children had been killed and those who survived would carry psychological scars for years. My thoughts once again returned to Galle and nine-year-old Tharesh Liyanage. Two weeks after the tsunami, Tharesh's mother's body still hadn't been found and in an attempt to get closure, the Liyanages decided to go to the Galle hospital to meet forensic pathologist, Dr Rohan Rowanapura.

By coincidence, I too was visiting Dr Rowanapura at this time and noticed a subdued Tharesh entering the forensic pathologist's hospital. The Liyanages wanted to check Dr Rowanapura's records to see if Ishwarie Liyanage's body had ever been found and brought to the hospital. Since he was the last person to see her alive and was aware of the clothes and jewellery his mother had been wearing, it was left to Tharesh to try to identify her through the pictures on Dr Rowanapura's computer.

It was a delicate moment and a heavy burden for a nine-year-old to be saddled with. But this was the best way of making a correct identification. Realizing the sensitivity of the situation, Dr Rowanapura tried to make Tharesh comfortable by indulging in small talk with him. Then with great care, he only showed Tharesh pictures of what he thought could be his mother's clothes. Tharesh leaned forward in his chair, fidgeting nervously with his hands. Then his eyes widened as he concentrated intently on the screen and, seconds later, he nodded his head vigorously. That's all Dr Rowanapura needed to know. Easing him gently off the chair, Galle's forensic pathologist put his arm around Tharesh's shoulder and led him away from the computer.

We were lucky to be able to film this incredibly private moment and I felt embarrassed to approach the family. But, to my surprise, Udyoga Liyanage, Tharesh's father, did want to talk and expressed his gratitude for Dr Rowanapura and his entire staff, who had by now even prepared a death certificate. Udyoga also readily agreed to let me talk to Tharesh, who was keen to tell me about his studies and his school. 'I want to become a scientist,' he said resolutely. The family's dignity in this almost unbearable moment of grief choked me up. I wondered how I would have coped with a situation like this if I were a nine-year-old.

For all the strength and resilience that he had displayed, Tharesh acknowledged that the tsunami had scarred him: 'Now when I hear the smallest sound I get scared and turn around,' he disclosed, reminding me that he had first realized that something was horribly wrong when he heard the sound of the roaring water. 'The sound of plates and dishes falling bothers me. When our school band plays and the cymbals clash, that sound bothers me. I feel nervous,' he said in a tiny voice. But in his own style, rather than dwelling on his problems, Tharesh was trying to deal with them: 'I am planning to buy books on earthquakes to see what exactly you can do to save yourself, like maybe hide under the table.'

About 60 km away, nine-year-old Basura Weerakoon was also trying to cope with the tragedy and get on with life. His parents and elder sister had perished on board the *Queen of the Sea* and their bodies had never been found. On 26 December itself Basura had been adopted by his father's brother, Sudath

Weerakoon, who is an architect. 'Our social system is fairly strong,' he explained. 'Here in Sri Lanka family ties matter and Basura is very attached to his grandparents who visit him regularly.'

Like most nine-year-olds, Basura loved video games, cricket and books. And now, just like Tharesh, he also found it very hard to deal with noise; so much so that even a ringing telephone could trigger off uncontrollable outbursts of anger in him. 'I still think about the tsunami all the time,' he told me. 'Whenever there is a loud noise I think the water is coming at us again.' Basura had also developed a hatred for the sea and, while travelling in a car along the coast, he always sat on the seat away from the water.

Basura's experience mirrored that of other younger children, who had grown up believing that the sea was a benign and friendly force. Raised with such a belief, it was hundreds of children who first rushed onto the beaches on 26 December, intent on grabbing thousands of squirming fish that were left on the sand as the sea retreated. Most of these children didn't even notice the waves roaring once again towards them. Crushed under the weight of the water, they died within seconds. Those who survived had seen their siblings, parents, other relatives and homes sucked out right in front of their eyes.

Shortly after the magnitude of the havoc caused by the tsunami became known, several community elders saw children swearing at the sea. Some were so angry that they even wanted to attack the water. One monk related an incident involving a child whom he saw going up to the sea and challenging it to a fight. With less than fifty psychiatrists for its entire population of nineteen million citizens, the Sri Lankan Government lacked the resources to provide adequate medical counselling. Also knowing full well that such counselling went against the grain of Sri Lankan culture, officials settled on a strategy of trying to reintegrate children with families and communities as soon as possible.

Given his tender age, Abhilash's doctors reasoned he was unlikely to face any such challenges. He would also have no memories either of his separation from his family or his trip to the United States. Shortly after he was reunited with his family, ABC's highly rated breakfast show Good Morning America flew them all to the US for an interview. It was an incredible experience for the Jeyarajahs who had never travelled on a plane before or even left their country. The trip wasn't without controversy though. Some questioned why one Sri Lankan family was being given special treatment when thousands of others had suffered equally. All this did not bother the Jeyarajahs. For them, their most cherished memories of the United States were the love and affection that they were showered with. And all that mattered to them was to ensure that their son grew up as a normal Sri Lankan child.

8

The Evil That Men Do

The video was chilling. Not only had these two men robbed a dead or helpless woman, they had come to blows over their spoils.

Dateline: Magona, southern Sri Lanka,
26 December 2004

LIKE THOUSANDS OF OTHER SRI LANKANS, PRIYANTHA Colombaarachi got up early on 26 December. It was Poya Day, one of the most auspicious occasions in the Buddhist calendar and the first thing he wanted to do was say his prayers. Walking through the clay-coated courtyard of his home, he made his way into the family's brightly lit prayer room to light a lamp at the feet of a golden painting of the Buddha. Thirty-three-year-old Priyantha prayed for wealth and prosperity. After years of civil war, the Sri Lankan Government and Tamil Tiger rebels fighting for an independent homeland in the northern and eastern parts of the country had agreed to a ceasefire that was still holding. The truce gave an unprecedented boost to economic activities like construction and, in the past few months, Priyantha, a building contractor by profession, had been reaping the benefits. There were more projects to work on, more overtime to be earned and, after years of strife, Priyantha wanted his country to forget its bitter past and focus on improving the living standards of its people. In the past few months, Sri Lanka's economy had recorded a healthy 5.3 per cent growth rate and Priyantha was desperately keen that this momentum be maintained so he could build a future for his twenty-seven-year-old wife and two young sons, Ishan and Kavishka.

After praying for both his family and nation, Priyantha walked back into the family's spacious home, set amidst a coconut plantation. He first woke his wife up and together they prepared the children for a special journey to one of Sri Lanka's holiest Buddhist sites – the Kataragama monastery – about 170 km away from their home in Magona, southern Sri Lanka. Accompanying them were his elderly parents and his elder brother's and sister's families. In all, at just past 6:00 a.m., fifteen members of the Colombaarachi family boarded a thirty-six-seater bus that Priyantha had specially hired for the journey. The rest of the seats were taken up by other friends and relatives whom he had invited for this festive occasion.

The mood was lighthearted as the bus pulled out of Magona, an hour's drive south of Colombo, and, within minutes, everyone was singing religious hymns. The Colombaarachis were a devout lot. For the past twenty-four years, they had made a similar pilgrimage to the Kataragama monastery on Poya Day. This time, just at the start of what would be their twenty-fifth visit, everyone on board was counting on the gods to bestow them with special favours and blessings.

Two-and-a-half hours into the journey, as hunger set in, Priyantha pulled over at a seaside restaurant for breakfast. As all the elders sat down to enjoy bread dipped in sweet tea, Priyantha attended to the needs of his elderly and ailing father. He offered him a pillow and led him back inside the bus so he could lie down and rest for a while. All the children, except for one-year-old Kavishka, rushed to the nearby beach, clapping and cheering as a few large waves rolled onto the shore. None of them had ever seen such huge waves, but it was a sight that didn't frighten them in the least. In fact, as the waves smashed into the rocks and drenched them in the process, they were all squealing and giggling in delight.

Priyantha and his wife barely noticed the frolicking children. The long drive had upset their younger son who was bawling his head off. In an effort to calm him down, the couple was contemplating taking him inside the bus, when they suddenly noticed they were standing in knee-deep water. Within seconds a huge, dark wave rolled ashore catching Priyantha off guard; he had a mental blackout. 'My mind stopped on me,' recalled Priyantha with a shudder. 'I didn't know what to think or how to react. The sea had come onto land and I was neck-deep in water.' Unaware of the children's whereabouts, Priyantha's first recollection of those frightful moments was of his parents struggling to stay alive. They were thrashing and struggling in the debris-laden water, with nothing to latch onto.

Aware of the fact that his parents lacked adequate strength and agility, Priyantha wanted to put them both aboard the bus so that he could drive them to safety. But the force of the water was so intense that the bus itself was pulled out to sea and the slightly built Priyantha, who didn't know how to swim, could barely move. 'My father then started yelling: "Help mother, she is being sucked out to sea."' Priyantha implored his father to try to cling onto a tree, but his frail health prevented him from doing so. At that time, Priyantha was no more than a few feet away from his parents and was immensely frustrated that he couldn't do more for them. 'The water was 15-feet high and my parents were being pulled out to sea. In twenty seconds they were gone and as they raced past me both were pleading and crying: "Son please help us." Priyantha's mother was only fifty-five years' old. His father died on his sixty-fifth birthday.

The shock of seeing his parents sucked out to sea in a matter of seconds was more than what Priyantha could bear, and he passed out. When he regained consciousness, the water level had dropped to about 6 feet and, twenty minutes later, after he had reoriented himself, he began a frantic search for the rest of his family. After walking for about a kilometre, he found the body of his brother Samantha. Although an expert swimmer, Samantha had suffered multiple head injuries. 'With him dead, I knew there was little chance of finding all the others alive,' reasoned Priyantha. A short while later, two policemen helped him fish out the body of his thirty-seven-year-old sister Nilunkha from a lake. Then he found his wife's body and, together with his brother-in-law, he half-carried, half-dragged the dead to an air force camp, 4 km away.

After leaving his wife's and sister's bodies there, Priyantha returned to locate his wailing elder son, five-year-old Ishan, and his ten-year-old nephew Harsha, both of whom had outsmarted the wave by quickly climbing onto a building. Harsha's twin sister, Harshini, had also survived by clambering up a tree.

By 6:00 p.m., except for the bodies of his parents who had been washed out to sea, Priyantha had found the bodies of all his family members and deposited them at a local hospital. A day that had started with prayer and religious fervour had ended in the death of nine members of his family, including his wife, a one-year-old son, parents, brother, sister-in-law, sister, one niece and a nephew. Of the fifteen members of the Colombaarachi family who had left home in the morning, only five had survived and one, Priyantha's eighteen-year-old sister was still missing. Among the survivors were his brother's children – the ten-year-old twins Harsha and Harshini. They had lost their parents, grandparents, younger brother, two cousins and an aunt all within fifteen minutes. Adding to Priyantha's inconsolable grief was the behaviour of those who lived in the area. 'Some people came to help,' he said. 'But they robbed my dead family members of their jewellery and cash. I didn't really care about the money. All I wanted was my family members back alive.'

Priyantha was also worried about his eighteen-year-old sister. There had been no word about her. But the encouraging news was that no one had seen her being dragged out to sea either and he continued to cling to hope. Late that night, with the authorities fearing another tsunami, all the survivors of the Colombaarachi family were airlifted to Colombo. At 3:00 a.m. the next day, Priyantha managed to call a friend, who picked him up and the two drove back to the hospital in Galle so that they could claim all the bodies and complete the last rites.

A grief-stricken Priyantha was in for an even bigger shock when he reached the hospital. Unable to deal with such a large number of corpses, the doctors had transferred his family members' bodies to another medical facility. By the time Priyantha reached the other hospital, it was pitch dark. In the absence of electricity, Priyantha borrowed a flashlight and started the most difficult mission of his entire life. 'It took me more than an hour to look at 1000 bodies and find my family,' he sobbed. 'I recognized my son from the shoe he was wearing.'

The time now was 7:30 p.m. and Priyantha had to persuade the overworked and strained doctors to hand over the bodies. It wasn't easy because the medical staff had just been ordered to begin mass burials and were reluctant to hand over decomposed bodies, but an angry Priyantha refused to give in. 'I shouted and fought with them to get my bodies back,' he noted chillingly. 'I then loaded them onto a truck and wanted to drive them home, but a local politician approached me and told me there was no point in taking them back because they were in such a poor state.' At 10:15 that night, with just his friend for emotional comfort, Priyantha buried the bodies in a mass grave. But he didn't have the heart to put his one-year-old son Kavishka's body in with all the others. He lovingly carried him in his lap during the long drive back home. When the tsunami struck, Priyantha couldn't do anything to help his younger son and had been wallowing in guilt ever since. But now that he was back in control, the most important thing in the world for him was to bring his child home and give him a proper burial.

About 70 km away, freelance photographer Ajanta Samarawickrama was taking a bit of a breather from the frenzied pace of the past two days. When the tsunami had roared into town, Ajanta had the professional instincts and the presence of mind to scurry to the highest building he could find, which was next to the bus stand in Galle. He then switched on his video camera and managed to capture some of the most sensational and frightening eyewitness shots of the tsunami from anywhere in the world. Just hours after arriving in Galle I had met up with Ajanta and convinced him to sell me this video, which was later aired repeatedly on CNN (see also Chapter 2).

The first time I had watched Ajanta's images I was facing a tight deadline and concentrated mainly on grabbing pictures that displayed the awesome power of the tsunami. But even then, one image of two men fighting over a woman stood out in my mind. It was hard at that point to establish clearly from that shaky video if this woman was dead or alive. Also, lacking both the proper context to the pictures and the time to talk to the photographer, I had abstained from using that section of the video. In the aftermath of all he had shot and seen, Ajanta too had forgotten about the two men. But a few days later he found his mind returning to those haunting images.

Ajanta had actually filmed a heinous crime being committed. His first picture in this section of the video showed a young, short man wearing just a sarong carrying the limp body of a petite woman. Moments later, the individual had pried something off the woman's body, but even before he could pocket what he had taken, a taller, more belligerent man in a sarong and open shirt confronted him. In the ensuing altercation, the smaller man was forced to drop the woman to the ground. As her head smashed against the concrete, the taller man walked away with his booty: a thin gold chain.

The video was chilling. Not only had these two men robbed a dead or helpless woman, they had come to blows over their spoils. Ajanta's images showcased human greed and a callous disregard for others in their most naked and evil form. As he peered at what was happening through his viewfinder, Ajanta felt a wave of repulsion sweeping over him. How could these people behave this way? he wondered. For him these images were harder to film than the ravages of the tsunami itself and, at one point, he seriously contemplated putting his camera down. 'I wanted to stop filming,' he recalled. 'I just wanted to rush there to stop that madness.' Frustrated he couldn't do more, Ajanta got his chance a few days later when he enlarged the images of the men and published the photographs in a local newspaper.

The response was overwhelming. A grieving nation was incensed, forcing the police to launch a high-level probe. In order to tap into the outrage that the story had generated, I dispatched a crew to meet Galle's senior superintendent of police, Hatpavana Lasantha de Silva, who was contemptuous of the looters: 'At a time of national crisis, I'm sure they are sick in mind. They suffer from various mental diseases.' As luck would have it, while we were at the station itself, police officers brought two handcuffed suspects in for questioning. Our cameras rolled on the action, giving us the picture of the day, and this was just the beginning. Police recovered a gold chain from the men and remanded them to custody, promising to press charges of theft and murder as soon as possible. 'These are sadistic sort of crimes that have happened at a time of crisis,' remarked Superintendent de Silva. 'This has happened when people have been struggling to survive and there is a presidential directive to take the toughest possible action against such behaviour.'

The arrest of the two suspects was big news in Galle, further boosting sympathy for the dead woman, who was later identified as thirty-five-year-old Deshika Kalyani. The day the tsunami struck, Deshika was accompanying her niece to a sewing class. They were due to catch a bus from Galle's main bus stand, but never completed the journey. With no news of the two women, Deshika's family, led by her sister Nella Aryawati, had been searching in vain: 'We looked for them everywhere and visited all the police stations and hospitals in the area.' Then, on 28 December, the family saw the gruesome footage of the two men and their fight over Deshika's chain on national TV. Recognizing the

Galle bus stand in these images, Nella approached senior police officials, who asked her to check the pictures of the dead at Galle's hospital. Trembling with fear, Deshika's family made the journey to Galle and identified her from the dress she was wearing.

The pain and numbness felt by Deshika's story was also shared by others. A Colombo couple, who refused to believe that their six-year-old missing daughter had been killed, put out advertisements in the newspapers, asking for any information that could lead them to their child. The couple and other family members received several calls, with one caller repeatedly asking for money before he would divulge any information.

Around this time there were local rumours that another fifteen-year-old girl, whose parents had been killed and home washed away, had been raped. Details on the case were hard to come by and, after hours of research, all I could establish was that she was probably in a child-care centre in the Galle area. Locating the girl and trying to verify this story was comparable to finding a needle in a haystack, but given the huge outcry over what happened to Deshika, my instincts told me we had to try to locate her. The question was how? We tried calling local journalists, but drew a blank. Next, we contacted child-care agencies like UNICEF, which also had no information about the girl. We had reached another dead end, but as was his habit and just when we needed him most, the smiling Wasantha Wijendra walked back into our lives.

With his array of influential contacts and his formidable local knowledge, Wasantha soon traced

'The Shrine': Buddhist monks visit Peraliya (southern Sri Lanka) to pay their respects to the more than 1000 people killed in this train, which was swept off the tracks by the tsunami.
(*Courtesy: The Sunday Times*, Colombo, Sri Lanka.)

The emotional Jeyarajahs reunited with their son Abhilash (Baby 81),
Kalmunai, Sri Lanka. (*Courtesy*: *The Sunday Times*, Colombo, Sri Lanka.)

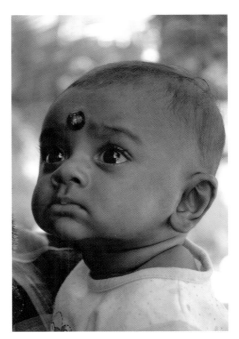

Baby 81, a symbol of hope around the world, and Sri Lanka's most famous infant.
(*Courtesy*: *The Sunday Times*, Colombo, Sri Lanka.)

Undertakers carrying coffins of unidentified tourists at a cemetery in Colombo, Sri Lanka. (*Courtesy*: Associated Press/Eranga Jayawardena.)

A Sri Lankan hero: Forensic pathologist Dr Rohan Rowanapura, who fingerprinted and took DNA samples of over 700 bodies in record time at Galle, southern Sri Lanka. (*Courtesy*: Nalaka Karunarathna.)

Volunteers cremating bodies at Nagapattinam, southern Tamil Nadu. (*Courtesy*: Associated Press/Gurinder Osan.)

the girl to a child-care agency in Galle itself. Editor/ producer Rohit Gandhi was tasked to do the interview and he uncovered yet another horrific story. The fifteen-year-old girl and her sister were at home when the tsunami struck, forcing them to seek shelter on their roof. When they clambered down an hour later, their parents had vanished. Traumatized and confused, the girls trekked to their stepmother's parents' home, where their grandmother asked them to spend the night. As she related her story the young victim broke down: 'At night when I was changing my clothes he (grandfather) came and touched me and started feeling me but I was able to push him away. In the morning, I got up early at about 7:30 a.m. and ran away from there.'

Such criminal acts were isolated events, across a nation in which hundreds of thousands of Sri Lankans had done so much to help each other. But they did have a huge impact in Galle, where public anger was so intense that some citizens decided to take the law into their own hands. Several looters were beaten black and blue by mobs. And one man believed to have robbed a corpse was stabbed to death.

Three days had now passed since the tsunami had struck and Priyantha Colombaarachi was still trying to locate his missing sister. He finally found her at the Galle hospital, where she tearfully recounted how a stranger, who had promised to reunite her with her family, had raped her. 'This man tied my hands behind my back,' she narrated, sobbing. 'I struggled to push him away. I also begged him to take me to my parents but he smothered my face and screams with his shirt.' Given that this suffering had been caused not by nature but by humans themselves, I decided to file a story on the subject, titling it 'The Evil That Men Do'. It ran every hour for a twelve-hour stretch on our network.

Swamped by so much bad news, Sri Lankans were desperate for some uplifting stories and an opportunity would soon present itself on 8 January, when a frail, old man was rushed to Galle hospital. Rumours soon spread that he could be a tsunami survivor, prompting our Colombo stringer Iqbal Athas to call me, while I was still out at sea on a fishing trawler. As we talked, I felt a surge of adrenaline flow through my tired body. After almost two weeks of serving up a steady diet of depressing news, this development presented a good chance to try to change the tempo of our coverage by providing a riveting and inspiring story. Wrapping up our shoot, I raced to the hospital, reaching there late in the evening along with a pack of hungry reporters.

Scrambling up a flight of stairs, we all made our way to a first-floor ward, where fast asleep in one of the corner beds was an emaciated, delirious and tiny man with a heavy stubble and an untidy mop of hair. His breathing was laboured and loud, giving him the appearance of a character in a horror movie. As I bent over his bed for a closer look, I noticed his scrawny knees were scrunched right up to his chest, and that he could not have weighed more than 40 kg. Doctors who had first examined him told me he appeared to be sixty years old and had a fractured forearm. When he was admitted, this mysterious patient was suffering from pneumonia, had a low urine output and was severely dehydrated. My own assessment was similar, but a little more succinct: it looked like he had been through hell.

Junior doctors speculated he could have been caught and trapped in debris for days because the other survivors whom they had treated recently were also suffering from similar symptoms and ailments like dehydration and pneumonia. Since it had rained a fair bit after the tsunami, these doctors also believed it was theoretically possible for him to survive for almost fourteen days on rain water alone. But senior hospital staff were more sceptical, pointing out that his story was too good to be true and suggested that a closer examination of the fracture would confirm not just the time of his injury but most likely his status as well.

It was an interesting situation and a story we could hardly ignore. But since the man still hadn't spoken a word and I couldn't rule out the possibility that he was perhaps a vagabond or homeless person, I adopted a cautious posture on air. I reported just the facts and told the anchors that we would come to know more details only after locating the person who had brought him to the hospital. A few hours later, we tracked down Karunya Ratna Guruge, a worker with a local political party, who revealed that the patient had been found in a neighbourhood that had been completely devastated by the tsunami and was accessible only by bulldozers. Since it was very late at night, we decided to visit that area the next morning. All we could do for now was maintain a vigil along with dozens of other visitors by the man's bedside.

As the hours passed, more and more reporters descended upon the hospital. Realizing the media's keen interest in their patient, doctors increased their level of care. A bevy of nurses hovered around the man, who by now had mumbled that his name was Sirisena. With hopes building that Sirisena could talk any minute, no efforts were spared to make him comfortable. Fresh linen and blankets were ordered for the star patient and bottled oxygen was also provided to ease his breathing. Just as intrigued by this mysterious man as the waiting horde of reporters was a nurse, who forcibly tried to open his heavy eyelids. She failed, managing only to invite another loud snore from Sirisena, who now was probably the most pampered patient in the country. Every time he turned, reporters scrambled to his bedside with notebooks and cameras on the ready. But Sirisena wasn't ready to reveal his past. Not yet.

With so much mystery surrounding Sirisena, it was but natural for show producers to start expressing great interest in the story. On 9 January, we set up our *live* equipment and reported that Sirisena had just revealed he had two children. But before the doctors could probe any further, he had gone back to sleep. Later in the day, the doctors gave him a dose of anaesthesia and put a cast on his arm. We transmitted his latest pictures and comments from doctors as interest continued to build within the system. Starting at 6:30 p.m. CNN USA too wanted a flurry of live shots and I crossed my fingers, hoping that Sirisena would finally say something meaningful.

In case he didn't, my back-up plan was to squeeze as much information as possible from Karunya Ratna Guruge, the volunteer who had brought him to hospital. With Karunya leading the way we went back to the neighbourhood where Sirisena had been found. The roads leading up to the area were still full of debris and we drove past several bulldozers to arrive at a spot where every single home had been demolished. The putrid smell of chemicals hung in the air and Karunya led me to a drain. 'I found him here with only his head showing above the water,' he declared. Sirisena had been naked and so weak that he'd slumped into his rescuer's arms, who now emphatically announced: 'I am convinced he's a survivor. I am very happy. This is a good occasion in my lifetime. I will never forget this.'

Nor would the millions following his story. Three days after he had been admitted, Sirisena still hadn't said a word. Perhaps he didn't want to. Some people recalled seeing him walking around after the tsunami. More revealing perhaps was the police's speculation that he could be a looter who got trapped inside the building he had set out to rob. As reporters got wind of the police's fears they dropped his story. Sirisena just wasn't the hero they were looking for.

But the Colombaarachi family was still attracting a fair bit of media interest and I decided to drive down to their home in Magona, about 50 km south of Colombo. When I met him, Priyantha was trying to get on with his life, but with the entire family now dependent on him, he wasn't sure where he would get the resources to bring them up and look after the educational needs of his dead brother's children.

The government had provided him $100 for every family member who had been killed, an amount Priyantha felt was a cruel joke. What was also very difficult for him to deal with was the constant questioning of his nephew and niece Harsha and Harshini. 'The children often ask me where their parents and grandparents are,' he said forlornly. 'They want to know when they will be reborn.'

As we sat and talked in his courtyard, family members fussed over us, regularly bringing us soft drinks. Even though we weren't thirsty, we accepted them with gratitude and thanks. The Sri Lankans are caring people and feel insulted if you waive their hospitality. At lunchtime, one of the children in the household scrambled up a tree and brought us a few coconuts each. As we drank their sweet water, I felt a huge lump in my throat. This family was deep in grief and finding it hard to cope with life, yet even the youngest among them was being the perfect host.

Even though he had resumed work, Priyantha was still depressed and finding it tough to live in his ancestral home, which contained so many memories of all his loved ones. 'If I had the money I would move out of here,' he declared. He also confessed that the tsunami had changed him and his attitude towards life and work forever: 'Earlier, all I wanted to do was make money. I used to come home at 2:00 in the morning, but now I return home early. I have so many duties and I want to enjoy time with those in the family who are still left.' Before leaving I asked Priyantha to take me to the family's prayer room, where I asked him what time he would be saying his prayers that day. 'We won't,' he said, with a resigned shrug. 'The tsunami swept away our faith.'

9

The Shrine

For many Sri Lankans this train is now a shrine — a symbol of their suffering. A place, where it seems, this entire country's grief comes together.

Dateline: Peraliya, 26 January 2005

EXACTLY ONE MONTH HAD PASSED SINCE THE TSUNAMI struck and to mark this solemn anniversary, I decided to visit the site of the train wreck: the spot where more than 1000 men, women and children had perished. For millions of Sri Lankans, Peraliya still marked the epicentre of the country's grief and I felt it would provide a sense of the sombre national mood. I was also keen to photograph the massive reconstruction effort in the area. So, accompanied by my team, I reached my destination at about 4:00 p.m.

The first thing we noticed was the heavy traffic. There was hardly any place to park and dozens of cars and buses laden with travellers from across the country were converging on the scene. Many families came with children and packed lunches in tow, which surprised me because I had half expected to walk into an incense-burning prayer ceremony. What I hadn't counted on was hundreds of people walking briskly to get their first glimpse of a train that was now the country's most well-known tomb.

Joining the large crowd, we walked past some security guards and then a few seconds later I was standing by the *Queen of the Sea*. It had taken hundreds of specially trained rescue workers, army tanks and bulldozers to drag the overturned wagons from a shallow bog onto a small section of railway track that was, remarkably, still intact. All the coaches had been placed in the correct order, and facing the direction of the train's intended destination – one it never reached – was the steel-blue Canadian-built locomotive engine.

Large chunks of the engine were missing, but as I walked alongside, I shuddered. It must have taken an unimaginable amount of energy to nonchalantly lift and fling something so huge, so heavy and so imposing in appearance. Walking down the length of the train, I noticed signs warning people not to touch or pick anything from inside the coaches. All the mud-brown coaches were mangled and dented, and, as I stopped to look at them, images of those last frightening moments played out in my mind's eye. I could almost hear and see the black thundering water slam into the coaches causing unimaginable fear and panic. I could also visualize other gruesome scenes: tiny hands clutching at the wagon's steel window bars and wide frightened eyes peering at me from within the shadows of the train. Accompanying all these images were loud agonizing screams that covered me in a cold sweat and kept me glued to the same spot for almost fifteen minutes.

As I began to walk again, the horror of what happened here continued to assault my senses. Still lying in piles along the track were the footwear and clothes of passengers. I stopped dead in my tracks when I came upon the overturned muddy shoe of a young passenger. The child, I estimated, must have been four years old. The same age as my older daughter.

The sound of clicking cameras awakened me to the presence of others in the area. People were craning their necks to look inside the wagons; some were inspecting the track, showing their children where they thought the waves had first hit and taking pictures of the bedraggled coaches. Yet again, I felt puzzled, but then realizing I was perhaps missing something, I let my professional instincts take over and observe what was happening more closely.

The introspection immediately cleared my first impressions. Yes, there were a lot of people here, many had children and food with them, but average Sri Lankan families come to worship at temples in similar fashion. And the closer I looked, the more I could understand the depth and intensity of the visitors' feelings. People had come here to pay their respects. Most families walked about in hushed silence. No one touched the train or went inside it. People treated it like a sacred site. Seconds later, I recorded my 'standup' or a brief on-camera segment. It took minimal effort and the words just spilled out of me:

> For many Sri Lankans this train is now a shrine – a symbol of their suffering. A place, where it seems, this entire country's grief comes together.

One month after the tsunami, feelings here were still very raw, with many Sri Lankans being reminded of all that the country had lost. The terrible tragedy brought home the realization that the island had lost almost an entire generation of children. It took Sri Lanka's bloody civil war eighteen years to kill almost 65,000 people. In just a few hours, the tsunami had killed about 30,000. More than any place that I had ever visited, Peraliya was living proof of humankind's frailty when faced with the awesome fury of nature.

None of the people I mingled with and talked to were grieving. By this time, most had identified their loved ones, picked up their soggy belongings and moved onto rebuilding their shattered lives. The majority of Peraliya's current visitors had heard about the train through the media and many, like business executive Dayaratna Chandrashekhar, talked about this spot in the same hushed tones that most Americans reserved for the destroyed World Trade Center towers. 'When I see the train,' remarked Dayaratna, 'I think about the 1000 people who lost their lives here and it is about the biggest tragedy in one place in Sri Lanka.' Commenting on the train's abiding national legacy, another visitor, Danister Wirasinha, summed up his thoughts this way: 'In my living time I am not going to forget this nor will other Sri Lankans.'

Just a few feet away, local resident Hikkaduwa Rohan had brought his wife and four-year-old daughter with him. As he inspected the coaches, he talked about providence and fate: 'If the train had been just a few minutes early or late none of this would have happened.' Hikkaduwa had no qualms about bringing his young daughter to the site, explaining that her teacher had, in fact, asked her to paint an image of the train, a project he wholeheartedly supported because it would build awareness among children of the nation's worst-ever natural tragedy.

As a tribute to, and in remembrance of, those who died, Hikkaduwa wanted the train to remain at the same spot. But others had strong reservations: they pointed out the best course of action for the government would be to move it out and forget about the past. 'If the train was kept here,' commented Danister Wirasinha, 'we would continue to return for years and years, and younger generations would continue coming and remembering. That's not good. It's better to shift the train from here as soon as possible and forget [about it].'

It wasn't just visitors who had strong feelings about making the train a memorial. Local residents, many of whom had loaded children and relatives on the coaches only to have them swept away, felt it wasn't right to keep the train there because it constantly reminded them of their grief. Fisherman Kaluarchi Chandasa (see Chapter 4) was not at home when the tsunami struck, but his brother had put several visiting family members and children on board the train and clambered on himself, thinking they would be safer there. This decision cost him his life. Seven other members of Kaluarchi's family also perished, and eventually only the fisherman's wife and one of his three children survived. As he sat by the train, bemoaning his fate, Kaluarchi begged: 'Just tell the ministers to get this grief and train out of my face.' The government ultimately settled on a compromise, removing the engine and five coaches from Peraliya. Three coaches were left behind on a narrow section of track parallel to the main line as a memorial to those who died.

A few weeks later, on 20 February 2005, the government reopened the southern railway line and survivors from the *Queen of the Sea* were invited to board a brightly painted blue and yellow train at Colombo, called the *Galle Princess*, for a ceremonial trip to Peraliya. Travelling with railway officials, politicians and fellow survivors on board the flag-bedecked train was the guard of the *Queen of the Sea*, Wanigarathna Karunathilaka.

A twenty-year veteran of the railways, Wanigarathna was overjoyed with the government's decision to reopen the tsunami-shattered railway line. A hard-working man not prone to public displays of emotion, Wanigarathna was keen to put the pain of the past behind him and to get on with life. For him, the restoration of the service was a highly meaningful and symbolic act, showcasing to the rest of the world that the country was moving from mourning to building its future.

But as the *Galle Princess* approached the coaches of the *Queen of the Sea*, parked on a parallel track, the guard's steely demeanour melted and he vividly recalled every single moment of what happened on 26 December. It had been an uneventful ride till Peraliya, but when his train came to a halt, Wanigarathna noticed the water level climbing slowly and coming towards the railway track.

Within moments, water was sloshing around his knees inside the train itself. Outside, residents had started to panic and he noticed a girl screaming for help. Without a thought for his own safety, the *Queen of the Sea*'s guard pulled off his uniform, and clad just in his underwear, jumped off the train. Wanigarathna had lived all his life on a house near a river and wasn't scared of floods. Besides, at that point, he wasn't even aware it was the sea that had rapidly moved inland. However, the second he alighted from the train he noticed the huge waves and quickly yanked the girl off the tree and brought her back on board.

His thoughts then turned to the safety of the commuters. 'Passengers were getting down from the train. I requested them not to as the water level was high,' he recollected. Next, still in his underwear, he laboured his way through chest-deep water all the way to the front of the train. As he climbed aboard the 80-tonne engine to check on the safety of the driver and his assistant, they were deeply moved by his concern: 'The driver was wondering what to do. We had never experienced something like this and since this was such a unique situation I told him we would think of our next option when the water flowed away.'

Seconds later, he got down from the engine and jokingly told the driver and his assistant he would soon return, this time in his full uniform. While walking back to the rear of the train, he thought he was seeing things when he noticed a 30-foot wave come tearing in from the sea. His first thought was that no one would survive, but his safety training instincts quickly kicked in and he boarded one of the coaches, exhorting passengers to open their windows. But no one noticed or recognized him as he was still in his underwear and all he could do was watch as people prepared to deal with what they thought was certain death: 'The Buddhists were praying to Buddha, Muslims began praying to Allah and Catholics prayed to Jesus to try to save them.'

When the powerful wave smashed into the compartment, it keeled right over. However, keeping his cool, the guard opened a window leading to the roof of the train and helped at least twenty people scramble out and swim to safety. Moments later, the entire wagon was hurled right off the tracks and into a lagoon some 30 metres away. Gathering the survivors around him, Wanigarathna accompanied them to the high ground of a nearby temple. A smile broke across his weather-beaten face when he got there. Standing with the rest of the survivors was the girl whom he had earlier pulled off a tree and onto the train. 'I was pleased to see that she had cheated death twice,' he noted with satisfaction.

He was also heartened to find that his assistant had survived and they both teamed up to return to the train so that they could check on the remaining passengers. 'We took some strong wooden poles with us because the water level was still about 3-4 feet high and there were wells and pits everywhere.'

On the way, they ran into several other passengers whom he directed to the safety of the temple. Minutes later, they reached one of the wagons in which he saw at least fifteen bodies. He recognized one right away. 'It was the postman who always accompanied the train.' Later, they reached the engine, which, as already mentioned, had turned over. When Wanigarathna clambered aboard, he found the driver's body, but as he was unable to pull it out, he decided to rejoin the survivors back at the temple.

It was here that he ran into a familiar face, the stationmaster of the nearby Beruwalla Station: Nimal Premasiri. His own home had been destroyed and his wife and daughter had been killed, but Premasiri was busy trying to help the survivors, feeding them tea and cookies. Noticing Wanigarathna shivering in his underwear, Premasiri found him a sarong and advised him to rush to the closest police station. When he got there, Wanigarathna informed the officer in charge of what had happened to the train and was stunned when the policeman told him that they were receiving many such reports of death and destruction from across the country.

While millions turned to religion to try to comprehend what had happened, Wanigarathna didn't blame the gods. As he reasoned: 'This incident was caused by nature and wasn't created by gods. Some people died and some were saved. So life should go on. That is the power of karma.' Given all that he had seen and experienced, Wanigarathna entertained no thoughts of quitting his job. Proud of his long career in the railways, he wanted to continue serving his country and his people.

Unlike many other survivors, Wanigarathna felt no hatred towards the sea and his recent experience had just reaffirmed his belief that humans were helpless against nature. Still, recognizing the tremendous loss of life, he wanted the government to construct a proper memorial at the scene of one of the world's worst train tragedies. Like some other Sri Lankans, Wanigarathna too felt it was inappropriate to keep the last three wagons of his ill-fated train in Peraliya: 'The damaged rail compartments should be removed because when people pass this place they'll remember their parents, relatives, sons and daughters,' he advised.

Over the next few weeks, Peraliya was to become even a bigger draw for international journalists. They saw this place as an enduring symbol of the tsunami that had killed more than 30,000 people in this tiny island-nation. But their arrival in large numbers was creating problems for the grieving locals, who had never interacted with visitors. Most of the scribes were also unfamiliar with local customs and went about stomping around and photographing everything in the rubble, without appreciating the reality that what they thought was just debris was still someone's home. Till just a few days earlier, Peraliya's residents had lived and raised their children there and they felt that journalists needed to ask them for permission before they entered and stepped all over what was still a piece of their lives.

With schools shut, the neighbourhood children were equally distressed and appeared withdrawn. Noticing their predicament, Juliet Coomb, a thirty-two-year-old volunteer and photojournalist from Melbourne, sought the help of an interpreter to unlock their pain. 'I was amazed with my findings and this is what a group of children told me: ``The first few days we cried not due to the death of our families but fear of these big machines held by giants with white faces that shine bright lights in our eyes.'' '

Given such anxieties, Juliet came up with the idea of 'phototherapy'. This therapy involved giving children cameras and film so that they could be entertained, feel empowered and have access to an avenue to communicate their feelings. She had tried phototherapy earlier with Vietnamese street children in 1992 and had learnt that children can come up with great achievements, if given a chance. 'Kids don't understand why people run around with a camera,' she observed. That's why, she felt, they were bewildered. In the case of Peraliya's 484 children, she noted: 'They had never seen such things before and what got even more difficult for them was to be photographed and probed. They were questioning why so many people were intruding into their lives.'

Despite all these uncertainties, the children were quick to immerse themselves in their new project. They also took a shine to their talkative teacher, Juliet, who, in turn, was fascinated by their response: 'They got the little kids' perspective on the big picture, managing to crawl under things and get into nooks and crannies that adults could never dream of getting to.' Most importantly, the children were communicating their grief. One child showed Juliet pictures of the home of his schoolteacher, who was killed when the train's engine crashed right into his living room. Juliet was moved to tears when the child explained: 'I feel very sad I can't go to school because I have no teacher.'

Weeks after the tsunami, Juliet learnt that the children were still scared of going to the beach. She tried to allay their fears by organizing her photography classes right there and was taken aback when many children just shot extreme close-ups of the sea and the waves. 'I'm frightened of the sea,' one pupil told Juliet. 'It eats people and it may eat me up.' Another student of hers expended his entire roll of film photographing a rock. 'This is the last place I saw my relatives alive,' he explained.

Most children were so scared of the train that they only took its pictures from a distance. But thirteen-year-old Teshan went into the train and shot 'ghosts' using the simple technique of shaking his camera slightly just before pressing the shutter. Another orphan shot only silhouettes through the window, explaining his photography this way: 'I lost several members of my family and all I see are their ghosts.'

The children's pictures also reflected their confusion over why some things survived and some didn't. There were several snapshots of intact Buddha statues peering forlornly from among the rubble. Among Juliet's favourites was a snapshot of a Buddhist robe lying on a piece of twisted and tangled track. The robe's eye-catching orange colour stood out against the drab background, indicating that the children realized that only god or higher powers could withstand nature's might. Curiously enough, I too had reached the same conclusion when I first visited Peraliya. The dented wagons illustrated nature's awesome fury and humankind's helplessness when confronted by it. But being able to capture something so poignant in just one picture spoke volumes about the children's artistic eloquence.

Empowered with their new set of skills, the children soon decided to turn the tables on pesky hacks and trained their cameras on them. At one point, a group of twenty children surrounded a five-member camera crew and put the fear of god into them. 'They intimidated them, standing like a wall around them,' recalled Juliet, taking great delight in relating the crew's misery. 'They [the journalists] approached me for help and I asked them to be more thoughtful of what effect they had on others,' she recounted. Juliet ended her interaction with the crew by giving them another stern lecture. 'I told them that they shouldn't just walk in without even introducing themselves or even talking to people they photograph in their own language.'

A few weeks into the project, Juliet began noticing big changes in the children. 'When I first met them they were glum and you only got a smile out of them if you played a game.' Soon, along with photography, the children were also learning how to make puppets. 'It made them giggle, laugh, scream and shout,' observed Juliet, adding that what they enjoyed the most was making puppets that looked like the Western relief workers who were helping them. The children also opened up to her, discussing their ambitions to become doctors and engineers. None of them wanted to take up the more traditional activities such as fishing or farming, which taught her a lesson: 'We just can't send such children sewing machines and guess this will help girls sew themselves out of sorrow.' Juliet figured that these kids were very much part of the global world and their aspirations were being shaped by newer, more modern ideas than she had first anticipated.

With just a few days left for her departure, Juliet realized that she had actually been influenced more by those whom she had set out to change. 'They could smile while they were living in a hell,' she marvelled, appreciating their indomitable spirit to find the best things in life when they had been through the worst. They also worked very hard to keep Juliet happy and their behaviour led her to conclude: 'The people of Sri Lanka are very inspiring. I think they have an amazing attitude to get on with life and the Western world has a lot to learn from them because we get so easily put off by mundane things and believe others when they say we can't do so many things.'

As she wound up her project, Juliet had all her cameras returned to her. The children kept their pictures, which were among the few things they could really call their own as they huddled in their threadbare tents. Some of their pictures were purchased by the London-based *Independent*. The Royal Commonwealth Society also expressed serious interest in their art. Juliet has planned to use all the money from the sale of the pictures to help defray film and processing costs when she visits the children again. She also plans to write a book with the help of world-renowned Australian cricketer Shane Warne, in order to help Peraliya's youngest members with their future educational needs.

Reflecting on her weeks spent in Sri Lanka, Juliet wondered many times if she was smart enough to keep pace with the children. Their photography was so lucid and expressive that she was convinced that even after thirteen years in the business, she needed retraining.

I must confess I had similar thoughts. The children of Peraliya had retrained me not just about journalism but also life – how to live it and how to be dignified and resolute after having lost so much.

For that alone, I knew I would be visiting Peraliya, its three forlorn wagons and wonderful children again.

10

'The Miracle'

'...we found nine survivors: four men, three women and two children. The survivors' entire village had been destroyed and they had lived for days...on just jungle potatoes and wild boar. I thought it was a miracle...'

Dateline: Honolulu, 25 December 2004

IT WAS A DARK AND DREARY CHRISTMAS DAY IN Honolulu, but forty-three-year-old Dr Stuart Weinstein wasn't the complaining sort. He tinkered with his computer inside the operations room of the Pacific Tsunami Warning Center and said a prayer of thanks that he didn't have to be outside where the conditions were wet and miserable. Dr Weinstein was the lone scientist on duty that day and his job was to be on constant alert for any unusual seismic activity so that he could warn twenty-six Pacific countries and the US military of the impending threat of a tsunami. At about 3:00 p.m., just as he was settling into what he thought would be an uneventful day at the office, his attention was diverted by a seismometer, which had detected some activity. As he peered at the first raw data, Dr Weinstein noted that an earthquake had occurred near Indonesia, measuring perhaps 6.0 or 7.0 on the Richter scale. A few minutes later, more seismic information trickled in from Australia, but even before he could examine the new records, the center's 'digital event detector' beeped loudly, confirming that a seismic event had indeed occurred.

The earthquake alarm immediately brought another seismologist, Barry Hirshorn, to the center and he joined Dr Weinstein to pinpoint the exact location of the earthquake, which they discovered was just off the northern coast of Sumatra. The two scientists then quickly estimated the earthquake's magnitude as 8.0 on the Richter scale. At 3:15 p.m., roughly fifteen minutes after the seismic event, the center put out an advisory to twenty-six Pacific countries, including Indonesia and Thailand. That same message also stressed: 'There is no tsunami warning or watch in effect.' The warning, however, wasn't transmitted to any of the countries in the Indian Ocean simply because they were not under the Pacific-based warning system.

Twenty-five minutes after the first bulletin, the Pacific Tsunami Warning Center upgraded the intensity of the quake to 8.5. At 4:00 p.m., it released another bulletin, which emphasized the higher magnitude and mentioned that there was the 'possibility' of a tsunami occurring near the epicentre of the earthquake. 'We knew this was a big earthquake and there was a possibility North Sumatra could be hit by a tsunami,' reasoned Dr Weinstein, 'but we couldn't even think it would generate a tsunami that would travel as far as Thailand and Sri Lanka.'

Once the second bulletin had been issued, the scientists tuned into CNN and started scrolling the Internet for further information. It was while he was surfing the Net that Dr Weinstein came across wire reports of deaths in Phuket, Thailand, forcing him to recoil in shock and horror: 'Oh my God! This *is* a tsunami,' he thought. But he couldn't still fathom how an earthquake measuring 8.5 on the Richter scale had unleashed such a cataclysmic wave. It was only at 7:25 p.m., when the authoritative Harvard Seismology Group calculated the earthquake to be an 8.9, that Dr Weinstein realized that the event was powerful enough to unleash an intense tsunami. (In the coming days the earthquake's intensity was further revised to 9.0 and then 9.3, making it the second most powerful earthquake in history.) Since it was too late to warn Thailand, Indonesia, Sri Lanka or India, the scientists concentrated on warning other countries like Mauritius and Madagascar, which were still in the path of the monster waves. But the Pacific Tsunami Warning Center soon ran into a problem. It had no contacts in these countries and had to rely on the US State Department to contact embassies in Mauritius and Madagascar. It was also left to the State Department to directly call the governments of all other East African nations.

Over the next few days, the Pacific Tsunami Warning Center was censured by the media, and some scientists received emails labelling them as 'stupid' and 'moronic'. Dr Weinstein believed such attacks were baseless and unfair: 'People died because there was no warning system in the Indian Ocean and we could not just invent one. We did not also have any sensors in that area.' Further, he added, 'The Pacific Warning Center is not a warning system. We detect events, we make evaluations, then we issue bulletins relaying what we know. The clients who receive these products make a decision whether to evacuate or not. That's not a decision we make. It would have been very weird calling foreign governments and telling them to evacuate when we don't even do that in our own nations.'

Responding to the other criticism that they didn't contact the media and specifically warn them about the earthquake, Dr Weinstein stated that their bulletins were put out on a wire service that carried specific meteorological and oceanographic data. 'As far as I know, all major newspapers and wire services in the US go through this data all the time. I don't know what happened in the case of 26 December – maybe they didn't pay attention.' In hindsight, scientists at the center felt that there was nothing they could have done differently. 'It was a night of complete sadness and frustration,' remarked Dr Weinstein, who felt he did the best he could, given the information that he had. He continued: 'The earthquake struck the earth where a warning system was not operating. If it had happened in the Pacific, a warning would have gone out in fifteen minutes. Hundreds of thousands of people would not have died and we would have known much earlier about what was going on.'

The night of 26 December was one that no one at the Pacific Warning Center would ever forget and all the five scientists there, including Dr Weinstein, had learnt some hard professional lessons: 'We should forget about putting "Stop" signs after the accident. No ocean basin is safe and we have to think of a global tsunami warning system to protect all oceans.' Dr Weinstein was so pained and haunted by events that night he could not sleep at all: 'I saw this tragedy unfold hour by hour. And when I heard people had died I knew that was just the tip of the iceberg. The iceberg, I knew, would get bigger. This was not the way I wanted to go down in history, being on duty on a day like that. I would have rather gone down in history as being a member of a warning system that operated as it should have in the Pacific basin and saved thousands and thousands of people.'

Why then had no one even considered a tsunami warning system in the Indian Ocean? The answer was simple. Compared to the Pacific, which on average witnesses six tsunamis every 100 years and is a high-risk zone, seismologists point out there have been just two in South Asia over the past 120 years. The last one occurred in the Arabian Sea in 1945, killing 300 people. Prior to that there was a major tsunami in the Indian Ocean on 27 August 1883, when the island volcano of Krakatoa exploded with such monstrous ferocity that the sound could be heard 5000 km away. There were four blasts spread over a few hours that day and the last one is believed to have been the biggest explosion ever recorded in history. The volcano itself disintegrated and sank to the bottom of the ocean. When its searing magma came in contact with cold seawater, the result was a shooting cloud of steam, rock and ash that was hurled about 30 km into the atmosphere. Since Krakatoa itself was uninhabited, no one on the island was killed by the falling debris. But giant tsunami waves, some of them reaching an astonishing 135 feet, rolled out towards Java and Sumatra. They obliterated nearly 300 settlements and eventually killed 36,000 people.

Unlike in the Pacific, there was little official or political interest in setting up a tsunami warning system in the Indian Ocean. In 1967, a Canadian expert, Tad Murthy, had mooted the idea of such a system but was politely rebuffed by Indian authorities: 'If there's a tsunami once every sixty years it doesn't really concern the public,' he rationalized. 'Who remembers something that occurs with such rarity? Public memory is very short and the media and politicians tend to forget as well.' But the idea had crossed the mind of an Australian scientist, Phil Cummins. In October 2003 he was part of his country's delegation that attended a conference in Wellington, New Zealand, hosted by a little-known UN body, the International Coordination Group for the Tsunami Warning System in the Pacific. It was at this conference that Cummins proposed an expansion of the international network into other parts of Asia. The group's response was typically bureaucratic: it would require a change in the mandate of the organization. But rather than completely brush off the Australian's views, it was decided to set up a working group that would advance scientific arguments to buttress the case for an expansion of the tsunami warning system into the Indian Ocean.

After the meeting ended, Cummins uncovered historical evidence of a large 8.8 Sumatran earthquake that had spawned a tsunami in 1833. He then ran computer simulations, which showed that the tsunami would have ravaged the Sumatran shoreline east of the fault and would have spread rapidly westward towards other Asian countries. On 26 December 2004, something similar happened, but with even greater intensity. Watching these events unfold in Sydney was Cummins, who had still not formally presented his research: 'I felt very heartbroken to see it happen and felt if we had a few more years then we could have perhaps have made a real difference.'

But all was not lost. Many in the community of seismologists were encouraged by the response of world leaders and organizations after the tsunami. In January 2005, US President George Bush pledged to expand his country's tsunami warning system beyond the Pacific into the Atlantic and the Caribbean. The UN too took an initiative and promised a tsunami warning network would be created in the Indian Ocean by 2006 to be followed by a global network in 2007. In March 2005, five countries – India, Australia, Indonesia, Malaysia and Thailand – announced that they would be setting up their own warning systems and would share information with each other.

Of all the Asian countries, Canadian expert Tad Murthy believes India will be the first to set up its proposed $30 million system: 'There are no major technical difficulties and the major components, except the computer models, are in place. I am confident the system will be operational in 2007.' So how will it work? The system involves harnessing the country's already well-respected technological skills by deploying pressure sensors on the ocean floor that can detect a rise in the sea level. The collected data would then be transmitted to floating buoys and relayed via satellite to warning stations on the ground. Experts feel that smaller countries like Sri Lanka need not spend scarce resources to build such systems but can piggyback on information already available to the larger countries. It's a strategy that Sri Lanka, according to its foreign minister, Lakshman Kadirgamar, has found entirely acceptable: 'The experts are telling us that what we should focus on is not the high-tech aspect – we haven't got the money for it anyway – but how to quickly disseminate any information we are given. How to get our people evacuated without panicking them. We must have early warning systems of that kind, we are working on that. We are setting up a disaster management agency as well ...'

Even with an advanced system in place, which may soon be able to predict tsunamis in the Indian Ocean, protection and safety are by no means guaranteed. What's also needed alongside a good warning system, say the experts, is public awareness. 'If you had a system in place, would people pay attention to it?' questioned Dr Weinstein. He also pointed out that history has shown many people would still rush to witness an unusual natural phenomenon. In Phuket, on 26 December 2004, hundreds died when they made a dash to see the ocean receding, a phenomenon scientists call 'draw-down' and which almost certainly indicates a tsunami is imminent. According to Dr Weinstein: 'If this had happened in Hawaii people would have the awareness to stay away. But in Thailand a lot of people died and they didn't really have to. The draw-down indicated a tsunami and they should have taken that as a signal to run. What they didn't know hurt them.'

Three months later, on 28 March 2005, the earth shook again. Just like the 26 December earthquake, this one too had its epicentre just off the coast of Sumatra and occurred at a depth of nearly 30 km on a segment of the same fault line that had triggered the earlier tremor. The second quake was felt as far away as Thailand, Malaysia and Singapore – more than 700 km from the epicentre. Within moments of the tremor – it measured 8.7 on the Richter scale – I received a call from Atlanta, catching me once again on vacation. Luckily though, I was still in New Delhi and managed to assemble the entire bureau together in less than half an hour. Over the next few hours, we all began to closely monitor what was clearly another fast-unfolding news event.

In contrast to 26 December, what really stood out for me this time around was the level of international cooperation. Fresh from the lashing it had received from the media in the days following the last tsunami, the Pacific Tsunami Warning Center flashed a warning that the quake could cause a 'widely destructive tsunami' and coastlines within 1100 km of the epicentre should be evacuated. Unlike the first earthquake, scientists in Honolulu also took pains to ensure that every single Asian country was informed. Japan's Meteorological Agency too initiated similar action, immediately notifying Thailand, Indonesia, Sri Lanka, India, the Maldives and Malaysia. The US–Japan initiative highlighted a greater willingness to share critical data with countries whose own warning systems had yet to be established.

The response from national governments and people was just as speedy and encouraging. In

Indonesia's Banda Aceh, the capital of the Aceh province, eyewitnesses reported that the seismic activity lasted for about two minutes and knocked out the electricity, but thousands immediately poured out onto the streets and made a speedy dash for higher ground. By this time, tsunami warnings had been issued in Japan, Thailand, Malaysia, Sri Lanka and India. Television reports showed people being evacuated from hotels and hospitals in the province of Phuket, one of the worst-affected areas in the 26 December tsunami. In Sri Lanka, blaring sirens along the country's eastern coast ordered residents to evacuate immediately. And closer to the capital, Colombo, Buddhist temples switched on their loudspeakers to broadcast soothing religious hymns. Further north, in India, several coastal states issued tsunami alerts, and the Central Government, after calling an emergency meeting of relief officials, put the armed forces on heightened alert. In Chennai, police put up barricades on all roads leading to the coast. Residents in Nagapattinam, which bore the brunt of the last tsunami in India, needed no encouragement to move. Thousands fled within minutes of hearing about the first reports of an earthquake, seeking safety on higher ground.

Almost four hours had now passed since the tremors had first been felt and it was clear that other than the island of Nias, just west of Sumatra, where hundreds were killed, most parts of South Asia had been spared. It had been yet another adrenaline-filled night, and I joined thousands in praying for the families of those who had perished. But, like others in South Asia, I also felt an overwhelming sense of relief that the worst was over and another tsunami wasn't headed our way. The Indian and Sri Lankan Governments too felt the same and when they decided to cancel their tsunami alerts, I knew it was all right to send all bureau staffers home.

Greater public awareness was not the only positive outcome of the tsunami. Thirty-eight days after the 26 December tsunami, another amazing event – the discovery of nine survivors in the Andaman and Nicobar Islands – would capture the world. My initial reaction when the desk woke me at 11:30 p.m. to pass on the news was one of disbelief: 'It just can't be,' I thought, while firing up my computer to check the latest news dispatches from the region. The first report I read was from the Associated Press and it immediately grabbed my attention because it quoted a policeman, who had found the exhausted survivors in a forest. Not knowing what to make of his account, I scrolled back to the top of the news article and smiled as I read the name of the reporter on the story. Neelesh Misra is a good friend and, despite the late hour, I called him to check the story. Neelesh told me he had got to know the police officer, Inspector Shaukat Hussein, while earlier reporting on the tsunami from the region, and had received a call from him about the rescue just a few hours earlier.

Sensing my scepticism, Neelesh assured me the story was 100 per cent accurate, but I still asked him for the policeman's number. It was 2:00 a.m. when I woke up Shaukat Hussein in Campbell Bay on the island of Car Nicobar, but the groggy inspector readily agreed to share the details of his adventure: 'We were on a routine patrol on one of the islands in the morning and had walked about four kilometres when we came across a dead body. It was a sign there could be other people in the area, so we continued looking and couldn't believe our eyes when we found nine survivors: four men, three women and two children. The survivors' entire village had been destroyed and they had lived for days,' Shaukat told me, 'on just jungle potatoes and wild boar. I thought it was a miracle and felt very proud I could perform such a service. The survivors were all completely exhausted but soon after seeing us they all started crying. I didn't, but it was a very special moment.'

Happy that I had finally confirmed the story, I called the desk to offer up *live* shots from the bureau. For the next few hours, the Car Nicobar saga was the top story on both our domestic and international networks, prompting me to call Suhasini. I asked her, cameraman Rajesh Mishra and producer Maurya Gautam to gear up to take the early morning flight to the Andaman Islands. At 4:00 a.m., and only after the desk had signed off on the trip, did I tumble into bed – exhausted, but on cloud nine with this wonderful news.

Suhasini was excited to be part of the coverage plans, but grumbled when officials in the Andaman Islands told her that she would only be allowed one hour on the southern island where the survivors had been found. 'We were told that regardless of what time we landed, we would have to return before sunset because the runway at Campbell Bay had been badly damaged by the tsunami and the pilot needed full daylight to take off.' With a sinking feeling, Suhasini realized that she would get very little time to shoot the entire story. But there was no time to sulk. As soon as their plane landed, Suhasini and Rajesh commandeered a jeep reserved for senior officials and drove at breakneck speed to a camp where they met the survivors and their leader, Justin Edwards. On 26 December 2004, Justin was leading a small group to the village church located on top of a hill, when they saw the tsunami obliterate their place of habitation. Struck by the speed of the wave and the ferocity of nature, the entire group scurried to reach higher ground, but soon lost their way. For the first few days, they were sure that somebody would come looking for them, but as time passed hope of a rescue dwindled. Justin and the others walked for hundreds of kilometres through destroyed forests and even swam across small rivers.

Initially, they survived mainly on coconut water. And then, miraculously, they met a man from one of Nicobar's famed indigenous tribes. He showed them the different kinds of berries they could eat in the wild. He also taught them how to make a fire, and the most difficult part, how to kill and eat wild boar. To keep everyone's morale up, Justin made a calendar from sticks and stones. Eventually, thirty-eight days later, when they heard the sounds of a police motor boat, Justin exhorted the others to begin shouting at the top of their lungs. 'We were completely exhausted, but we put every last ounce of our energy into screaming for help. We had spent so much of our time praying and were happy that our prayers had at last been answered. We truly believed the policemen had been sent by god.'

Suhasini spoke with the youngest survivor in the group, a girl called Clara. 'My parents died in the tsunami', she said. 'I spent most of the last month just thinking of them. Now I don't know what I will do next.' All the survivors had lost their entire families, but after six weeks in the jungle, they had formed a tight bond amongst themselves. While she was speaking with Clara, Suhasini noticed the whole group stood closer around her. Their body language conveyed a protective intimacy and warmth that could only have come from sharing each other's grief after going through such an overwhelming experience together in the jungle.

Encouraged by the publicity and goodwill generated by the rescue of these nine survivors, authorities stepped up their search and rescue operations in the area. Thousands were still missing in these islands, located about 200 km from the epicentre of the quake, but, in the coming days, when officials failed to find any more survivors, it signalled the end of our tsunami coverage. I was glad that we had ended our stint on a bright and positive note. I also felt a tremendous surge of pride for being part of a news organization that had spared no effort or money in putting together coverage that had both moved and motivated millions around the world to provide help to all those who needed it so desperately.

The response from our viewers around the world was a key factor that pushed us to devote over 600 hours to the story across all our networks. 'CNN is hands down the best place to see and hear coverage on the quake/tsunami,' a viewer emailed. At the height of our coverage, we had eighty staff members grouped into twenty teams that were deployed across Asia and for us in the field, every single email meant that more people cared. The response from viewers and from other media organizations galvanized the drained and emotionally exhausted crews in the field to continue to push themselves. Noted the respected *Wall Street Journal*: 'CNN in particular has been fabulous. News ennobles them. It's as if the anchor sits straighter knowing they do have a purpose beyond being the aural screensaver on our TV.'

For insiders, like supervising editor Eli Flournoy, what really mattered on this story was CNN's news-gathering spirit: 'When a story like this happens, it's important to recognize the contribution of hundreds of people. People who were on location could have said: "I'm on vacation." But they didn't. In this situation, like in so many others, it was our people who started calling in – our people were on it, and we at the desk didn't have to think about dragging people in. For me, what mattered most was the mindset – of everyone being ready – and this was regardless of whether they were on vacation or how much sleep they had. None of that mattered. It was these things that made the difference.'

The story also marked a rite of passage for a new technology initiative in the company known as 'DNG' or Digital News Gathering. For three years CNN had been investing in new laptop computers that were a one-stop shop to edit pictures, transmit stories via satellite phones and also do *live* hits. The new technology was lightweight, easy to use and, compared to the earlier transmission method of using satellites, was also much cheaper, giving us greater lasting power on a long-running story like the tsunami. In the early days, even when this technology was still in its infancy and had teething problems, the New Delhi Bureau was quick to embrace it. The experience gained in the process was to later come in handy during the tsunami story. We already knew that one of DNG's biggest advantages was its versatility. Therefore, equipped with just four boxes of gear, we could give our viewers information from several different locations rather than confining ourselves to just one spot. In the tsunami's immediate aftermath, we loaded up our DNG gear onto boats, small planes and helicopters to bring *live* pictures from Indian ships involved in Sri Lanka's largest-ever humanitarian operation. Later, to show viewers how their compassion was making a difference and helping to save lives on the ground, we quickly relocated our equipment to capture footage of US Marines and hundreds of relief-laden aircraft that had arrived from all corners of the world.

One of our DNG teams, led by Stan Grant, also made it inside Tamil Tiger rebel territory to provide what was possibly the most moving coverage from all of Sri Lanka. None of this would have been possible without the vision of CNN International's senior management, which appointed Paul Ferguson to equip every bureau with this revolutionary technology. 'During the tsunami,' explained Paul, 'we had more cameras in the field than at any other time in our history. Such a presence gave us more than just video shots; we had people on the ground who were listening to victims and telling us their stories.' But most importantly, CNN International's senior vice-president, Tony Maddox, believed DNG field crews used the technology to transmit 'ferocious' eyewitness video images that brought alive the horror of what had really happened.

Just like Vietnam changed the concept of covering war, the tsunami changed the concept of broadcasting disaster. With new technology at one's command, real-life images of what had happened just a few hours earlier could be beamed instantly across the globe. Within a matter of hours, people connected with what we saw. Millions felt overawed and vulnerable, realizing that this calamity could just as easily have affected them. Reporters covering the story felt the same way. Stan Grant felt that journalism itself had evolved from being removed and distant to becoming something more human: 'We were part of the story, we were equally vulnerable. The kids who died could just as well have been ours. What we saw wasn't one army against the other. What we witnessed was random, brutal...we realized we could all have been affected.'

Suhasini too found that the objectivity that most reporters normally relied on just wasn't valid anymore; not after the stories she had heard: 'Two days after the tsunami, I met a man and his neighbours who went back to find their children. This must have been so heartbreaking, but he described how they went around the beach pulling the buried bodies of children out of the mud and how they had to wipe the sand off the faces to try to identify them. Then if they didn't find whom they were looking for, they would bury the children back in the same spot. I think neutrality does get blurred in these situations because their pain quickly becomes your pain and there's no question whose side you are on.'

These changes in our reporting style were being keenly noticed by CNN's senior management. Commented Tony Maddox: 'The tsunami did mark a gradual change in our business. The old-fashioned part of me gets uncomfortable if I see different reporters editorializing but there is nothing wrong with showing the human side, and responding. People clearly get deeply moved. If our reporters show how they are moved and do it properly, that can be quite moving for the audience.' Chris Cramer too liked the new style of reporting: 'I think audiences understand impartiality; they understand calm and cool but they also understand sensitive reporting. They don't expect you to burst into tears; the tsunami wasn't a licence to burst into tears, but we also had to realize that keeping a stiff upper lip could be interpreted by our audiences as us not giving a damn.'

Revolutionary changes were also implemented on our Internet Website: CNN.com. Since the tsunami, we were receiving thrice our normal traffic and editors quickly set up a link, asking for eyewitness accounts. But as more and more people started writing in to ask for help in locating loved ones, editor Amanda Barnett promptly shifted gears: 'We quickly moved from a perspective of [reporting] what happened to helping. We asked people to email us, and asked others to look to see if they recognized any of the names or pictures. This was about putting people in touch with each other and we just stepped away and let people connect.'

This was the first time that CNN.com. had gone beyond merely reporting the news, and the results were encouraging. More than 100 people across more than a dozen countries were able to find a friend or family member through the service, which soon also included a link to a page on which staffers had posted a list of reputable organizations that were accepting donations. The outpouring of emotion and the volume of mail – CNN was getting about ten emails a minute – made Amanda realize the important role that she and other staffers had to play: 'There were no government agencies to help here. This was a void we could fill. There were mothers looking for sons, friends looking for friends. There were as many people writing back saying I saw so and so, or I'm alive. It was amazing to see how much people cared and how involved they were willing to be. The compassion was amazing. We are so accustomed not to getting involved, but the way we worked it out is we gave people the vehicle to help each other. This was like a community service and it really felt like we were doing some good.'

Over the next few days, CNN.com launched a feature (it was later called .com Desk) through which television viewers were shown reunions that were brought about by our website. In essence, this segment put CNN.com staffers on air to talk about the encouraging and inspiring stories coming out of the tragedy. Perhaps the most high-profile story showcased on this segment was once again that of Hannes Bergstrom (see Chapter 5). Soon after he was taken to a Phuket hospital by Americans Ron Robbin and Rebecca Beddal, doctors put out his picture on the Net and his family immediately recognized him. Later, watching Ron and Rebecca who were invited as guests on the Larry King show, a girl in the US was so taken in by their act of kindness that she immediately shot off a letter:

Dear Mr King,

My name is Missy McDonough and I am nine years old. I live in Englewood, Florida, and I have been watching the sad, horrible things that have happened to all the tsunami victims. My great-grandmother just recently passed away and left me some money. I want to help as many people as I can and I want to send $100. I just watched your show tonight and it had Ron and Rebecca on it. They were the ones who saved the little boy who was wrapped in blankets. They said that they were giving money right to the people there who needed it. How can I send my money to them so they can give it to people who need it most? Could you please let me know?'

CNN.com journalist Veronica de La Cruz responded in a flash and immediately put Missy on the phone so that she could talk with the couple. She then recorded parts of their conversation to be played back on CNN, where she also reported that the money Missy had donated would be used by Ron and Rebecca to feed a Thai family for a few months. Veronica was not only touched by Missy's gesture, but was also extremely pleased with the role that CNN.com had played in bringing people together: 'When we started asking viewers to send their appeals, the Website became an "instant community" for people around the globe: people who were waiting for word on missing friends or relatives. In many instances, I know their feelings of helplessness and grief were replaced by hope and inspiration, simply through the kindness of strangers. People were logging on and writing in just to say "hang in there", "we are praying for you" or "everything is going to be okay". I was in awe of the kindness of strangers. I was in awe of the power of the Internet.' Veronica also never felt that she had crossed the line on the story: 'You have a responsibility as a journalist, but you have a responsibility as a human being too. You realize that you are part of a process and you just want to help. It's hard not to.'

After witnessing such an enormous surge of 'people power' on the Net, CNN.com editors are now working on technical solutions to make their site more interactive. They believe a new phase of CNN.com will soon evolve – one that will be more community and people based. Chris Cramer too has pledged that he will try to do everything to make CNN a much more helpful tool for viewers in case of a tragedy: 'We would be happy to engage in and to join in on any meaningful debate and conversation about how we might use our channels to publicize authoritative government-sponsored warnings. We would be perfectly happy to engage in serious discussion about that. We won't conceal from audiences what we know but we must realize that many of those who died listened to other forms of radio and TV. We also recognize that every broadcaster has that responsibility.'

For all the change that the tsunami brought about in our reporting style, we were criticized by one of India's leading newspapers for showing too many dead bodies. Wrote the *Indian Express* on 30 December 2004: 'Why has Southeast Asia's biggest tragedy become every American network's ghoulish Disneyland party? Has disaster finally found its paparazzi?' Responding to the criticism, Chris Cramer retorted: 'I'm respectful of anyone's criticism and just because a large number of people have died does not give a licence to engage in opportunistic journalism. But it would be irresponsible to edit around images and to sanitize them in such a way that we air the grief and spare the tragedy. That would be absurd and disgusting. We are not in the business of protecting our audiences from unpleasantness.'

The newspaper article angered many CNN correspondents. This was a challenging story and we all felt the *Indian Express* had failed to grasp the core of our coverage, which was to showcase the immense suffering of millions across Asia. Stan Grant, who covered northern Sri Lanka, best summed up our collective feelings about such denigration: 'What we did wasn't for our personal glory; it wasn't for the glory of CNN. It was the need to make sense of what happened. The commitment was not for ratings, but it was purely to give dignity to the so many lives that were lost.'

Our coverage eventually inspired thousands of people around the world. The Sri Lankan president, prime minister, foreign minister and high commissioner to India all thanked CNN for opening the floodgates of relief to their country. Such comments lifted my teams exhausted spirits, but what mattered to me most and will always be part of my most cherished memories was the impact we had on viewers like nine-year-old Missy McDonough. Soon after she donated $100 to Ron and Rebecca, Missy went from door-to-door collecting more charity and eventually raised $1626. Four hundred dollars of that money came from one woman alone, who had heard of her efforts on a local radio station and decided to jump in and help.

As I look back and ponder over my most challenging assignment to date, I realize there's not much I would have done differently. What we managed to achieve was possible only because of teamwork and the help of some of the warmest and most wonderful people I have ever encountered in my life. How can I ever forget the generosity and compassion of Wasantha Wijendra, whose car I had first commandeered in Galle? Forensic pathologist Dr Rohan Rowanapura's diligence and dedication to help his people pointed to the highest possible standards of professionalism, which I shall always try to emulate. The children of

Peraliya taught me about resilience and the ability to overcome odds. Their struggle has touched me so deeply that I'll continue to visit them and hopefully they can continue to teach us all valuable lessons about self-respect.

Rather than dwell in a state of despair, hundreds of the survivors I met wanted to get on with their lives. They symbolize the tenacity of the human spirit and I feel privileged to be sharing their stories. My professional experience recorded the fury of nature. But more significantly, it also brought home the power of people. Individuals like the Indian naval doctor, Lieutenant Commander Gopalan Parthasarathy, come to mind. Even though he was unaware of the fate of his own family, Commander Parthasarathy volunteered to rush to help his neighbours in trouble. It was such selflessness and sacrifice that soon proved to be the vanguard for the world's largest-ever relief operation.

As I watched the arrival of relief planes from countries as poor as Bangladesh, I fully understood the meaning of the term 'the world is a village'. In their darkest hour, people all over the world had reached out to the Sri Lankans and, as their president pointed out, it was such support that gave them the courage to endure.

The tsunami has changed me, as it has so many others. I think I'm more sensitive now, and am beginning to realize that there's more to life than one's professional fulfilment and financial security. My family, which always meant so much to me, now matters even more. As for life in general, I take it as it comes and try not to let minor disappointments faze me.

On the work front, I've come to see that journalism isn't only about the timely transmission of accurate information. Although this is essential to the profession, responsible reporting should cut deeper, providing a more profound understanding of events around us.

During our coverage of the tsunami, my colleagues and I tried to bring to light the humanity that prevailed amid the terrible tragedy, in the hope that these stories would inspire compassion and support. The response was overwhelming. News stories can make a difference, I guess.

Publisher's Acknowledgements

The publisher and the author pledge all proceeds from this book towards the rehabilitation of tsunami victims. We are grateful to the following for providing their services free of cost in the making of this book:

Associated Press
CNN
Walid Hneini
Ilaksha Studio
Indian Navy
India Today
Nalaka Karunarathna
Nikita Overseas Pvt. Ltd.
The Sunday Times, Colombo, Sri Lanka
Thomson Press (India) Ltd.
TIME Magazine
Unicef India

Their support and generosity are deeply appreciated.

How the Deadly Waves Sprea[d]

SCOPE OF THE TRAGEDY

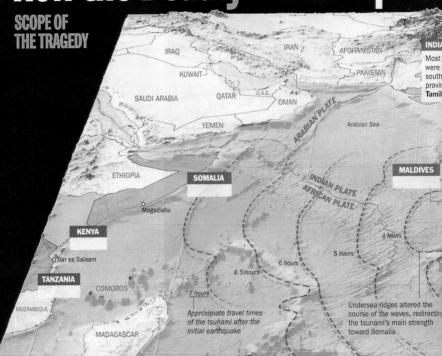

IRAQ

KUWAIT

SAUDI ARABIA

QATAR

U.A.E.

OMAN

YEMEN

IRAN

AFGHANISTAN

PAKISTAN

INDIA

Most
were i
south
provin
Tamil

ETHIOPIA

SOMALIA

Mogadishu

KENYA

Dar es Salaam

TANZANIA

COMOROS

MOZAMBIQUE

MADAGASCAR

ARABIAN PLATE

Arabian Sea

INDIAN PLATE
AFRICAN PLATE

MALDIVES

4 hours

5 hours

6 hours

6.5 hours

7 hours

Approximate travel times of the tsunami after the initial earthquake

Undersea ridges altered the course of the waves, redirecting the tsunami's main strength toward Somalia

WHAT CAUSES A TSUNAMI?

A tsunami (a Japanese word that translates as "harbor wave") is triggered by a vertical disturbance in the ocean, such as an earthquake, landslide or volcanic eruption

1 The disaster was caused by a massive **earthquake** off the coast of Indonesia, where two **plates** of the earth's crust grind against each other

BURMA PLATE

INDIAN PLATE

Stress builds as one plate pulls down on the other

2 About 1,200 km
edge of the Burr
plate snapped, f
a **massive displaceme**
of water in the
Indian Ocean